Museum of Anthropology
University of Michigan
Technical Reports
Number 15

RESEARCH REPORTS IN ANTHROPOLOGY
Contribution 10

The Garnsey Spring Campsite:

Late Prehistoric Occupation in Southeastern New Mexico

by

William J. Parry
John D. Speth

with contributions by

Regge N. Wiseman
Stephen A. Hall
and
Virginia Popper

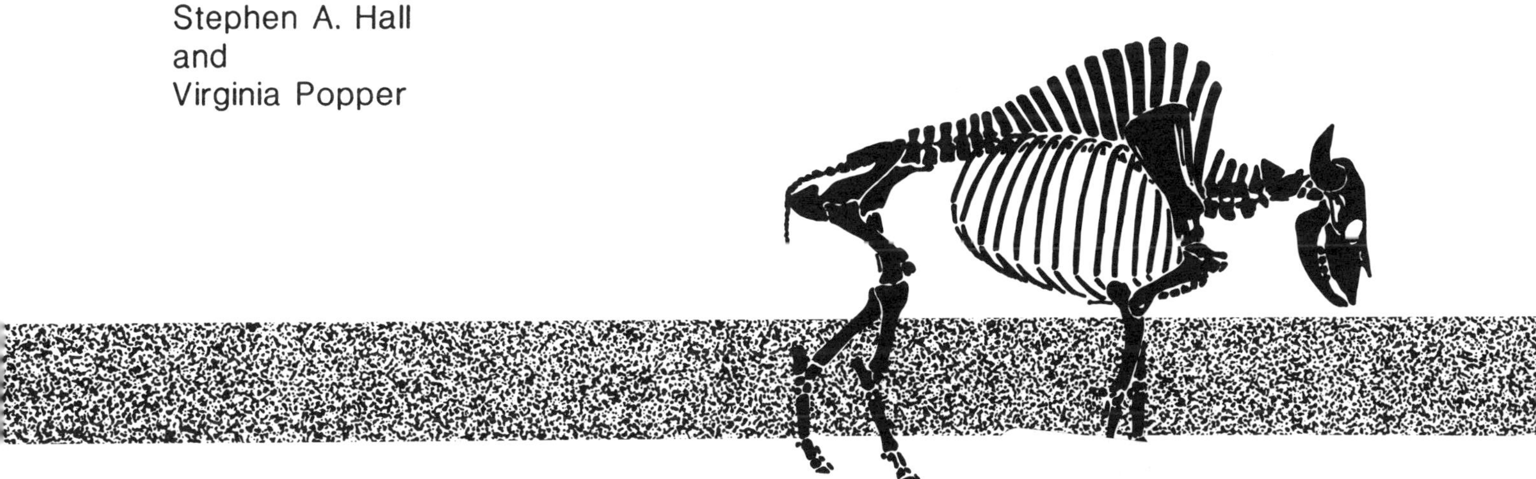

Ann Arbor
1984

Printed in the
United States of America

ISBN 0-932206-99-9

TABLE OF CONTENTS

LIST OF TABLES

LIST OF FIGURES

ACKNOWLEDGMENTS

Research at the Garnsey Spring campsite (LA-18400) was conducted under Federal Antiquities Act Permit No. 77-NM-037, issued to the University of Michigan by the Department of the Interior and administered by the Bureau of Land Management in the State of New Mexico (Roswell District). Funding for the research was provided by the National Science Foundation (BNS 78-06875). Additional support came from the Horace H. Rackham School of Graduate Studies and the Museum of Anthropology, both of the University of Michigan.

We would like to acknowledge our gratitude to the many people who helped us during the project. First and foremost are the Garnseys, Elmer and Jane, who graciously welcomed us on their ranch. We are also grateful to Richard I. Ford, Director of the Museum of Anthropology at the University of Michigan, for his help and encouragement throughout the course of the research. Numerous other people have also helped us immeasurably along the way. These include Ann Ramage, BLM District Archaeologist in Roswell, Leo Flynn, Manton Botsford, Dan Harrison, Dave Snow, and Dedie Snow. Finally, we would like to thank the members of the field crew who labored under rather difficult conditions at the campsite and the bison kill.

Clement Meighan and his associates at the University of California in Los Angeles graciously undertook the obsidian hydration analysis, and Fred W. Nelson of Brigham Young University did the source determinations for us. Most of the line drawings and many of the photographs of artifacts were done by Katherine Clahassey. Thomas R. Rocek and Claire McHale assisted in the unenviable task of entering and proofreading the endless tables in the appendix. Mary Hodge masterfully handled the final editing and production of the volume.

1. INTRODUCTION

The Garnsey Spring site (LA-18400) is an aboriginal campsite near a permanent spring only a few hundred meters west of the Garnsey Bison Kill (LA-18399; see Speth and Parry 1978, 1980; Speth 1983). We decided to work at the campsite specifically because its location and many of the artifacts on the surface suggested that it might be a processing locality associated with the kill. Limited excavations at the campsite in 1977 and 1978 showed, however, that while it may have overlapped in time with the kill there was no convincing evidence of a direct functional relationship between the two sites. Excavated artifacts and scanty faunal remains from the campsite point instead to a wide range of habitation and maintenance activities and the procurement of a variety of animal species throughout much of the late prehistoric ceramic period, and possibly during late preceramic times as well. The bison kill, on the other hand, appears to represent a series of spring-season procurement events occurring over a relatively short period of time around A.D. 1450. Moreover, work at the kill site indicates that processing activities took place on the floor of the Garnsey Wash, close to where the animals had been killed. There is no convincing evidence at present that portions of field-dressed bison were transported to the campsite for additional processing. The reader should bear in mind, however, that poor faunal preservation at LA-18400 precludes any definitive assessment of the functional relationships between the two sites.

The small-scale excavations at the campsite revealed that the deposits were shallow and badly disturbed. The combined effects of deflation, erosion, and heavy rodent disturbance made recognition of natural stratigraphic levels virtually impossible. Moreover, we encountered very few undisturbed cultural features such as pits or hearths, and no structures. Thus, the campsite yielded very little material in clear datable contexts. As a consequence, we terminated work at the campsite and focused our efforts entirely on the nearby bison kill.

Despite the obvious limitations of the campsite, we feel it imperative that we create a permanent record of the information recovered by our work. We do so in the hope that as knowledge of local and regional prehistory improves these data will prove useful. We should also point out that further work at the campsite might still prove fruitful. Resistivity surveying, augering, or judicious use of a backhoe may reveal subsurface structures that we failed to detect in our limited testing of the site. Such structures, should they exist, are more likely to contain stratified deposits with better preservation of organic remains.

This report, like its counterparts for the Garnsey Bison Kill (Speth and Parry 1978, 1980), is intended to provide a detailed descriptive record of the basic data and field observations in a format that can be produced relatively quickly and inexpensively. Included in this report are extensive appendices providing inventories of recovered materials. It must be kept in mind that this report is preliminary in nature, and that our interpretations and conclusions are likely to require substantial revision in the future.

2. SITE DESCRIPTION

Introduction

The Garnsey Spring campsite (LA-18400) is about 20 km (12 mi) southeast of the city of Roswell, Chaves County, New Mexico (Figs. 1 and 2). The site is on Bureau of Land Management land about 0.8 km (0.5 mi) northeast of the southeast corner of Bottomless Lakes State Park (NE 1/4 of the SW 1/4 of Section 35, T. 11 S., R. 26 E., Bottomless Lakes 7.5 minute quadrangle, topographic series), and approximately 350 m northeast of the principal excavations at the Garnsey Bison Kill (LA-18399; see Speth and Parry 1980).

Fig. 1. Location of Garnsey Spring campsite and other late prehistoric sites in southeastern New Mexico.

The campsite is situated on a gently sloping terrace overlooking a small unnamed draw (henceforth Spring Draw), a tributary of the Garnsey Wash (Figs. 3-6). The site is bounded on the south and southeast by the steeply sloping sides of this channel. An even smaller gully bounds the site on its west side, while the gently rolling hills of the Mescalero Pediment lie to the north and east.

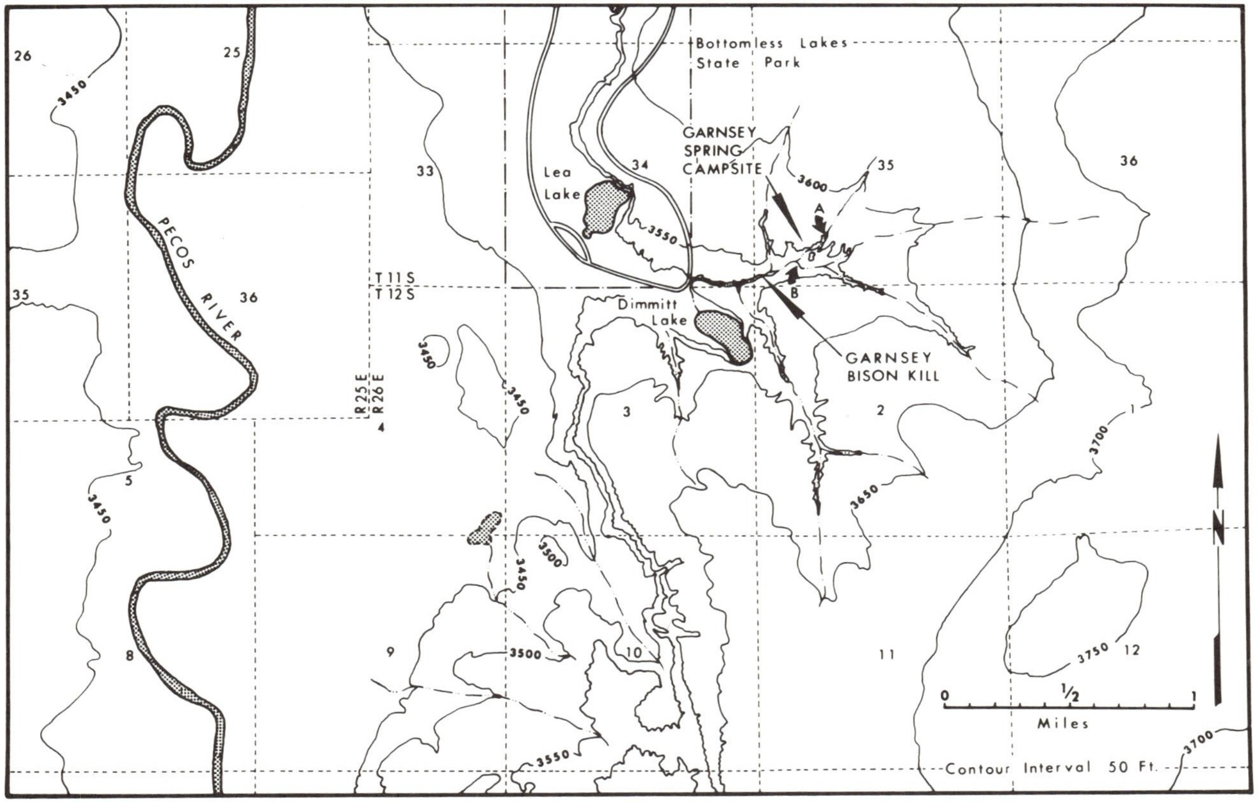

Fig. 2. Bottomless Lakes area, New Mexico, showing location of Garnsey Spring campsite and Garnsey Bison Kill (adapted from USGS Bottomless Lakes 7.5 minute quadrangle, topographic series). A, pictograph rockshelter at head of Spring Draw; B, location of "Garza" hearth on south bank of Garnsey Wash.

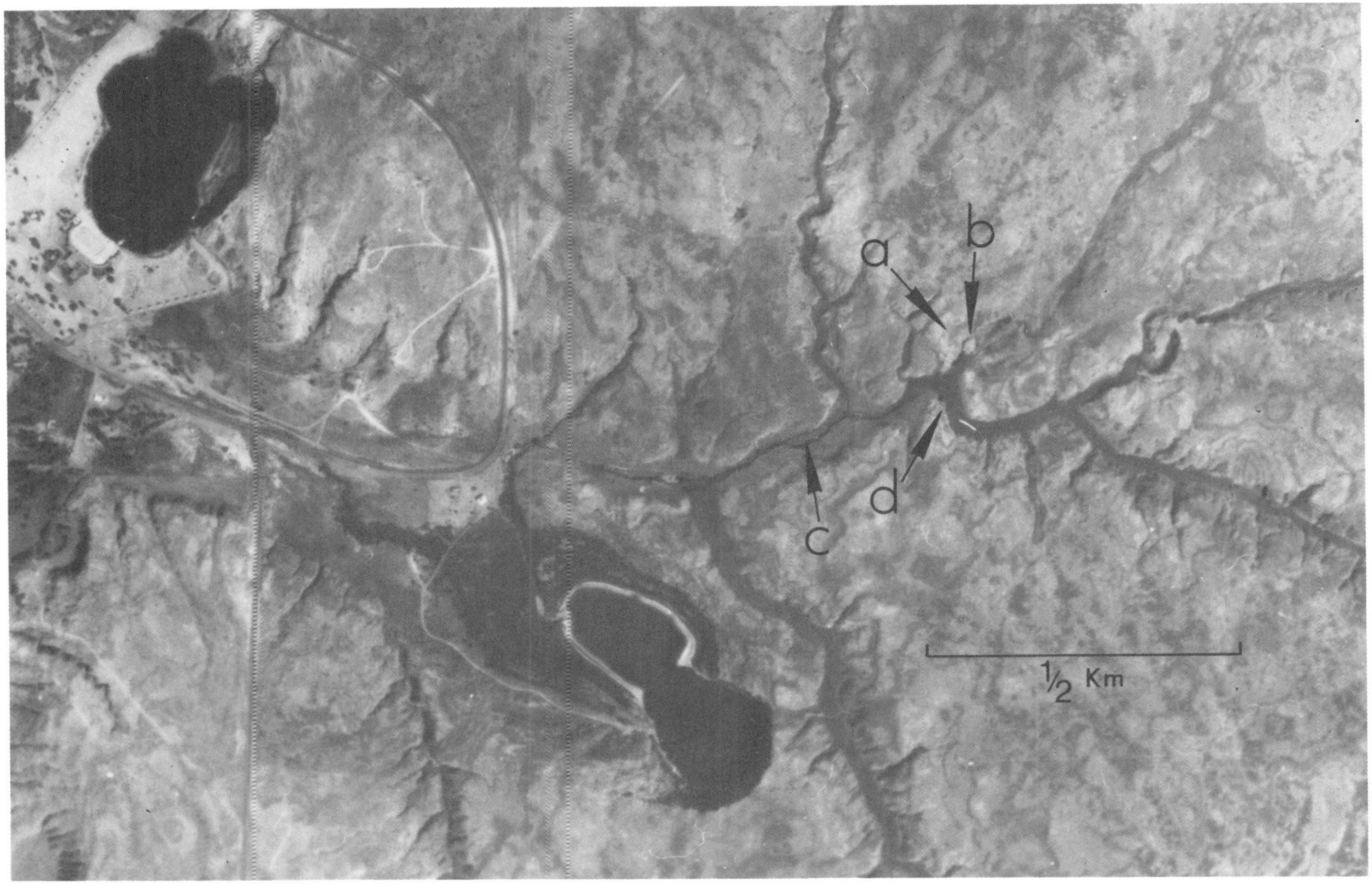

Fig. 3. Aerial photograph of Dimmitt Lake, Lea Lake, and Garnsey Wash (enlargement of BLM-ARS series; date 09-30-73; image 7-51-21; original negative scale 1:31,680). a, Garnsey Spring campsite; b, pictograph rockshelter; c, Garnsey Bison Kill; d, "Garza" hearth.

Fig. 4. Low altitude aerial view of Garnsey Wash (foreground) and Pecos Valley (background). Photographer facing west. a, excavation of bison processing areas at Garnsey Bison Kill; b, spring; c, pictograph rockshelter; d, Trench A (western 4-m^2 block) at Garnsey Spring campsite; e, "Garza" hearth. Photo taken July 1978.

Fig. 5. Low altitude aerial view of Garnsey Spring campsite. Photographer facing west. Left arrow, pictograph rockshelter; Right arrow, Trench A (western 4-m^2 block). Photo taken July 1978.

The channel of Spring Draw is usually dry, but water occasionally runs through it after spring and late summer downpours. After a flood, water seldom stands in the channel for more than a few hours before being absorbed into small sinkholes and solution cavities that abound in the underlying gypsum bedrock (Permian Artesia Group; see V. Kelley 1971). Spring Draw enters the Garnsey Wash about 130 m south of the campsite. Located at the junction of the two channels is a perennial spring which seeps from a low bedrock outcrop in the floor of the wash, providing a permanent source of water (Fig. 7). Today the relatively saline water is suitable only for cattle, but prior to recent lowering of the water table and extensive overgrazing the spring probably provided an important source of fresh water. The section of the Garnsey Wash downstream from the spring has been described in detail in Speth and Parry (1980) and Speth (1983).

Fig. 6. Low altitude aerial view of Garnsey Bison Kill. Photographer facing southeast. Center, main excavation in bison processing areas on floor of Garnsey Wash; Left arrow (black), "Garza" hearth on south bank of wash; Right arrow (white), location of pollen section (see Chapter 9). Photo taken July 1978.

Local Vegetation

Modern vegetation on the site consists predominantly of grasses, especially black grama (*Bouteloua eriopoda*) and tobosa (*Hilaria mutica*), broken by patches of snakeweed (*Gutierrezia sarothrae*). A variety of shrubs, including honey mesquite (*Prosopis juliflora*), four-wing saltbush (*Atriplex canescens*), apache plume (*Fallugia paradoxa*), prickly pear (*Opuntia* spp.), and yucca (*Yucca* spp.) dot the landscape, and dense stands of sacaton grass (*Sporobolus airoides*) grow in the bottoms of adjacent draws. Small stands of salt cedar (*Tamarix pentandra*) occur throughout the Garnsey Wash.

Fig. 7. Spring on floor of Spring Draw near junction with Garnsey Wash. Photographer facing northeast.

Local Climate

The climate of the area today is semiarid. Roswell receives approximately 295 mm (11.62 in) of rain annually (Houghton 1974:802). Winters are relatively dry, with the entire time from November through March accounting for only 58 mm (2.28 in). Therefore over 80% (237 mm or 9.34 in) of the average annual precipitation occurs during the seven months from April through October. The rains come in two distinct periods, the first in May followed by a slight decline in June. The principal rainy season occurs in July, August, and September. These three months average approximately 132 mm (5.21 in), or nearly 45% of the annual rainfall. These late-summer rains generally come in the form of afternoon and evening thunderstorms, noteworthy for their great variability in intensity, frequency, and spatial occurrence. Hail may also occur.

The average annual precipitation values in southeastern New Mexico and the Southern High Plains do not differ greatly from values recorded in many parts of the Southwest or in the Central and Northern High Plains (see Court 1974: his Fig. 11). Looked at more closely, however, there are certain aspects of the precipitation pattern in the Southern High Plains that differ from those in surrounding areas and that may have been very important to human groups utilizing the region. First, a lower proportion of the total annual precipitation falls during the winter months in southeastern New Mexico than in other areas of the

Southwest, and peak summer rainfall comes somewhat later in the season. Second, the average ratio of median precipitation to mean precipitation in the Southern High Plains (less than 75%) more closely resembles values in southern Arizona and the Great Basin than values on the Colorado Plateau or in the Central or Northern Plains (Court 1974:212). Finally, the coefficient of variation of annual precipitation for the period 1931-60 (over 40%) is higher than anywhere else in the Southwest or Plains (Court 1974:211).

Summers in Roswell are warm. Average daily maxima exceed 32°C (90°F) from June through August. Daytime highs above 38°C (100°F) are common. Winters are mild. The average daily high, even in January, the coldest month, is about 13°C (55°F). Average minimum daily temperatures drop below freezing from mid-November through mid-March, but temperatures rarely reach -18°C (0°F). The average length of the frost-free season is 206 days, from 7 April through 30 October (Von Eschen 1961:51).

The Site

Cultural materials (including burned rock, chipped stone, and pottery sherds) are presently exposed on the surface of the terrace over an area of more than 20,000 m^2. However, most material is confined within a relatively narrow zone along the southern edge of the terrace (an area of about 5200 m^2; see Fig. 8).

When we began work at the campsite, relatively little recent disturbance was obvious, but the site was well known to local collectors and had been surface-collected for many years. It was especially known locally as a place where projectile points could be found in abundance. One Roswell collection that we examined and photographed contained over 50 more or less complete specimens, and other collections from LA-18400 undoubtedly exist. In addition to picking up artifacts on the surface of the site after rains, collectors were observed scraping the surface deposits with small garden trowels and passing the sediment through screens. Despite years of heavy collecting, points and other artifacts are still exposed after each rain.

The bias introduced by collecting activities is hard to assess. It is possible, for example, that the notable scarcity of ground stone artifacts is due to their removal by collectors rather than a reflection of the nature of prehistoric subsistence activities at the site. (The authors on several occasions were shown piles of grinding stones, manos, and metates incorporated into collectors' backyard rockgardens that had been systematically culled from local prehistoric sites.) Clearly, collector-produced bias has to be kept in mind when evaluating surface collections from sites in southeastern New Mexico. We were shown several sites, including one small pueblo, where continued heavy collecting had reduced surface visibility to zero, and we suspect that many ceramic-bearing late prehistoric campsites in the region have been transformed by selective collecting into "Archaic" flake scatters.

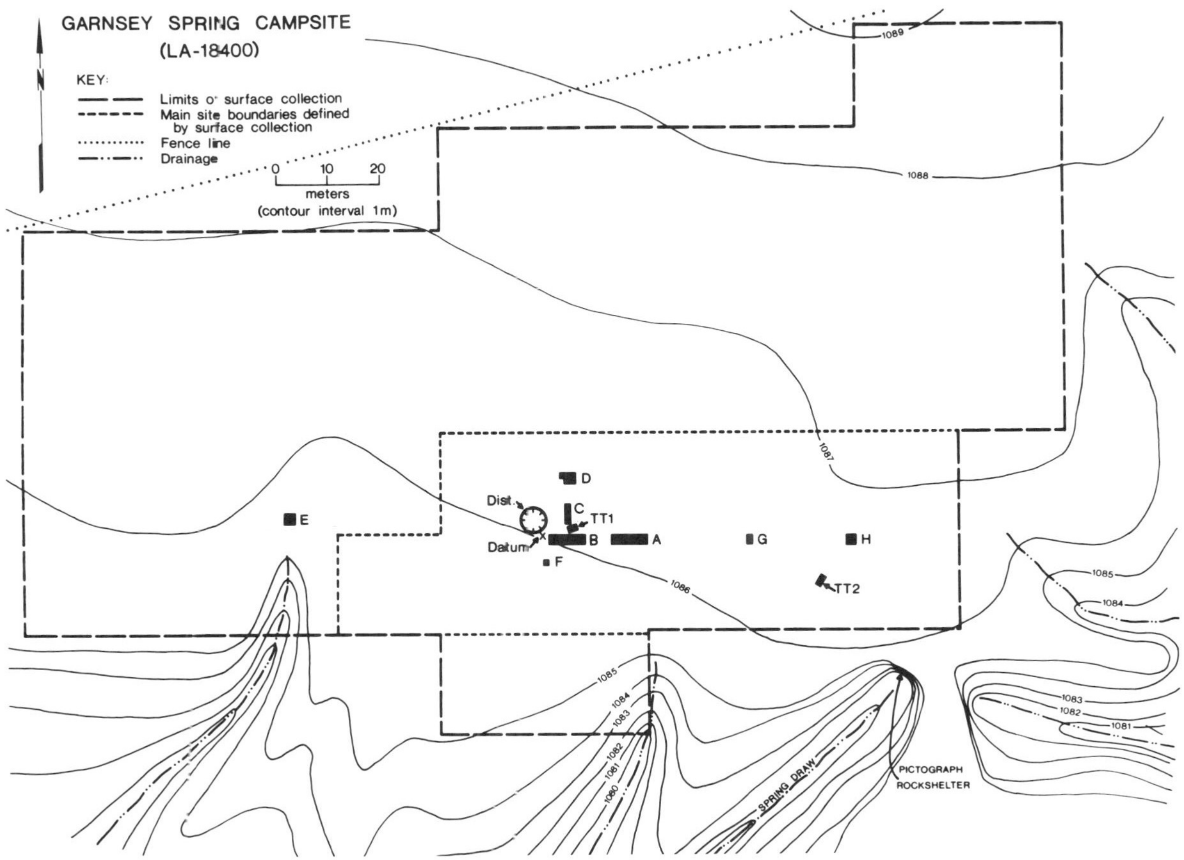

Fig. 8. Contour map of Garnsey Spring campsite, showing location of principal excavation units. TT1 and TT2, 1977 test trenches; A-H, 1978 excavation units.

Despite collector disturbance at LA-18400, we decided that the most efficient method of determining approximate site boundaries and delineating subsurface distributions of material was to systematically surface-collect the entire site area. This has also reduced site visibility, at least temporarily, and may help to decrease the level of vandalism.

We gridded the entire site into 20 x 20 m squares and collected all artifacts visible on the surface (see Fig. 9). Limits of the grid system correspond to the absolute limit of artifact scatter as determined by a quick preliminary survey. We found it necessary to use relatively large grid units, owing to limitations of time and personnel available for this phase of work.

The surface distribution of debitage is presented in Figure 10. Density contours for debitage were interpolated from grid counts using the SURFACE II computer graphics program (Sampson 1975). Most debitage tends to be concentrated in a relatively narrow band along the southern margin of the terrace. A second small concentration occurs at the extreme eastern margin of the site. Site boundaries have been arbitrarily drawn at the point where the density of debitage on the surface falls below 10 pieces per 100 m^2. The site limits defined in this manner enclose an area of about 5200 m^2, which includes nearly 70% of the artifacts recovered from the surface.

The spatial patterning of artifacts both within and beyond the boundaries established in this manner are shown in Figure 11a-f. Interpretation of these surface distributions is hampered by the large size of our sampling units, and especially by the small number of finished tools and other diagnostics remaining on the surface after years of amateur collecting.

The spatial distribution of most artifact classes parallels that of debitage. Highest concentrations of items are found in the south and taper off to the north and northeast. There are several minor deviations from this general pattern, however. Projectile point fragments, for example, tend to be concentrated in the southeastern part of the site, east of the area of preserved midden deposits. Cores, on the other hand, are concentrated around the midden in the southwestern part of the site. The distributions of both points and cores extend beyond the area in which flakes are concentrated, and nearly 35% of the cores occur in areas of low debitage density on the northern margins of the site. It is curious that the distribution of cores should differ from that of debitage.

Unfortunately, although these spatial data do reveal some degree of internal site patterning, they are inadequate to permit a more detailed investigation of their temporal or functional significance. As will become more apparent below, we encountered similar difficulties with the excavated sample, owing to extensive disturbance of what we had anticipated were in situ midden deposits.

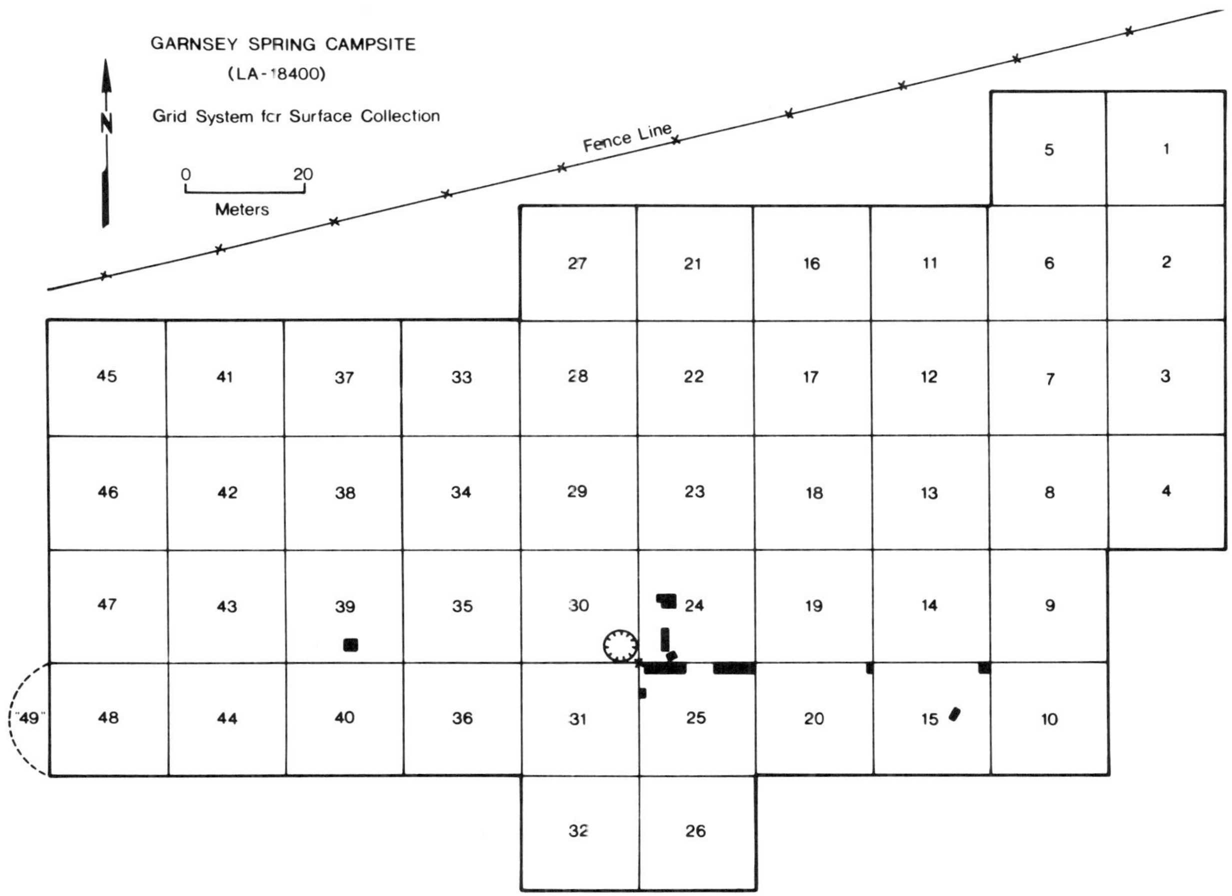

Fig. 9. Grid system used to surface collect Garnsey Spring campsite (each grid unit 20 x 20 m; units numbered sequentially from 1 to 49).

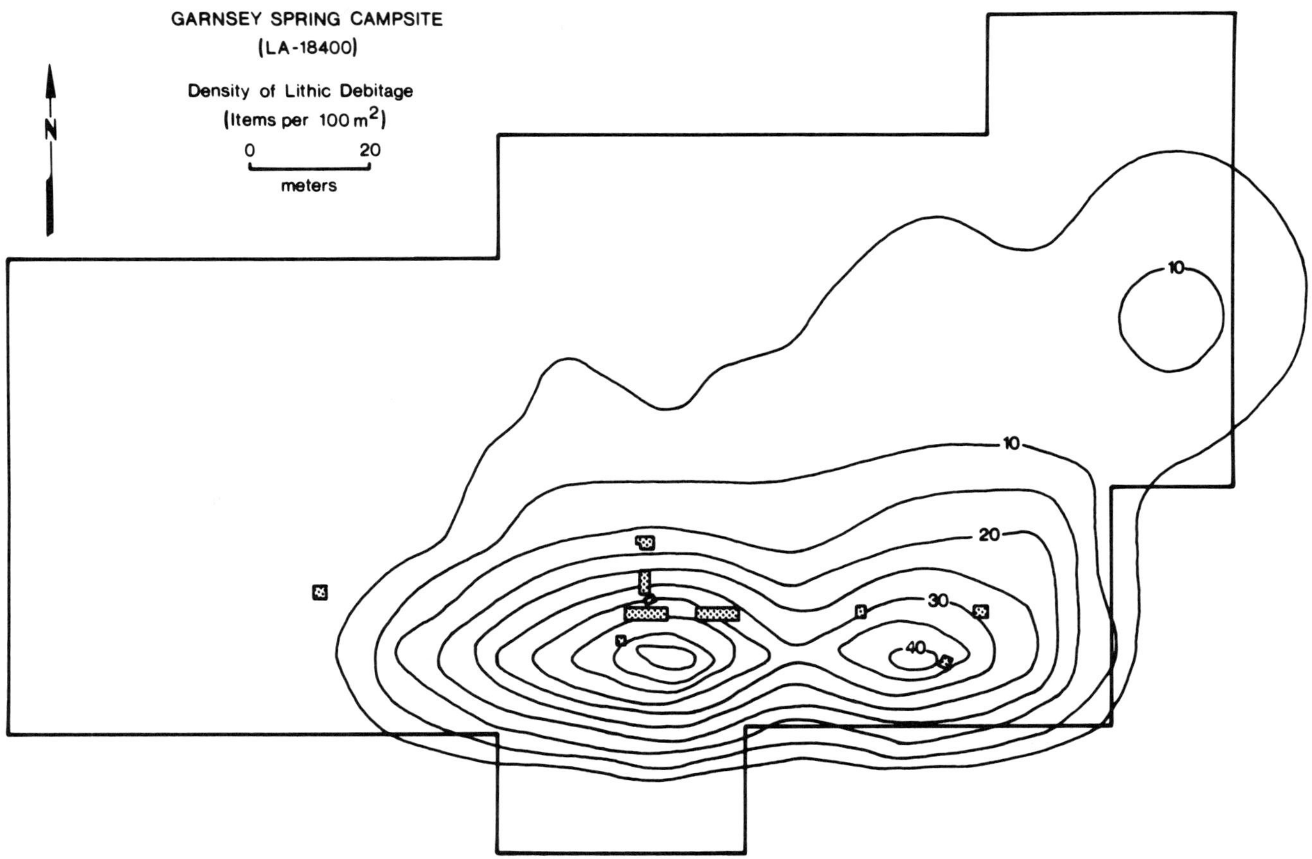

Fig. 10. Surface density of lithic debitage at Garnsey Spring campsite (excavation units indicated by stippling; contour interval 5 items per 100 m^2)

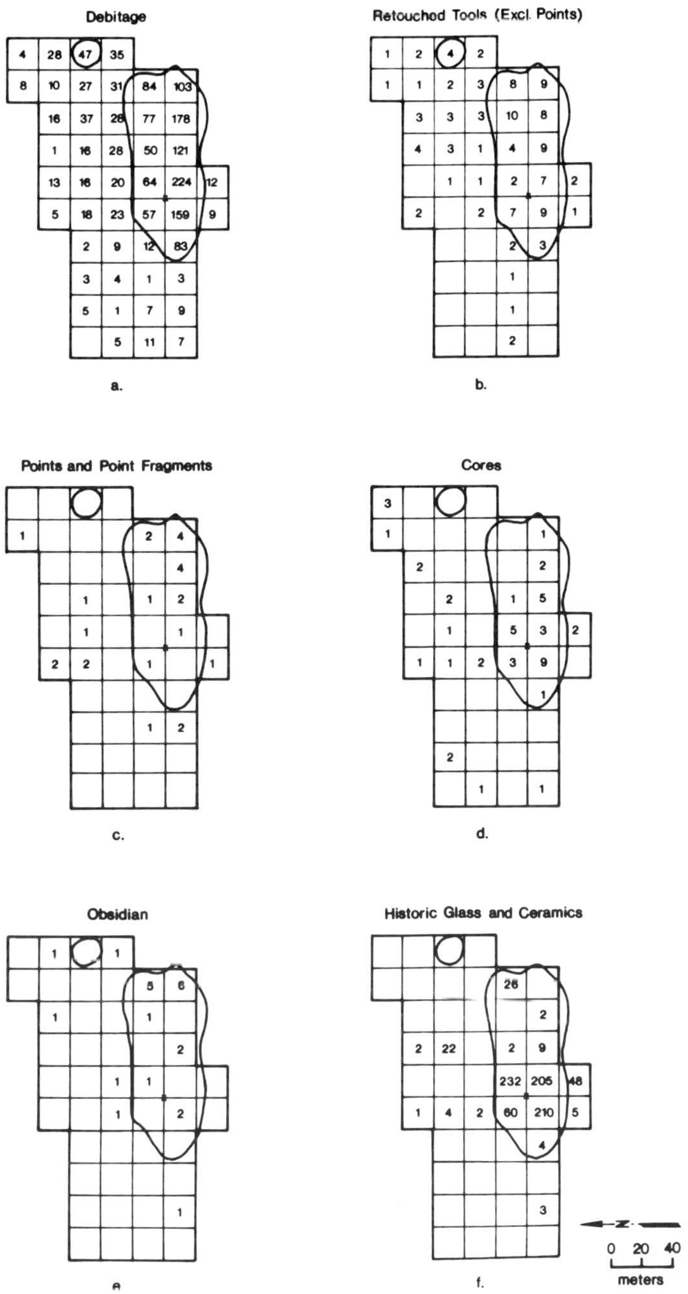

Fig. 11. Distribution of major artifact classes by 20-m grid units on surface of Garnsey Spring campsite (areas encircled by solid line have 10 or more pieces of lithic debitage per 100 m^2; "x" denotes 500N520W datum).

In addition to prehistoric remains, the surface of the site in the vicinity of the datum is littered with modern glass and china sherds, as well as a few scraps of hardware, rusted metal cans, and nails (see Fig. 11f). These fragments cover an area of about 400 m^2, concentrated immediately to the south and east of the datum, and reflect a brief occupation of the site during the early 20th century. Structures erected during this occupation appear to have been relatively insubstantial and constructed entirely above ground, resulting in no significant subsurface disturbance. The only subsurface disturbance that may relate to this occupation is a small pit just west of the datum.

Additional evidence of prehistoric and aboriginal historic utilization of the site area is provided by a series of incised and painted pictographs within a small overhang at the southeastern corner of the site (Figs. 12-16). This "rockshelter" was formed by headward erosion of Spring Draw, which has cut back into the soft gypsum bedrock. The roof of the "rockshelter", which covers an area of about 12 m^2, is formed by firmly cemented, tan alluvial sediment ("caliche") that overlies bedrock at this location. The pictographs are found on a flat, relatively unweathered slab of gypsum in the northwest wall of the shelter. The first two pictographs (from southwest to northeast) are abstract anthropomorphic figures, formed by rectilinear incising. Both have their appendages highlighted by red paint, and the interior of the second is filled in with black paint (Fig. 14). Then follow three human "stick" figures, also formed by rectilinear incising with appendages in red (the first two are not illustrated; the third may be seen in Fig. 15). The middle figure appears to be holding a tall decorated staff in each hand. Unfortunately, these figures have been badly damaged by recent vandalism. Superimposed over the last figure is an abstract incised horse (Figs. 15 and 16), carved in heavier lines than the other figures. There is no evidence that paint was used to highlight the features of the horse. No cultural remains other than the pictographs were observed in the shelter, and the nature of the floor (consisting of a jumble of gypsum blocks) would seem to preclude habitation under the overhang.

Fig. 12. View of pictograph rockshelter at head of Spring Draw. Photographer facing east-northeast. Pictographs on left (northwest) wall of shelter.

Fig. 13. Interior of pictograph rockshelter. Pictograph panel on rock wall to left (arrow).

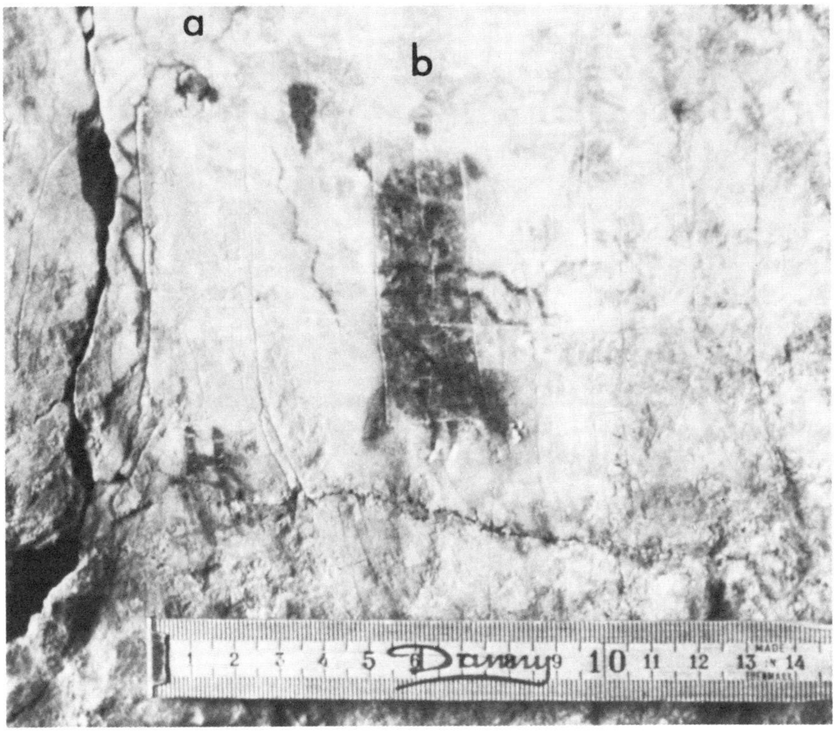

Fig. 14. Anthropomorphic figures, formed by incising and painting. a, appendages highlighted by red paint; b, appendages highlighted by red paint and interior filled with black paint.

Fig. 15. Incised horse superimposed over incised human figure.

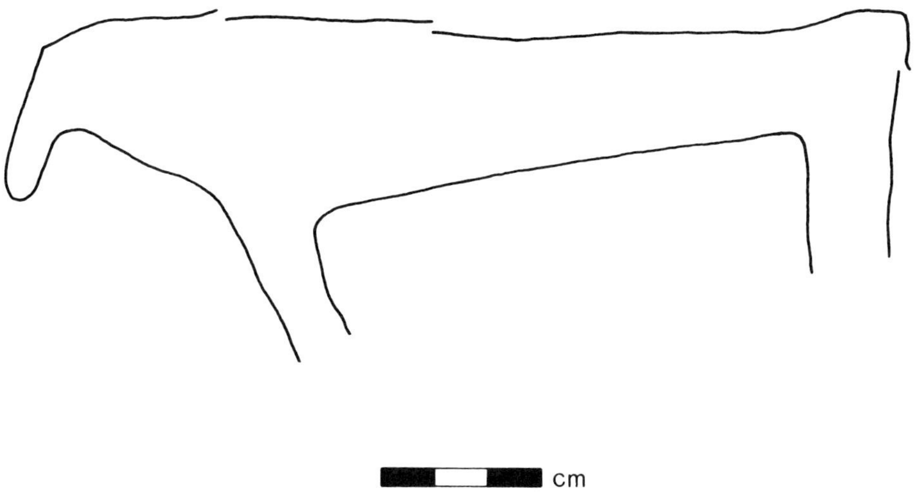

Fig. 16. Line drawing of incised horse (see Fig. 15).

3. EXCAVATION PROCEDURE

The Garnsey Spring campsite was first visited by the authors in the summer of 1977 during excavations at the nearby Garnsey Bison Kill. At the time of that visit a small side-notched triangular arrow point (Washita point) was discovered on the surface. The close proximity of the site to the bison kill, and the presence of Washita points at both sites, led us to speculate that the campsite might represent a processing station directly associated with the bison kill.

Subsequently, two small (2 x 1 m) test units (TT1 and TT2) were opened at the campsite to inspect the stratigraphy and to assess the preservation of organic remains in the deposits (Fig. 8). The first unit (TT1) was placed adjacent to the small 20th-century pit that had exposed at least 30 cm of ash-rich deposits. Excavation of this test unit confirmed the presence of deposits of some depth, but the lack of visible stratigraphy, evidence of extensive rodent disturbance, and the wide variety of point and ceramic types, warned us of the complexity of the site. We were encouraged, however, by the abundance of wood charcoal and bone fragments in the ashy matrix, suggesting relatively good organic preservation. Bone fragments included one identifiable bison bone and several small fragments of burned large mammal bone, further suggesting that the site might represent a bison processing station associated with the kill. Later excavations indicated that Test Trench 1 was anomalous, as no other excavation unit produced a comparable density of organic remains.

Test Trench 2 was located in the eastern half of the site in a relatively dense surface concentration of chippage, near the spot where the Washita point had been found. This part of the site proved to be completely deflated and no subsurface remains were encountered.

On the basis of the results of Test Trench 1, we decided that more extensive testing of the site was warranted, and we returned in the summer of 1978. Excavations were undertaken by a crew of three persons between 30 June and 10 August. During that interval eight noncontiguous test units, totaling 48 m^2, were opened. Excavations in both seasons totaled 52 m^2, representing only about 1% of the site area.

The 1978 test excavations were directed toward three primary objectives. These were to further assess the nature and condition of the deposits; to obtain adequate cultural material in association with charcoal to permit the establishment of a firm chronological framework for the site; and to recover a sample of floral and faunal remains adequate to determine the nature of subsistence activities at the site and the seasonality of occupation. With this information we hoped to assess the relationship between the campsite and the bison kill, and to expand our general knowledge of late prehistoric subsistence-settlement systems in the area. If the site proved reasonably intact, we anticipated conducting excavations on a larger scale in the future to investigate the spatial patterning and association of cultural materials and features.

The 1978 excavations themselves were not focused specifically on problems of spatial patterning, so no effort was made to employ a random sampling strategy. Instead, excavations were concentrated in areas that appeared to have relatively deep deposits, dense concentrations of artifacts, and good potential for organic preservation. Unfortunately, owing to the absence of clear-cut stratigraphy, heavy disturbance of the deposits, the scarcity of cultural features such as pits and hearths, and poor preservation of organic remains, adequate samples were not obtained and no additional excavations were undertaken. Given our primary commitment to the bison kill, we did not open any large-scale trenches at the site with a backhoe, a procedure that might still prove productive in the future.

All excavations at the campsite were gridded in 1-m units. During the 1978 excavations the site was gridded in a north-south direction, using a base line oriented to magnetic north. The datum point was arbitrarily designated as the northeastern corner of square 500N520W, and all other squares were numbered from this reference point. The two test units opened in 1977 were excavated prior to establishment of the grid system and have been designated simply as TT1 and TT2 (see Fig. 8).

Due to the lack of visible stratification in the cultural deposits, excavation proceeded by arbitrary horizontal 5 cm levels. Diagnostic artifacts found in situ were mapped in place, providing additional stratigraphic control. All excavated sediment was screened through 1/4 inch mesh. In addition, numerous matrix samples were processed by flotation and screened through 1/16 inch mesh to recover smaller faunal and floral remains (see Chapter 6). With the exception of two deeper tests, excavation was terminated at the contact with the sterile subsoil.

4. STRATIGRAPHY AND CHRONOLOGY

The campsite and surrounding area are underlain by gypsum and siltstone bedrock of the Permian Artesia Group (V. Kelley 1971). Bedrock is exposed at the surface over most of the western and northern portions of the site. In the eastern half, bedrock is overlain by culturally sterile, firmly cemented tan alluvial silts ("caliche") of probable pre-Holocene age. These deposits attain a maximum thickness of 4 m in the vicinity of the pictograph rockshelter at the southeastern edge of the site. These silts form the present surface over most of the eastern part of the site.

Intact midden deposits seem to be confined to an area about 30 m in diameter immediately east of datum in the central part of the site. These deposits, which overlie the sterile alluvial silts, average 20-30 cm in thickness and consist of gray-brown colluvium with ash, charcoal, scattered burned rocks, and a variety of artifacts. In a few places the midden is capped by up to 10 cm of sterile brown colluvium. Typical sections through the midden are illustrated in Figure 17. Excavations were concentrated in this portion of the site, as this apparently is the only area that preserves in situ cultural material. All other areas of the site that we tested were completely deflated and produced no subsurface remains.

No stratigraphy could be discerned within these midden deposits, neither during the course of excavation nor upon subsequent examination of exposed profiles. The contact between the gray-brown midden sediments and the underlying tan sterile silts, however, was easily recognizable. Innumerable rodent tunnels and dens were obvious below the contact but none could be traced into the overlying midden where many undoubtedly originated. As a result of this heavy disturbance, the contact between the two layers was extremely irregular. Although the dens and tunnels were no longer visible, the midden clearly had been churned by burrowing animals.

Trampling by humans or large herbivores probably has also disturbed the midden deposits. Experiments have shown that trampling of unconsolidated sediments, such as those of the campsite midden, can cause dramatic vertical movement of artifacts (Stockton 1973; Cahen and Moeyersons 1977).

Analysis of vertical distributions of artifacts from the campsite midden provide clear evidence of disturbance. One indication is the presence of several early 20th-century artifacts at depths up to 30 cm below the present surface. In addition, sherds from single prehistoric vessels were often spread over a range of depths, including two conjoinable sherds from a St. Johns Polychrome bowl that were separated vertically by more than 15 cm, and other sherds (not conjoinable, but probably from the same bowl) that were separated by up to 25 cm. Furthermore, the vertical distributions of different types of artifact bore little, if any, discernible relation to their presumed

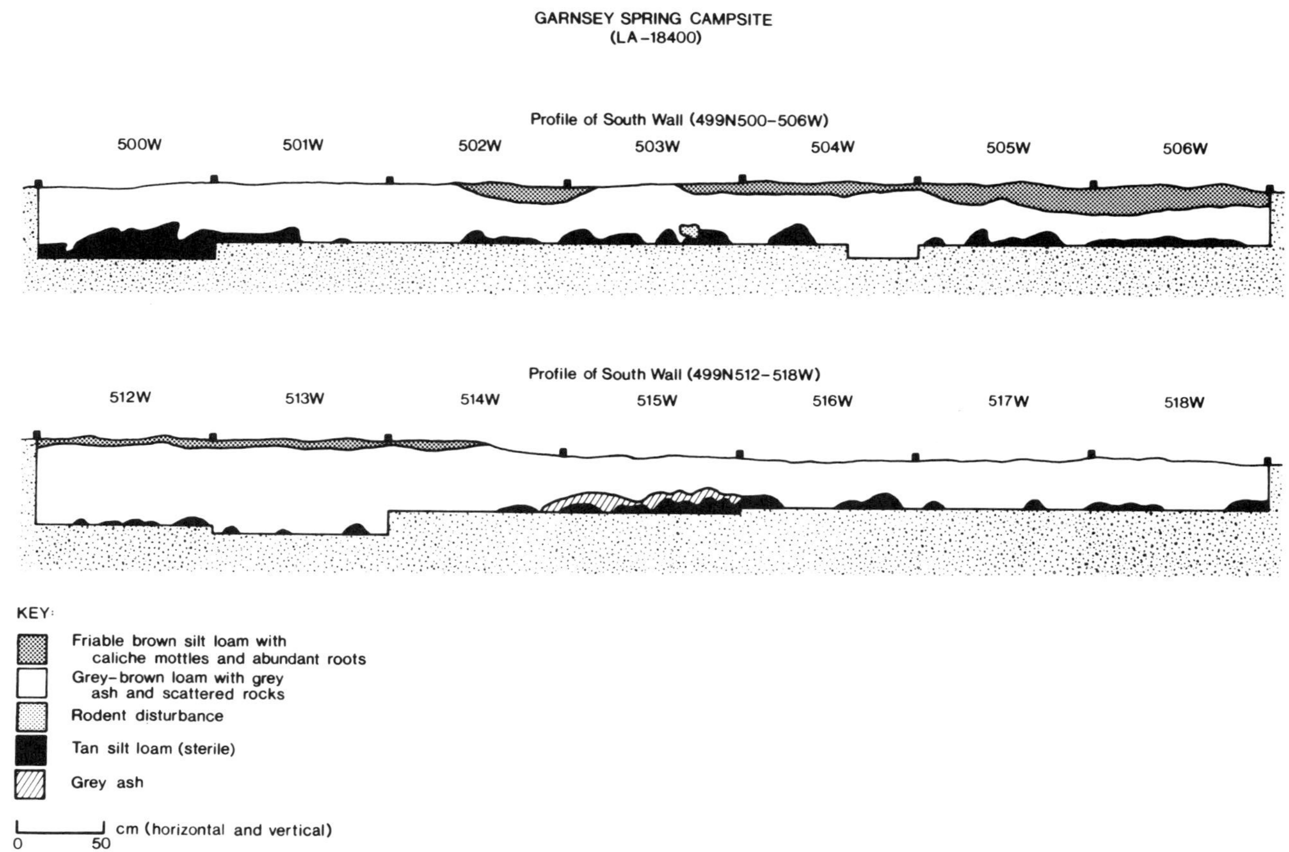

Fig. 17. East-west stratigraphic sections of principal campsite midden deposits. Upper diagram, Trench A; Lower diagram, Trench B (see Fig. 8 for location of trenches).

chronological placements. Virtually all classes of artifact were found in all levels of the midden. In almost every case, regardless of artifact type or age, specimens were found in highest concentration in the shallowest level, and decreased in density with depth (Fig. 18).

Stockton (1973) obtained a similar vertical distribution of specimens experimentally in an attempt to simulate the effects of trampling. In his experiment sherds of red glass were spread out on a level sandy surface and covered with 5 cm of sand. The deposits were then indiscriminately trampled for a day and excavated by 2-3 cm levels (Stockton 1973:116). Glass fragments had penetrated to a depth of 16 cm, well below the zone that was visibly churned. Stockton observed both upward and downward migration of fragments. The density of fragments decreased rapidly with depth below the original surface on which the fragments had been placed (Fig. 19).

We devised a simple computer simulation to further investigate the downward displacement of artifacts that might be produced by trampling. The assumptions underlying this simulation were that:

(1) all items initially rested on a single surface;

(2) each item moved once;

(3) the distance each item moved was a random number between 0 and 40 cm (40 cm below modern surface is the maximum depth at which artifacts were observed in the excavated units at the campsite);

(4) each item moved downward at a randomly selected angle to the surface between 0° (horizontal) and 90° (vertical).

The simulation was run twice, with 200 items per run. Generation of random numbers and subsequent trigonometric calculations of net vertical movement were carried out using MIDAS, a data analysis program of the Statistical Research Laboratory of the University of Michigan (Fox and Guire 1976). The resulting distribution of items for each run is presented in Figure 20. Comparison of Figures 18, 19, and 20 shows that the vertical distribution of items generated by the computer simulation corresponds fairly closely to distributions observed in Stockton's experiments and at the Garnsey Spring campsite. These results are compatible with the suggestion that the vertical distribution of objects at the campsite may be largely the result of random downward displacement of artifacts from one or more surfaces due to trampling and other types of disturbance.

In reality, the situation at the campsite is probably more complex. Two radiocarbon samples, consisting of pooled charcoal fragments from two different arbitrary stratigraphic levels in the midden yielded substantially different dates that are in proper stratigraphic order (see below). In addition, two intact cultural features were recovered in the basal level of the midden (Chapter 5). As these features could not have migrated downward, it is clear that the vertical distribution of material in the site cannot be accounted for entirely by random

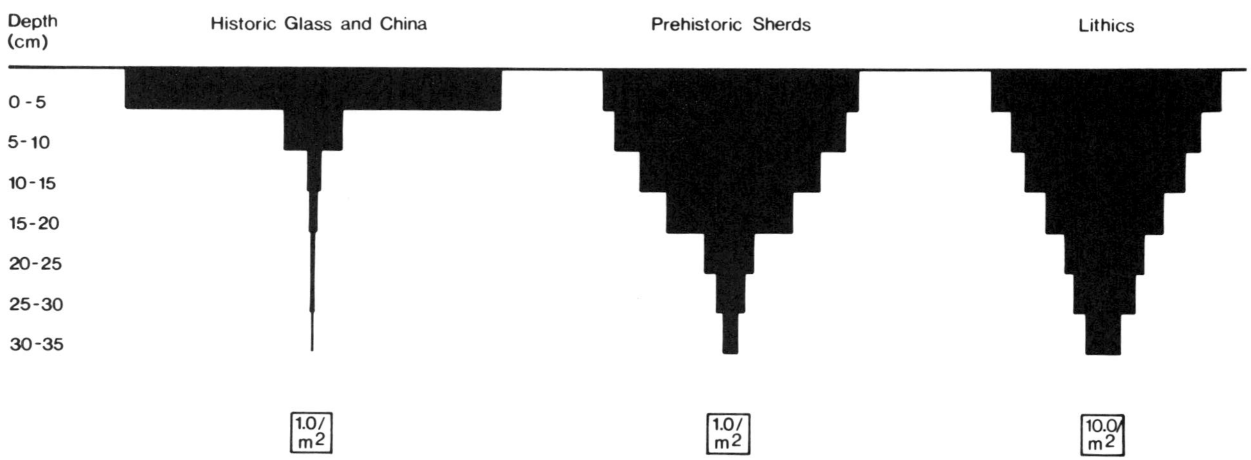

Fig. 18. Vertical distribution of historic and prehistoric materials at Garnsey Spring campsite.

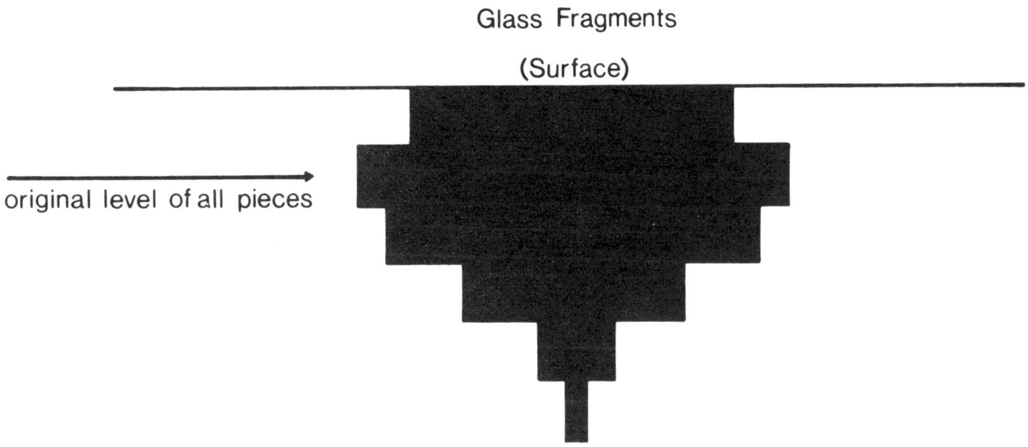

Fig. 19. Vertical distribution of glass fragments in experimental study of trampling (after Stockton 1973).

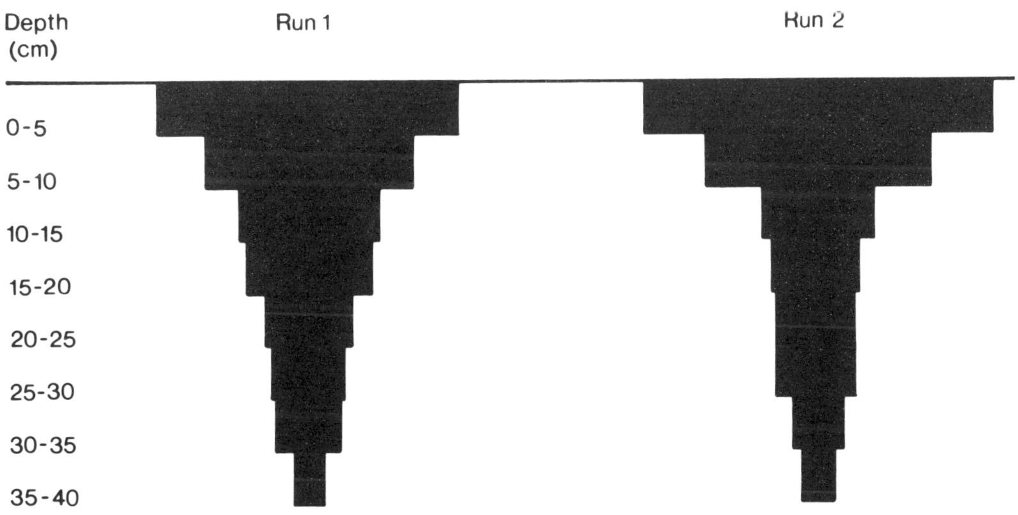

Fig. 20. Hypothetical vertical distribution of artifacts generated by computer simulation of trampling (2 runs).

downward displacement. However, disturbance and movement of artifacts probably has been sufficient to obscure most stratigraphic relationships within the site.

During the preliminary small-scale testing of the campsite in 1977, we encountered no in situ datable cultural features with associated diagnostic artifacts. Thus, to obtain some indication of the age of the midden deposits, we pooled the largest pieces of wood charcoal in each arbitrary stratigraphic level in Test Trench 1 and submitted two of these samples to Geochron Laboratories (Cambridge, Mass.) for radiocarbon dating. Prior to submission, approximately 20% of each sample was examined and identified; only mesquite (*Prosopis* sp.), a C_3 plant, was present in the analyzed portions (Syvertsen et al. 1976; Eickmeier 1978). As a consequence, the dates were not corrected for ^{13}C fractionation. Subsequent charcoal analyses at the campsite revealed that four-wing saltbush (*Atriplex canescens*), a C_4 plant, occurred in virtually every sample (see Appendix B) and therefore may have been present in the radiocarbon samples from Test Trench 1. If so, the resulting dates, uncorrected for carbon isotope fractionation, may be too young by as much as a century or more.

At the time we submitted the samples, we did not fully appreciate the extent to which the midden had been disturbed. Given the apparent homogeneity of the deposits, we expected the dates from two directly superposed arbitrary levels to yield more or less comparable results. However, as Table 1 shows, this was not the case. The dates are in proper stratigraphic order, but the means differ by more than half a millennium (note, however, that the ages nearly overlap at two standard deviations).

In hindsight, the two dates from TT1 are unreliable and should best be ignored. The fact that they are in proper stratigraphic order does offer some encouragement that the midden may not be totally churned. But the absolute values of the dates may be averages of older and younger pieces of charcoal that have been pooled into the same composite sample.

In 1983 we decided to submit two additional samples for radiocarbon dating to help clarify the chronology of the site. The first sample consisted of chunks of wood charcoal (mostly four-wing saltbush, *Atriplex canescens*) collected in 1978 from the east half of Feature 4, a basin-shaped hearth at the base of the midden in square 512N515W (see Chapter 5). This hearth, unfortunately, had no diagnostic artifacts in direct association, but its contents were undisturbed and its stratigraphic position suggested that it might provide a reliable date for the early phase of occupation at the campsite. With correction for carbon isotope fractionation, a necessary step because four-wing saltbush is a C_4 plant (Syvertsen et al. 1976; Eickmeier 1978; Downton 1975), the date from Feature 4 is A.D. 850±40 (A.D. 885±55 with MASCA correction). This value is surprisingly similar to the date obtained previously from the lower part of the midden in TT1 (Table 1).

A second wood charcoal sample comes from an isolated, shallow, basin-shaped hearth ("Garza" hearth) exposed at the surface on the left or south bank of the Garnsey Wash, directly across the wash from the campsite (see Figs. 2, 3, 4 and 6). A total of 15 lithic artifacts were collected from the surface within a radius of about 2 m around the hearth. No archaeological materials were visible on the surface beyond this zone. Nine of the specimens were tools, including 2 chert arrow point fragments (1 Garza point and another small, unidentifiable specimen), 2 chert scrapers, 1 sandstone scraper, 1 chert retouched flake, and 3 chert utilized flakes. With the exception of the points, all tools have steep edges (mean edge angle, 71°; range, 50°-100°). The remaining 6 artifacts are unmodified flakes (4 chert and 2 quartzite). No fire-cracked rocks, animal bones or pottery were present. A very limited range of activities is suggested by the small assemblage of mostly finished tools.

Although the association between hearth and Garza point is less than ideal, the sample was run in order to provide an age estimate for this highly distinctive point type and to bracket the most recent aboriginal use of the campsite area. The wood charcoal was not identified prior to submission of the sample. However, in the event that saltbush or other C_4 species were present in the sample, the date was corrected for ^{13}C fractionation (Table 1). With MASCA correction, two different ages are possible (A.D. 1470-1520 or A.D. 1640). Both placements are plausible on the basis of available information. A more recent calibration scheme developed by Stuiver (1982) eliminates the earlier age range and suggests a date of about A.D. 1640±50. Another recent but more conservative calibration scheme presented by Klein et al. (1982) places the date between A.D. 1480 and A.D. 1666. The campsite Garza date is very similar to two dates reported by Johnson et al. (1977) from levels containing Garza points at the Lubbock Lake site in the Texas Panhandle (A.D. 1635±50 and A.D. 1665±60). Taken as a group, the campsite and Lubbock Lake dates suggest that the most likely temporal placement of the Garza point is within the protohistoric period, although a slightly earlier appearance cannot be ruled out.

Owing to the lack of reliable stratigraphic and chronometric control, the chronology of the prehistoric materials at the site must be inferred through typological comparisons of artifacts with materials from other sites in the region. Unfortunately, such comparisons are severely hampered at present by the general lack of dated materials from Roswell and elsewhere in southeastern New Mexico and the Texas High Plains.

The ceramics from the campsite have been analyzed by Wiseman (Chapter 8, this volume) and compared with dendrochronologically dated materials from sites to the west. On the basis of these comparisons, Wiseman suggests that several occupations are represented within the interval A.D. 900-1400. Recent discoveries of brownware ceramics dating early within the first millennium A.D. in the El Paso area (Whalen 1978:60; 1981) and in the Texas Panhandle (Willey and Hughes 1978) open the possibility that some of the campsite brownwares also substantially predate A.D. 900. This seems unlikely, however, given the radiocarbon date from Feature 4 at the base of the midden.

Table 1
Radiocarbon dates from Garnsey Spring campsite

Provenience	Lab.[1] No.	Age[2] (±1 S.D.)		^{13}C Fractionation[3]	Age[4] (±1 S.D.)	MASCA[5] Corrected Age Range (±1 S.D.)
		B.P.	A.D.			
TT1 (5-10 cm)	GX-5100	660±125	1290±125	n.a.[6]	--	A.D. 1290±100
TT1 (10-25 cm)	GX-5101	1205±120	745±120	n.a.[6]	--	A.D. 775±135
512N515W (Feat. 4)	Beta-6605	930± 40	1020± 40	-14.89	A.D. 850±40	A.D. 885± 55
"Garza" Hearth	Beta-6693	320± 50	1630± 50	-27.87	A.D. 1670±50	A.D. 1470-1520; A.D. 1640

[1] GX, Geochron Laboratories, Cambridge, Mass.; Beta, Beta Analytic Inc., Coral Gables, Fla.
[2] Old (Libby) half-life (5568 years); not corrected for ^{13}C fractionation; age referenced to A.D. 1950.
[3] Carbon isotope fractionation values (per mil) measured relative to PDB standard.
[4] Corrected for ^{13}C fractionation; old half-life (5568 years).
[5] Determined according to procedures in Ralph et al. (1973); new half-life (5730 years).
[6] n.a., not analyzed.

A variety of projectile point types was recovered from the campsite (Chapter 7). One of the most common forms is a broadly corner-notched, expanding stemmed dart point with convex base (see Figs. 28 and 32 below). These points resemble Leslie's "Carlsbad" type (Type 8-D), which he attributes to the local Late Archaic (preceramic or aceramic) period and tentatively places sometime prior to A.D. 950 (Leslie 1977:133). Unfortunately, since no absolute dates are available for the Carlsbad point, this placement must be regarded as tentative.

Other point types from the campsite reflect ceramic period occupations (i.e., post-A.D. 900). Among these, the Washita point, with notches relatively low on the blade and concave base, is the most common form (see Bell 1958). Variants of the Washita point become extremely common in the Southern Plains and Southwest after about A.D. 1200, and persist into the aboriginal historic period (Johnson et al. 1977).

Interestingly, no triple-notched Harrell points (Bell 1958) were recovered in our excavations at the campsite, nor were any observed in the collection from the site made by a Roswell amateur. In contrast, at least two are included in the small sample of points from the nearby bison kill (Speth 1983), and Harrells are commonplace in amateur collections from other late prehistoric sites in the area. Their absence at the campsite points to a possible period of nonuse of the locality and further decreases the likelihood that the campsite and kill are functionally related.

Given the absence of Harrell points at the campsite, their dating becomes of considerable interest. Unfortunately, the chronological placement of the Harrell is controversial. Harrell-like points are found over a vast area of interior North America, extending from the Northern Plains in Canada to the Central Highlands of Mexico and from the Mississippi Valley to California. In the eastern part of this range, the Harrell may be very early. For example, at Cahokia in Illinois, triple-notched points resembling Harrells (Cahokia points) appear by about A.D. 900-1000 (Fowler and Hall 1975; Perino 1968). In the Northwestern Plains, by contrast, triple-notched points are late, not appearing until the very late prehistoric or protohistoric period (Reher and Frison 1980).

The Harrell point also appears to be relatively late in southeastern New Mexico and the Texas High Plains. For example, excavation by one of us (JDS) at the Henderson Site, a small pueblo just southwest of Roswell (Fig. 1), has produced over 300 arrow points. The vast majority of these are Washitas. Only 1 point is triple-notched, and it was found in surficial deposits. On the basis of ceramics, and a series of radiocarbon and archaeomagnetic dates (unpublished), the Henderson pueblo dates between A.D. 1200 or 1250 and 1400. The Harrell point, therefore, presumably postdates the occupation of this village.

The Garnsey Bison Kill, which lies directly east of the pueblo on the opposite side of the Pecos Valley, yielded both Washita and Harrell points and is dated on the basis of more than a dozen radiocarbon dates to about A.D. 1450-1500 (Speth 1983).

Triple-notched points first make their appearance in extreme southeastern New Mexico in the latter part of the Ochoa period (Robert Leslie, personal communication). While not yet firmly dated, the Ochoa appears to be a relatively late phenomenon, probably developing after A.D. 1300. Harrell points therefore probably do not make their appearance until about A.D. 1400 or later.

Harrell points are common on sites in the High Plains region of the Texas Panhandle. They apparently show up for the first time in substantial numbers sometime between about A.D. 1425 and A.D. 1525, based on their association with Rio Grande glazewares C and D at sites such as Tierra Blanca near Hereford, Texas and Blackburn near Canyon, Texas (Spielmann 1982).

On the basis of these observations, we very tentatively suggest that the triple-notched Harrell point in southeastern New Mexico is a late form, not appearing until perhaps A.D. 1400 or slightly later and persisting at least into the protohistoric period, if not longer (see Johnson et al. 1977).

A few Garza points were recovered from the campsite. As discussed earlier, these may first appear in the early 16th century or late 15th century and persist into the protohistoric or early historic period (early to mid-1600s; see discussion above and in Johnson et al. 1977). Historic occupation of the Garnsey Spring campsite is also indicated by the incised figure of a horse in the pictograph rockshelter (see Figs. 15 and 16 above), and by a surface find of a possible aboriginal gunflint in the vicinity of the main excavation units.

In summary, the presence of "Carlsbad" points and a radiocarbon date of A.D. 885±55 (MASCA-corrected) from the base of the midden point to occupation of the Garnsey Spring campsite beginning about A.D. 900 or earlier. The site was utilized, at least intermittently, until about A.D. 1400 and probably again in the 16th or 17th century, following a brief period of nonuse in the fifteenth and early sixteenth century. The period of nonuse is suggested by the absence of triple-notched Harrell points and of Glaze B and later ceramic types (see Wiseman, Chapter 8, this volume). Finally, manufactured items dating to the late 19th and 20th century reflect brief, recent Anglo- or Hispanic-American settlement of the site area.

5. FEATURES

Four prehistoric cultural features were found during excavations at the Garnsey Spring campsite. Two of these (Features 2 and 4) are small basin-shaped hearths, while the other two may be remnants of disturbed roasting features. The "Garza" hearth, a shallow basin-shaped feature located across the Garnsey Wash from the campsite, is also described below.

Feature 1: This feature was located in unit 500N502W, extending into unit 499N502W and possibly also into unit 500N501W. It consisted of an irregular but clearly bounded lens of gray ashy sediment, about 60 cm in diameter, that extended from 5 cm to approximately 9 cm below the modern surface. At the southeastern edge of the lens, and slightly deeper (8-12 cm below modern surface), was a small cluster of seven fire-cracked rock fragments. A single Chupadero Black-on-White sherd and a chert flake were found within the ashy lens.

Feature 2: This feature was located in unit 500N504W, extending slightly into adjacent unit 500N503W. It was a clearly defined circular basin, approximately 30 cm in diameter and 8 cm in depth (Figs. 21 and 22a-b). Feature 2 was first observed in the basal level of the midden, about 29 cm below modern surface, and extended into the underlying sterile subsoil to a maximum depth of 37 cm below surface. The pit contained black ashy fill with small fragments of charcoal (*Atriplex* sp., *Prosopis* sp., and *Forestiera* sp.), as well as numerous tiny fragments of burned small mammal bone, including 1 identifiable cottontail rabbit phalanx (*Sylvilagus* sp.). No artifacts were recovered from this feature.

Feature 3: This feature was located in unit 511N515W, extending slightly into 511N514W. Feature 3 was a concentration of 16 large fire-cracked rocks within the midden fill, extending from 17 to 28 cm below modern surface. The surrounding matrix was indistinguishable in composition and artifact content from midden fill elsewhere in this unit, and no diagnostic items could be specifically associated with the feature.

Feature 4: This feature was located in the basal level of the midden in units 512N515W and 512N516W. It was a circular basin, 34 cm in diameter and 12 cm in depth, extending from 30 to 42 cm below the modern surface (Figs. 22c-d and 23). The bottom of the feature, which cut into the sterile subsoil beneath the midden, was slightly reddened. The pit contained dark gray ashy fill with numerous large chunks of charcoal (*Atriplex* sp. and *Prosopis* sp.). One chert flake was found in the fill and a number of tiny chert chips were recovered in the flotation sample from this feature. A radiocarbon date of A.D. 885±55 (MASCA-corrected) was obtained on wood charcoal from this feature (see Table 1 above).

Fig. 21. Feature 2 (basin-shaped hearth) at Garnsey Spring campsite. Trowel points north; half of feature fill removed.

<u>"Garza" Hearth</u>: This feature was exposed at the surface in a shallow veneer of colluvium capping the left or south bank of the Garnsey Wash about 130 m south of the campsite (see Figs. 2, 3, 4, and 6 above). The hearth, situated about 10 m back from the edge of the wash, was an unlined, shallow basin 40 cm in diameter and 10 cm in depth. The fill consisted of reddish colluvium with fine grey ash and small (ca. 2-5 mm) flecks of wood charcoal. No artifacts or bones were found within the hearth. Fifteen lithic artifacts, including a slightly damaged Garza point (see Fig. 29i below), were found on the surface within a radius of about 2 m around the hearth (see discussion in Chapter 4 above). No artifacts were found elsewhere in the general vicinity of the hearth. The hearth fill was dry screened through a tea strainer to recover the charcoal. No other botanical materials were found. The charcoal yielded a radiocarbon date of A.D. 1670±50. MASCA correction produced two possible ages, an earlier range of A.D. 1470-1520 and a younger date of A.D. 1640. Other calibration schemes (Stuiver 1982; Klein et al. 1982) yield similar results (see Table 1 and discussion in Chapter 4 above).

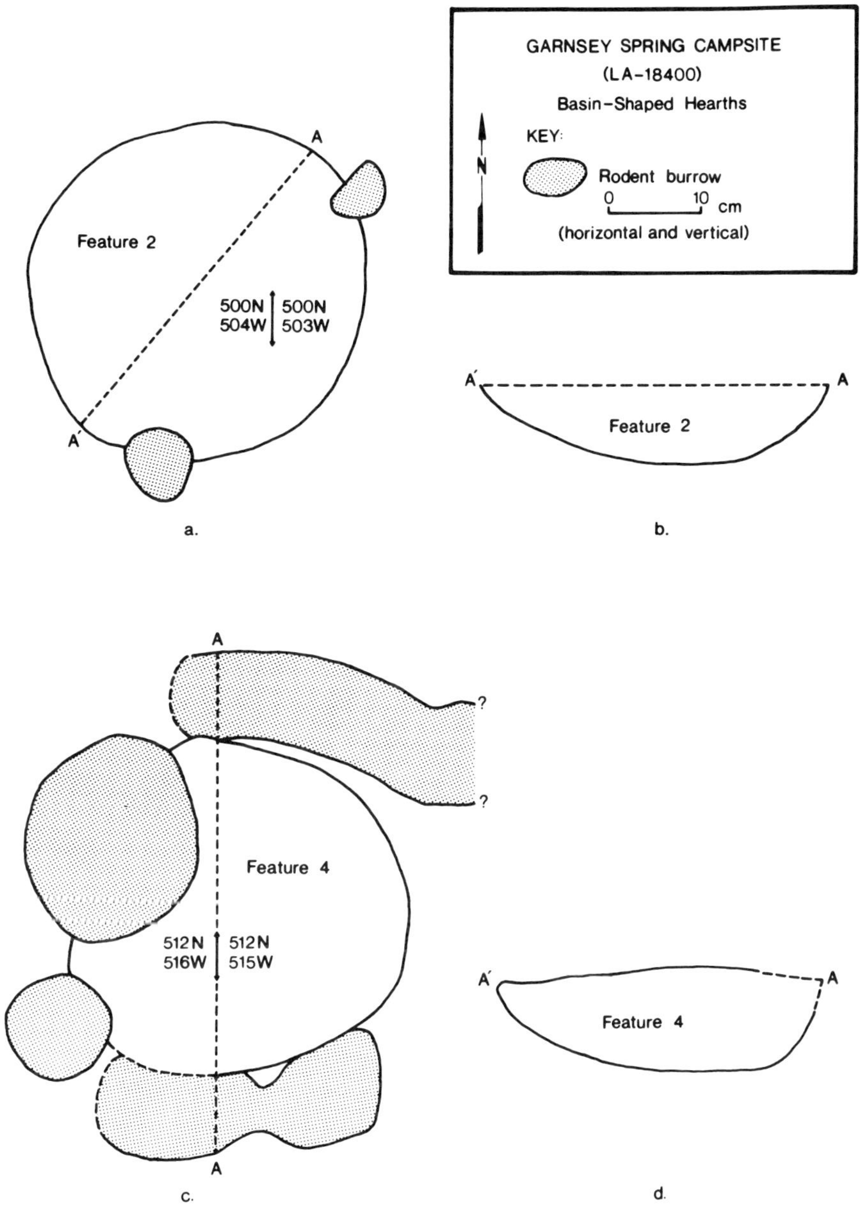

Fig. 22. Plan view and section of Features 2 and 4.

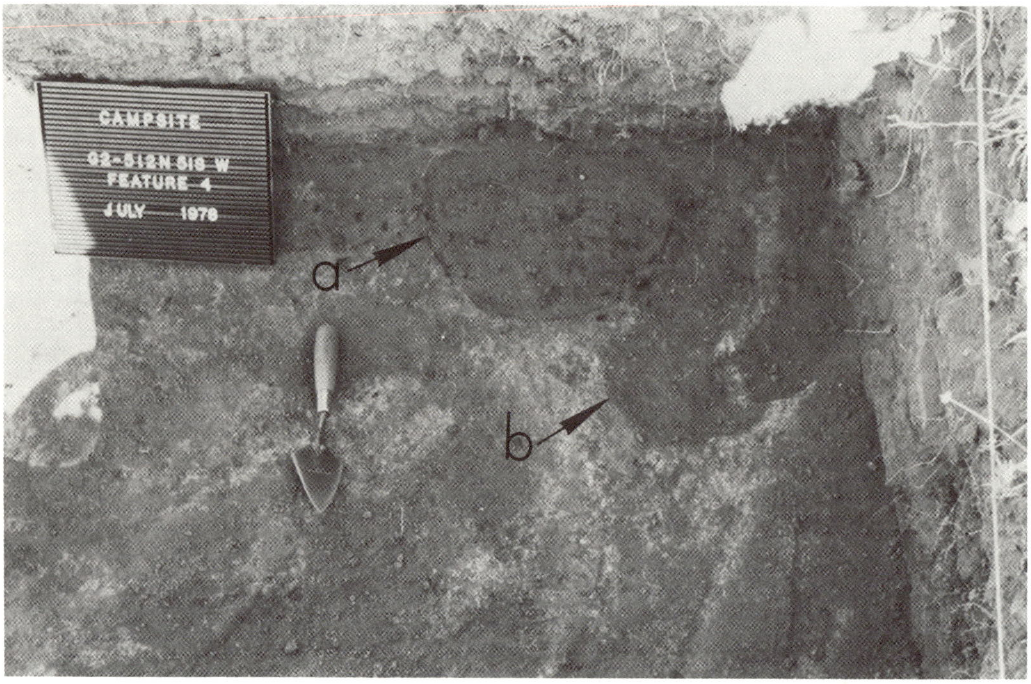

Fig. 23. Feature 4 (eastern half) at Garnsey Spring campsite. a, feature; b, rodent burrow. Trowel points east; feature extends into unexcavated unit to west.

6. FAUNAL AND FLORAL REMAINS

One of the objectives of the excavations at the Garnsey Spring campsite was to obtain samples of faunal and floral remains adequate to determine the nature of subsistence activities and, if possible, to determine the season or seasons of occupation. All bone and charcoal fragments recovered by screening (1/4 inch mesh) were bagged separately and saved. In addition, 25 samples of midden matrix, totalling approximately 150 liters, were collected from various locations throughout the excavations and processed by flotation, using techniques proposed by Minnis and LeBlanc (1976). Light fractions of flotation samples were separated through 1/32-inch mesh screen, while heavy fractions were processed through 1/16-inch mesh screen. We hoped with this procedure to recover seeds and other small floral remains, as well as microfauna.

Preservation of floral and faunal materials was generally very poor throughout the excavated areas of the site. Bones were badly fragmented and most unburned pieces were severely weathered and corroded. The density of bone was low throughout the midden (see Fig. 24), and it appears that much of the original fauna may have decomposed. This observation is supported by the relatively high proportion of tooth enamel fragments, which comprise 23% of the total faunal assemblage (Table 2). As teeth are resistant to weathering, their abundance probably reflects the decomposition of a significant proportion of the faunal remains.

Only two identifiable bone specimens were recovered in flotation samples. Most identifiable material was recovered in screening. It is likely that small animals are underrepresented in the faunal sample, since a disproportionate number of their bones may have been lost in screening (Thomas 1969). The paucity of identifiable small fauna in the flotation samples, however, indicates that the overall density of microfauna present (or preserved) in the deposits may have been very low to start with.

Large mammal bones may also be underrepresented. In Chapter 4 we suggested that the vertical distribution of artifacts probably reflects extensive disturbance of the soft midden deposits by trampling. Studies by Yellen (1977) and Gifford (1978) suggest that, under certain conditions, trampling will result in the incorporation of small bone fragments into the sediments, while larger bones remain on the surface where they are destroyed by carnivores, weathering, trampling and so forth. As a result, subsurface bones are uniformly small in size, tending to consist mainly of whole, identifiable small animal bones and small unidentifiable fragments of larger animal bones.

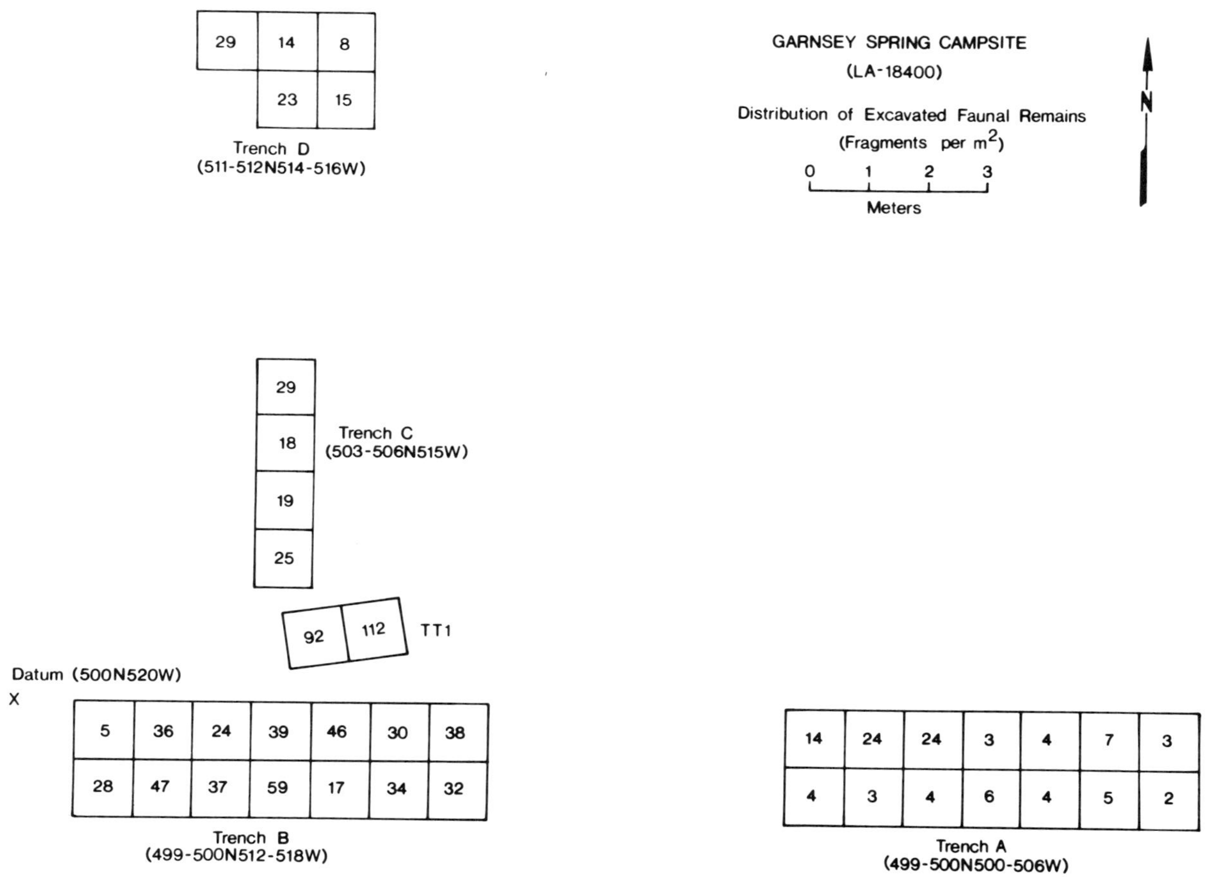

Fig. 24. Distribution of excavated faunal remains by grid square (fragments per m^2).

This description accurately characterizes the assemblage from the campsite, and we suggest that weathering and trampling have resulted in selective destruction of larger bones, leading to an underrepresentation of large mammals. Thus, the limited faunal sample from the site may be highly biased and any attempt to quantify these data is extremely risky.

Table 2
Inventory of faunal remains from Garnsey Spring campsite (excluding flotation samples)

Identification	No. of Specimens	Weight (g)	MNI[1]
Bison bison (Bison)	2	33.2	1
Large mammal (cf. *Bison*)	4	44.2	-
Odocoileus/*Antilocapra* (Deer/Antelope)	2	3.0	1
Medium mammal (cf. *Canis*)	1	4.1	1
Lepus cf. *californicus* (Jackrabbit)	16	6.0	2
Sylvilagus spp. (Cottontail rabbit)	9	1.6	2
Rodent	2	0.4	2
Mollusc	6	4.3	1
Unid. medium or large mammal	35		
Unid. small mammal	28		
Unid. tooth fragments (medium or large ungulate)	226	294.7	-
Unid. small bone fragments	650		
TOTAL	981	391.5	

[1]MNI, Minimum number of individuals

Preservation of botanical remains at the campsite was also poor. Small fragments of wood charcoal were thinly scattered throughout the midden, tending to be concentrated 15 cm to 30 cm below the surface. Charcoal pieces in shallower levels may have been broken apart by weathering and trampling, producing a vertical distribution pattern somewhat different from the pattern that characterized most of the artifacts (see discussion above). No carbonized botanical remains other than charcoal were found in any analyzed sample (Appendix B).

Owing to poor preservation and small sample sizes, very little can be said with certainty about subsistence activities at the campsite. Only 36 identifiable bone fragments and no identifiable plant food remains were recovered (see Table 2 above and Appendix A). Most of the identifiable bones are from rabbits, including both *Lepus* sp. (jackrabbit) and *Sylvilagus* spp. (cottontail rabbit). Many of the lagomorph bones are burned (8 or 50% of the jackrabbit specimens and 3 or 33% of the cottontail specimens). The frequency of burned elements suggests that many, if not most, of the lagomorph remains derive from aboriginal subsistence activities rather than from natural deaths of animals within the midden.

Bison and antelope or deer are represented by a few bones. Virtually all of the unidentified tooth enamel fragments derive from disintegrated teeth of medium to large ungulates, including bison. The abundance of tooth fragments suggests that ungulates may have been a relatively important component of the original faunal assemblage. Unfortunately, given the fragmentary nature of the sample, it is impossible to evaluate their actual contribution to the diet of the campsite inhabitants.

In addition to bones, several unworked fragments of freshwater mollusc shell were recovered. Finally, one small calcined, unidentifiable fragment of worked (cut and polished) bone completes the list of faunal remains.

All identified samples of wood charcoal are comprised primarily of four-wing saltbush (*Atriplex canescens*). Honey mesquite (*Prosopis juliflora*) and New Mexico olive (*Forestiera* sp.) are also common in the samples, and small amounts of juniper (*Juniperus* sp.), Mormon tea (*Ephedra* sp.), and buckthorn (*Rhamnus* sp.) were tentatively identified in some (Appendix B). All of these shrubs, with the exception of juniper, grow in the immediate vicinity of the site today. Scattered junipers can be found today along the west bluff of the Pecos Valley within 2 km of Garnsey, and these trees were probably the source of juniper wood for the campsite inhabitants. Juniper wood may also have been available in small amounts as driftwood in the nearby Pecos and Hondo Rivers. The nearest major stands are 80 to 100 km west of the site in the foothills of the Capitan Mountains. A few junipers also occur along the caprock escarpment 60 to 80 km east of the site. Both of these localities, however, are too remote from Garnsey to have been sources of firewood.

Charcoal samples from three deep sections of the midden were examined for temporal trends in species composition that might reflect paleoenvironmental changes. Although there is some variation in frequencies between levels and among units, no reliable patterns could be detected. It is likely that variability in the composition of the charcoal samples is largely, if not entirely, the result of cultural patterns of firewood selection by the prehistoric occupants of the site, combined with bias introduced by disturbance of the midden and by our methods of recovery. Although environmental changes undoubtedly occurred (see Chapter 9, this volume, and Speth 1983), they cannot be detected with these data.

The vertical distribution of faunal remains also varies from unit to unit. In the initial test trench (TT1), and in a few adjacent areas, bones were concentrated in the uppermost 10 cm of the deposit. However, in most units, especially to the north and east of the datum (e.g., 511-512N514-516W and 499-500N500-506W), bones were most abundant between 15 cm to 30 cm below surface. As a result, bone density by level has a bimodal distribution (Fig. 25). This distribution does not correspond to any of the artifact distributions (Chapter 4), nor does it appear to have stratigraphic or chronological significance. Rather, it probably results largely from differential degrees of weathering and disturbance in different areas of the site. In addition, some of the bone fragments from the uppermost level (0-5 cm) in the vicinity of the datum may derive from the 20th-century occupation of the site, and may not pertain to the prehistoric occupation at all.

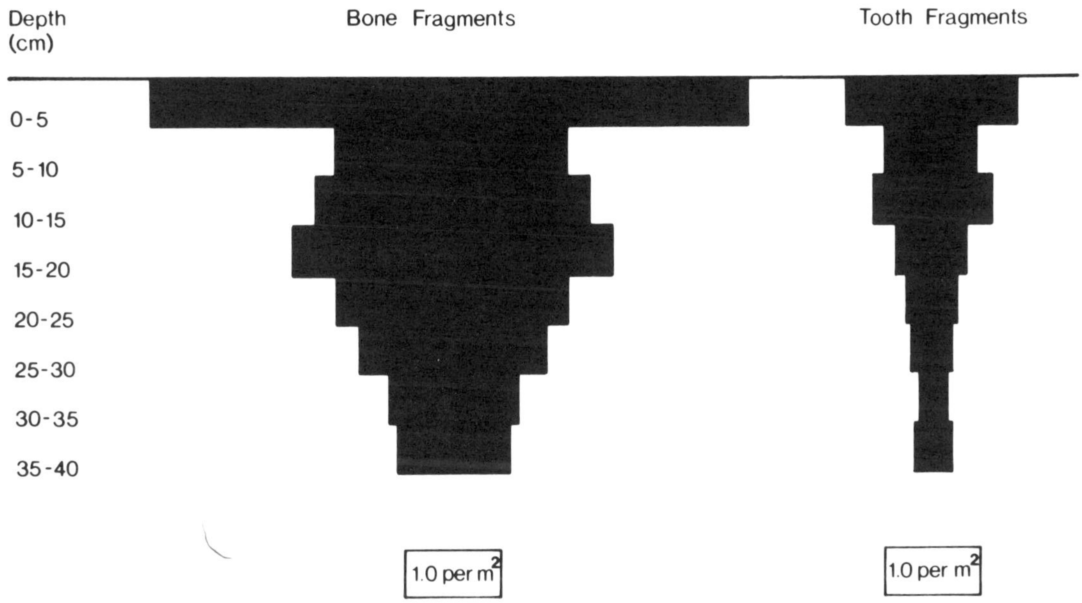

Fig. 25. Vertical distribution of bone and tooth fragments.

No direct evidence of seasonality is provided by the scanty floral and faunal remains from the Garnsey Spring campsite. However, several of the animal species represented in the faunal remains are known to exhibit seasonal variations in availability, permitting some tentative and indirect inferences regarding season(s) of exploitation.

Bison numbers in the Pecos Valley appear to have experienced seasonal fluctuations. Accounts of sixteenth-century Spanish expeditions which passed through the Pecos Valley in the summer and fall repeatedly observed bison tracks and bones, but no bison. Bison were not encountered west of the Llano Estacado in those seasons (see accounts in Hammond and Rey 1966:88-90, 207-209, 259-264). The Pecos Valley lies at the fringes of the historic bison range, and appears to have had marginal forage conditions during at least part of the late prehistoric period (Speth and Parry 1980:99, 124-125; Speth 1983). At the neighboring Garnsey Bison Kill, bison were hunted in March or April, probably immediately prior to their seasonal abandonment of the Pecos Valley area. The presence of bison bones at the campsite would also tentatively indicate occupation during the winter and/or spring, when bison were present in the area.

Hunting of rabbits also was a seasonal activity among historic Indian groups in New Mexico. The modern Tortugas (Tiwa) Indians of Las Cruces, New Mexico, hold communal rabbit drives in January (Beckett 1974). The Tewa of San Juan Pueblo hunt rabbits between October and February, although individual hunting may continue "until well into the spring, or until lice are found in their fur. The Tewa recognize that this makes them dangerous to one's health" (Ortiz 1969:113). The presence of disease-carrying vermin tends to preclude rabbit hunting during the summer months. Among ethnographic groups in the Southwest generally, rabbit hunting appears to have been most common in winter, and occasionally in the fall and spring as well. By analogy, therefore, the presence of rabbit remains at the Garnsey Spring campsite may also point to winter or spring (or, less likely, fall) occupation.

In sum, the presence of bison and rabbit bones at the campsite very tentatively point to occupation during the winter and/or spring. Obviously, additional occupations during other seasons are not precluded. Hopefully, future excavation and analysis of better-preserved late prehistoric sites will ultimately clarify the seasonal patterning of subsistence systems in the region.

7. LITHIC ARTIFACTS

Introduction

Lithic artifacts comprise the largest category of material remains from the Garnsey Spring campsite. Excluding surface finds, approximately 8140 lithic items were recovered from excavated units at the site, including 2 hammerstones, 62 whole and fragmentary projectile points, 75 other bifaces, 58 scrapers, 149 retouched flake tools, 143 utilized flakes, 72 cores, and approximately 7580 pieces of unmodified debitage. No manos, metates, or other ground stone tools were excavated, and only two small burned fragments were found on the surface (a piece of a thin sandstone slab metate and a possible one-hand mano of a nonlocal igneous material). A complete inventory of lithic artifacts is provided in Appendix C.

Raw Materials

A wide range of raw materials was employed in the manufacture of stone tools. Most specimens were chipped from fine-grained chert or chalcedony, of which numerous varieties are distinguishable on the basis of color and surface texture. The cherts and chalcedonies are similar in appearance to those recovered from the Garnsey Bison Kill. Although a wide range of variation is represented, the vast majority of these materials probably derive from gravels in the Roswell area or from bedrock sources in the limestone ridge country to the west of the Pecos Valley (Speth and Parry 1980:144-146; Speth 1983). A few specimens of Alibates and Tecovas cherts are the only ones that clearly derive from distant sources. In addition to the local cherts and chalcedonies, purple and tan quartzites (also locally available in cobble form from Pecos gravels) were used for the manufacture of a number of artifacts.

A surprising number of items were manufactured from nonvitreous, coarse-grained, highly weathered or patinated materials. These included very impure cherts, carbonates (limestone and/or dolomite), siltstone, argillite (claystone), basalt, and rhyolite. For the purposes of analysis, these materials were lumped into a single category, as weathering often prevented specific identification. A few specimens of vitreous, fine-grained igneous rock were placed in a separate category.

A small number of artifacts were chipped from obsidian. Obsidian is the only material present in the campsite assemblage that is clearly derived from a considerable distance away from the site. This material comprises 0.6% of the total chipped stone assemblage (51 of 8140 specimens), which is similar to the frequency of occurrence at the kill site (Speth and Parry 1980:145). The obsidian derives from at least three sources: Obsidian Ridge and Polvadera Peak, both in the Jemez region of north-central New Mexico; and an unknown source, perhaps also in the Jemez area (see discussion below). The presence of obsidian in the campsite and kill probably reflects low-intensity trade relationships with groups to the west and northwest (see Chapter 8).

Obsidian probably was brought to the campsite in the form of biface preforms and small cores, not just as finished tools. The small and highly fragmented assemblage of obsidian artifacts includes fragments of both finished and unfinished bifaces (including one Washita point), biface thinning flakes, tool retouch and resharpening flakes, and percussion flakes struck from small unprepared cores. A few flakes have unifacial retouch, but many flakes were used as tools without prior retouch. No obsidian decortication flakes were found.

Projectile Points

A total of 62 whole and fragmentary projectile points were recovered from excavations at the campsite. An additional 32 specimens were collected from the surface, and more than 50 others have been examined in an amateur's collection in Roswell. Considering that the site has been subjected to intensive point hunting by local collectors for decades, and that most of its area is deflated, the abundance of points that were still present on the surface and in the shallow deposits when we began our work was remarkable. Within the 52 m^2 opened at the campsite, the density of points exceeded one per square meter--a value 33 times greater than the comparable figure for the nearby bison kill. The abundance of points probably reflects numerous reoccupations of the campsite, as well as the frequent performance of tasks which involved the use or discard of projectile points.

Typology

A variety of projectile point forms was found, ranging from small "arrow points" to large "dart points." These have been classified into several generalized types, described below. All points recovered by the University of Michigan are individually described in Appendix C.

I. Basal-Notched Triangular Arrow Points (Type A of Appendix C). These points correspond to the Garza type of Runkles (1964; see also Perino 1968 and Johnson et al. 1977), and are characterized by unnotched triangular blades with weakly serrated straight edges, and concave bases with a single deep central notch. One specimen was found on the surface at the campsite (Fig. 29h). A second was found on the surface adjacent to the "Garza" hearth across the Garnsey Wash to the south of the campsite (Fig. 29i; see Figs. 2, 3, 4, and 6 above for the location of the hearth). A radiocarbon date from the hearth suggests that the Garza occupation of the campsite area occurred during the protohistoric or early historic period (see discussion above). Garza occupations at Lubbock Lake in the Texas Panhandle yielded very similar dates (Johnson et al. 1977). Metric attributes for the 2 Garza points are summarized in Table 3 (see Fig. 48 in Appendix C for definition of the attributes used in this and subsequent tables). Three additional Garza points were observed in the amateur's collection in Roswell (Fig. 26i-k).

Table 3
Metric attributes of basal-notched triangular (Type A or Garza) arrow points (N=2)

Measurement	N	Range
Axial length (cm)	2	1.56-2.62
Basal width (cm)	1	1.24
Thickness (cm)	2	0.23-0.39
Edge angle (°)	2	30-40

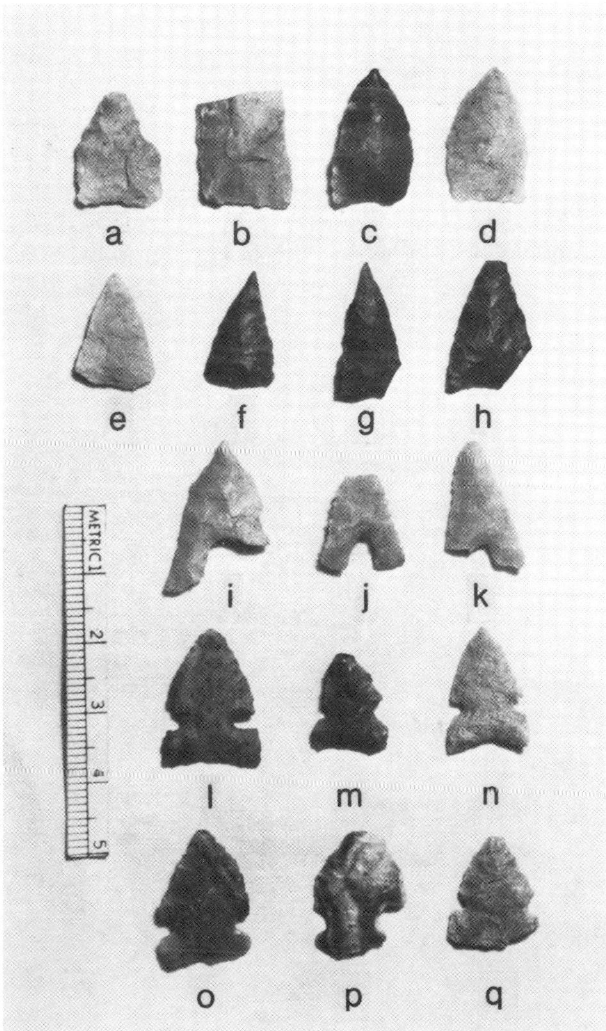

Fig. 26. Triangular arrow points from Garnsey Spring campsite in amateur's collection, Roswell, New Mexico. a-h, unnotched triangular (Fresno) arrow points; i-k, Garza points; l-q, Washita points.

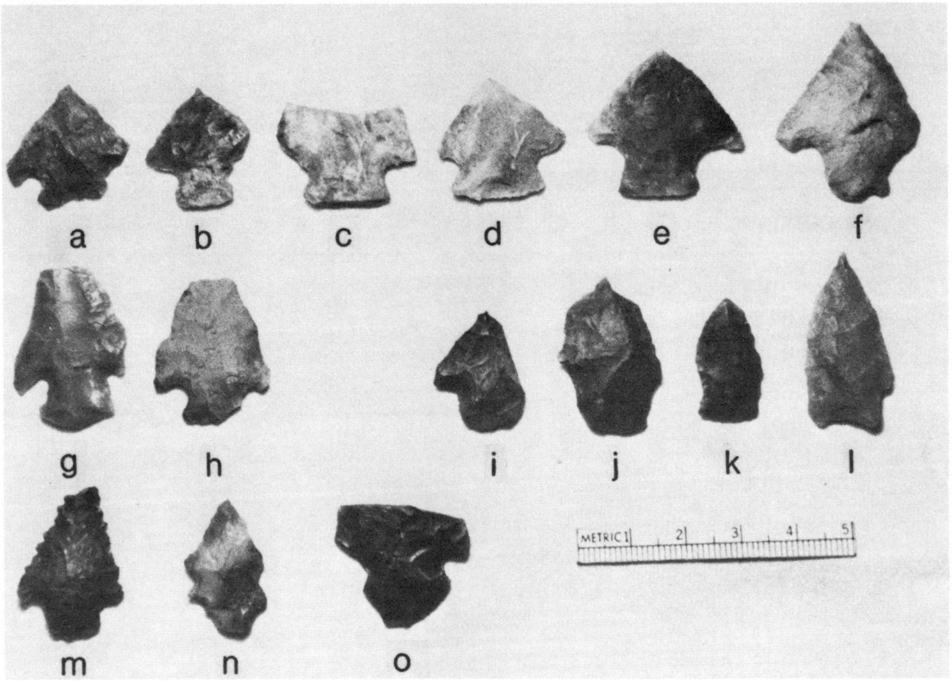

Fig. 27. Miscellaneous dart points from Garnsey Spring campsite in amateur's collection, Roswell, New Mexico. a-h, Ellis-like points; i-o, miscellaneous dart points.

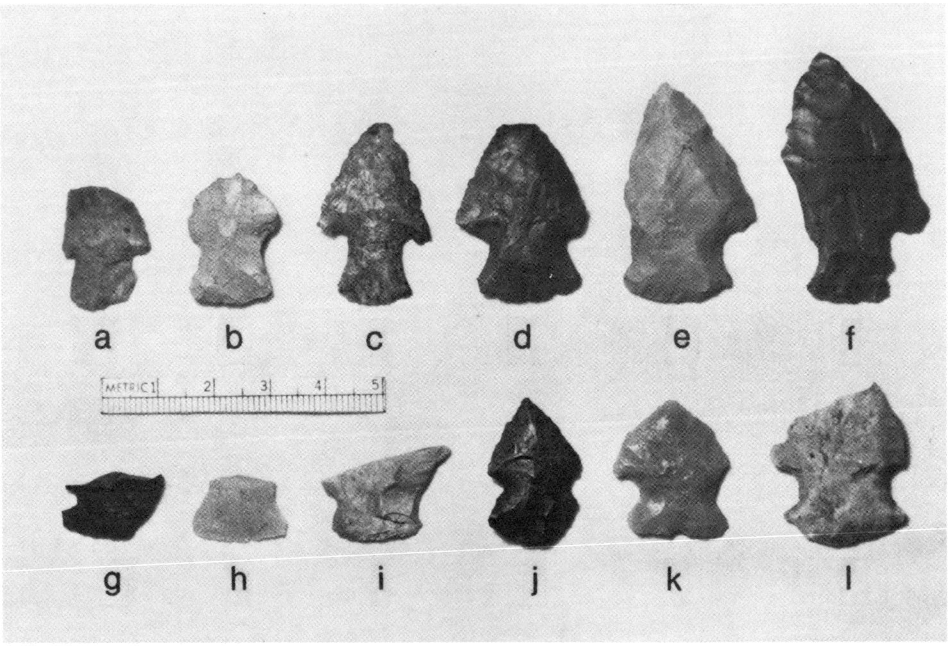

Fig. 28. Expanded-stemmed ("Carlsbad") dart points from Garnsey Spring campsite in amateur's collection, Roswell, New Mexico.

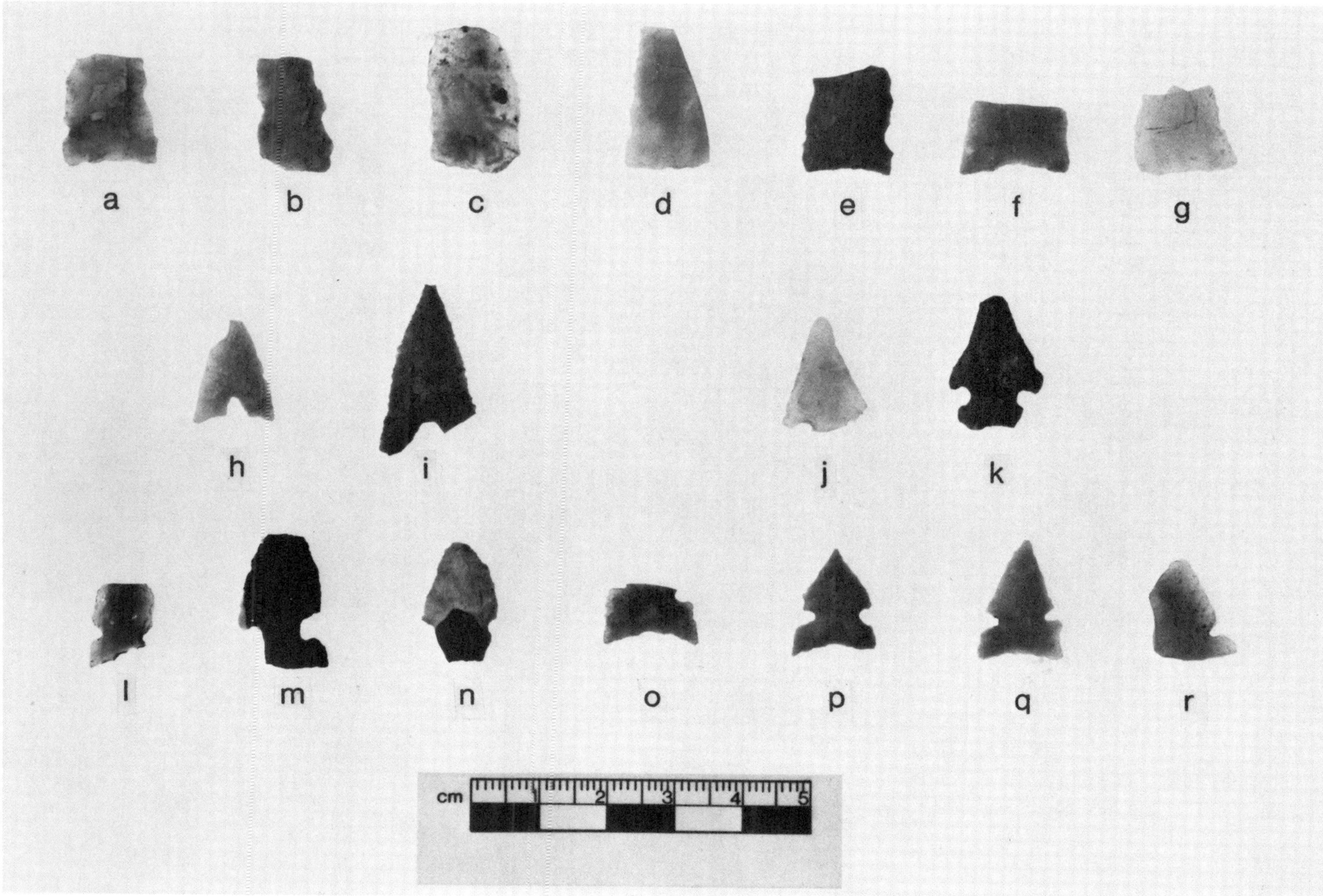

Fig. 29. Triangular arrow points from Garnsey Spring campsite in Michigan collection. a-g, unnotched triangular (Fresno) arrow points (Type D of Appendix C); h-i, Garza points (Type A of Appendix C); j-k, corner-notched arrow points (Type B of Appendix C); l-r, Washita points (Type C of Appendix C).

Fig. 30. Small broadly side-notched dart points (Type E of Appendix C) from Garnsey Spring campsite in Michigan collection.

Fig. 31. Miscellaneous dart points from Garnsey Spring campsite in Michigan collection. a, "Maljamar"-like point (Type J of Appendix C); b-d, indented-base dart points (Type I of Appendix C); e-k, barbed corner-notched dart points (Types F and G of Appendix C).

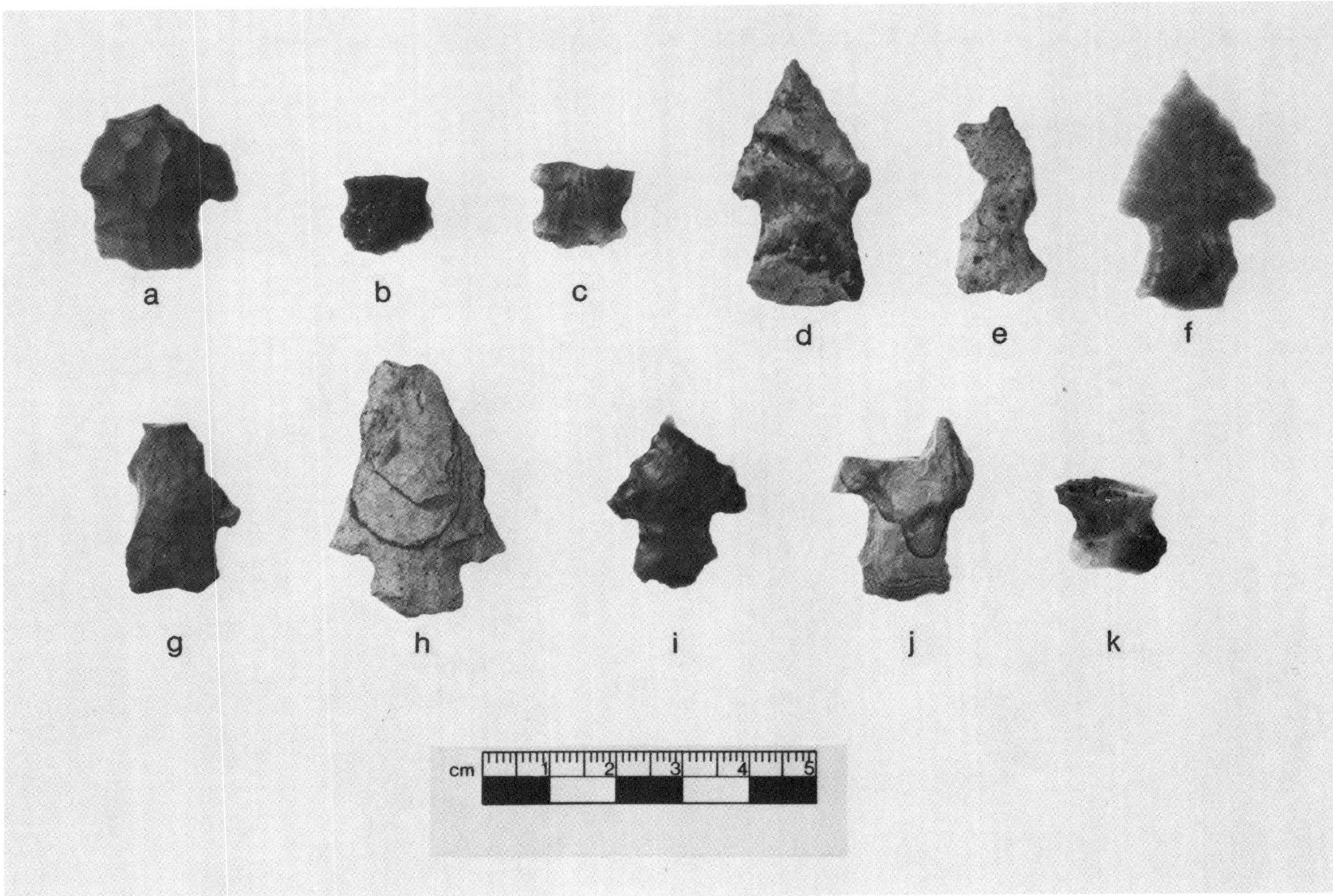

Fig. 32. Expanded-stemmed ("Carlsbad") dart points (Type H of Appendix C) from Garnsey Spring campsite in Michigan collection.

Fig. 33. Dart point stem fragments from Garnsey Spring campsite in Michigan collection.

II. Corner-Notched Triangular Arrow Points (Type B of Appendix C). The 2 points of this type, similar to Type 3-B of Leslie (1977), are characterized by triangular blades with straight or recurvate lateral edges, and narrow deep corner notches (Fig. 29j-k). Both specimens show heavy wear at the tip, and appear to have been used as drills or borers. Metric attributes for the specimens in the Michigan collection are presented in Table 4. None were seen in the amateur's collection in Roswell.

Table 4
Metric attributes of corner-notched triangular (Type B) arrow points (N=2)

Measurement	N	Range
Axial length (cm)	1	2.03
Blade length (cm)	2	1.49-1.57
Notch length (cm)	1	0.27
Tang length (cm)	1	0.63
Tang width (cm)	2	0.55-0.71
Shoulder width (cm)	2	1.30-1.43
Thickness (cm)	2	0.35-0.36
Edge angle (°)	2	60-70

III. Side-Notched Triangular Arrow Points (Type C of Appendix C). These points correspond to the widespread Washita type of Bell (1958), and fall within Leslie's (1977) Type 2 for southeastern New Mexico. Similar points were recovered from the Garnsey Bison Kill (Speth and Parry 1980), and are common throughout the region. (It should be noted that in Speth and Parry [1980] we used the term "Harrell" in the original broad sense of Suhm and Jelks [1962] to refer to both side-notched and triple-notched forms; in the present study we are following more current Southern Plains terminology, restricting the term "Harrell" to the triple-notched forms and "Washita" to the side-notched forms.) The Washita points from the campsite are characterized by triangular blades with straight or slightly convex lateral edges, and narrow deep side notches (Fig. 29l-r). Seven "typical" specimens have concave bases, and 1 has a deeply concave (V-shaped) base. In addition, there are 2 points with nearly straight bases and 2 with slightly convex bases. The latter 2, in particular, should perhaps not be included in the Washita type, because elsewhere in the Southwest small triangular arrow points with convex bases tend to precede in popularity the concave-base forms (see, for example, Holmer and Weder 1980:67). However, given the extremely small sample from the campsite and the overall similarity of these two specimens in other respects to the forms with concave bases, they have been included in the Washita type. Metric attributes for the 7 "typical" specimens in the Michigan collection are summarized in Table 5 (only concave-base points are included). An additional 6 Washita points were observed in the collection in Roswell (Fig. 26l-q).

Table 5
Metric attributes of side-notched triangular
(Type C or Washita) arrow points (N=7)

Measurement	N	Mean	S.D.	Range
Axial length (cm)	3	1.78	0.14	1.62-1.86
Blade length (cm)	3	1.08	0.12	0.95-1.19
Notch length (cm)	5	0.26	0.11	0.13-0.43
Tang length (cm)	5	0.74	0.09	0.67-0.90
Base width (cm)	3	1.34	0.07	1.28-1.42
Tang width (cm)	7	0.73	0.11	0.59-0.91
Shoulder width (cm)	5	1.07	0.13	0.92-1.25
Thickness (cm)	6	0.32	0.03	0.30-0.37
Edge angle (°)	6	33	4	30-40

IV. Unnotched Triangular Arrow Points (Type D of Appendix C). These points resemble the ubiquitous Fresno point described by Bell (1960), and Leslie's (1977) Type 1 for southeastern New Mexico. Seven specimens were recovered by the University of Michigan (Fig. 29a-g); an additional 11 were recorded in the amateur's collection in Roswell (Fig. 26a-h). Most specimens have triangular blades with straight or slightly convex lateral edges, no notches, and straight or slightly concave bases. Some of the specimens are finished points; most however probably are unfinished Washita point preforms. Metric attributes for the 7 Michigan specimens are summarized in Table 6.

Table 6
Metric attributes of unnotched triangular
(Type D or Fresno) arrow points (N=7)

Measurement	N	Mean	S.D.	Range
Base width (cm)	6	1.42	0.17	1.16-1.66
Thickness (cm)	6	0.36	0.07	0.26-0.44
Edge angle (°)	7	31	3	25-35

V. Small Broadly Side-Notched Dart Points (Type E of Appendix C). These points are similar to Type 5 of Leslie (1977), and are characterized by an ovate blade with convex lateral edges, broad shallow side notches, and a straight to slightly concave or convex base. Most specimens show traces of reworking and possible use as cutting tools. Metric attributes of the 6 Michigan specimens are presented in Table 7 (see also Fig. 30a-f).

Table 7
Metric attributes of small broadly side-notched (Type E) dart points (N=6)

Measurement	N	Mean	S.D.	Range
Axial length (cm)	4	2.33	0.32	2.08-2.76
Blade length (cm)	4	1.27	0.36	0.83-1.71
Notch length (cm)	6	0.64	0.16	0.43-0.89
Tang length (cm)	6	0.97	0.17	0.72-1.13
Base width (cm)	6	1.64	0.23	1.40-2.06
Tang width (cm)	6	1.36	0.15	1.12-1.53
Shoulder width (cm)	4	1.74	0.19	1.57-1.93
Thickness (cm)	5	0.59	0.09	0.53-0.72
Edge angle (°)	6	55	13	40-70

VI. <u>Barbed Corner-Notched Dart Points</u> (Types F and G of Appendix C). These points comprise a variable group of highly fragmentary specimens with broad blades, deep corner notches, and pronounced barbs (Fig. 31e-k). Some of the specimens resemble Leslie's (1977) Type 8-A, but typological comparisons are hampered by the condition of these specimens. Measurements are also largely precluded by their fragmentary condition.

VII. <u>Expanded-Stemmed Dart Points</u> (Type H of Appendix C). These points are similar to the informally defined "Carlsbad" type (Types 8-D and 9) of Leslie (1977). Most specimens are broadly corner-notched with expanded stems and convex bases; a few have broad shallow side notches, straight stems, or straight bases. Most specimens show signs of reworking and use as cutting tools, and the tips of 2 were also used for graving or boring. Metric attributes of 11 of the Michigan specimens are presented in Table 8 (see also Fig. 32). At least 12 additional "Carlsbad" points were observed in the amateur's collection in Roswell (Fig. 28). Numerous stem fragments were recovered from the campsite (Fig. 33); most of these probably are from "Carlsbad" points, although some may derive from corner-notched dart points (Types F and G above).

VIII. <u>Miscellaneous Dart Points</u>. A single example of a small, straight-stemmed dart point (Type J of Appendix C) that corresponds to one of Leslie's (1977) "Maljamar" point types (Type 10-A) was recovered in the excavations (Fig. 31a). Another distinctive point has serrated edges, narrow deep corner notches, and an indented base (Type I of Appendix C; Fig. 31b). Two other fragmentary specimens are corner-notched with deeply bifurcated bases (Type I of Appendix C; Fig. 31c-d). Among the dart points in the amateur's collection, 8 resemble the Ellis type (Bell 1960:32-33; see Fig. 27a-h); 7 others were too varied to be assigned confidently to type (Fig. 27i-o), although a couple of them resemble one or the other of Leslie's (1977) "Maljamar" types (his Type 5).

Table 8
Metric attributes of expanded-stemmed (Type H or "Carlsbad") dart points (N=11)

Measurement	N	Mean	S.D.	Range
Axial length (cm)	4	3.62	0.59	2.75-4.05
Blade length (cm)	4	2.30	0.60	1.64-3.09
Notch length (cm)	11	0.87	0.24	0.57-1.28
Tang length (cm)	11	1.21	0.27	0.80-1.70
Base width (cm)	10	1.49	0.14	1.30-1.80
Tang width (cm)	11	1.26	0.16	0.98-1.57
Shoulder width (cm)	6	2.23	0.38	1.59-2.68
Thickness (cm)	8	0.62	0.12	0.47-0.84
Edge angle (°)	7	56	9	45-70

Chronology

As noted in Chapter 4, projectile point chronology in the Roswell area is poorly known. As a consequence, it is tempting to compare the campsite materials with the much more securely established sequence of point types in Texas and Oklahoma (Suhm and Jelks 1962; Bell 1958, 1960; Perino 1968). However, given the present paucity of chronologically controlled data from southeastern New Mexico, we feel it is premature and perhaps inappropriate to rely heavily on such long-distance correlations. We have opted instead to compare several of the campsite varieties to the informal types recognized by Leslie (1977) for southeastern New Mexico. While Leslie's types have not yet been rigorously defined, and have been dated largely on the basis of their presumed associations with ceramics in surface collections, they nevertheless reflect point types which recur frequently in the area and provide at least a general indication of the span of time represented by the Garnsey Spring assemblage (see Table 9).

Functional Variability

Although the terms "projectile point," "arrow point," and "dart point" have functional implications, artifacts have been assigned to these categories on the basis of their morphology, not their function. All bifacially retouched specimens with a basal element that permits hafting, two sharp lateral edges, and an acute tip were classified as projectile points. The distinction between "dart points" and "arrow points" was made on the basis of overall size, haft-element size, and thickness. However, these morphological classes appear to cover a range of functions, and it is likely that many specimens did not serve primarily as weapon points. Evidence of this functional variability is provided by use-wear patterns and lateral edge angles, which are closely related to the functions served by the tools (Wilmsen 1968; Parry 1980).

Table 9
Estimated age of projectile point types from Garnsey Spring campsite

Point Type	Estimated Age (A.D.)	Michigan Collection		Amateur Collection		Total	
		N	%	N	%	N	%
A (Garza[1])	1500-1650?	2	4.7	3	7.9	5	6.2
C (Washita[2])	1200-1600+	11	25.6	6	15.8	17	21.0
D (Fresno[3])	1200-1600+	7	16.3	11	28.9	18	22.2
B (Type 3[4])	950-1200	2	4.7	0	0.0	2	2.5
J (Maljamar[4])	850-1000?	1	2.3	2?	5.3	3?	3.7
E (Type 5[4])	850-1000	6	14.0	4?	10.5	10?	12.3
H (Carlsbad[4])	pre- 950	14+	32.6+	12+	31.6+	26+	32.1+

[1] Runkles (1964); Perino (1968); Johnson et al. (1977)
[2] Bell (1958); Johnson et al. (1977)
[3] Bell (1960); Johnson et al. (1977)
[4] Leslie (1977)

The distribution of edge angles suggests that at least three distinct functional classes are represented by the projectile points (Fig. 34). One class includes all specimens categorized as side-notched or unnotched arrow points (described above as Types A, C, and D), which have a unimodal distribution of edge angles with a modal value of 30° and a range of 25-40°. These acute-edged specimens, like their counterparts from the Garnsey Bison Kill, show very little edge damage or wear along their lateral edges, but several have impact fractures at their tips. It is probable that these specimens do in fact represent projectile points. On the other hand, the two corner-notched "arrow points" (Type B) have much steeper lateral edges (60-70°) that exhibit heavy wear, particularly at the tip, in the form of small step fractures and pronounced abrasion and rounding. These two specimens unquestionably have been used as drills and do not appear suitable for projectile tips in their present dulled condition.

The distribution of edge angles of dart points differs from that of arrow points. Although there is some overlap, most dart points have steeper edges than do arrow points. Edge angles of dart points (Types E, F, G, and H) range from 40° to 70°; the distribution is bimodal with clear modes at 50° and 70°. While some variation in edge angles may be attributed to attrition and reworking of the points, the clear bimodality suggests that two functional groups may be represented. Most dart points in the sample show heavy wear on their lateral edges (step flaking, crushing, and abrasion) and many seem to have been resharpened or reworked. In at least two cases the tips have been reworked into "spurs" for graving or boring. In general, the "dart points" appear to have been used for a variety of heavy cutting, scraping, and piercing tasks, and probably did not serve exclusively, or even primarily, as

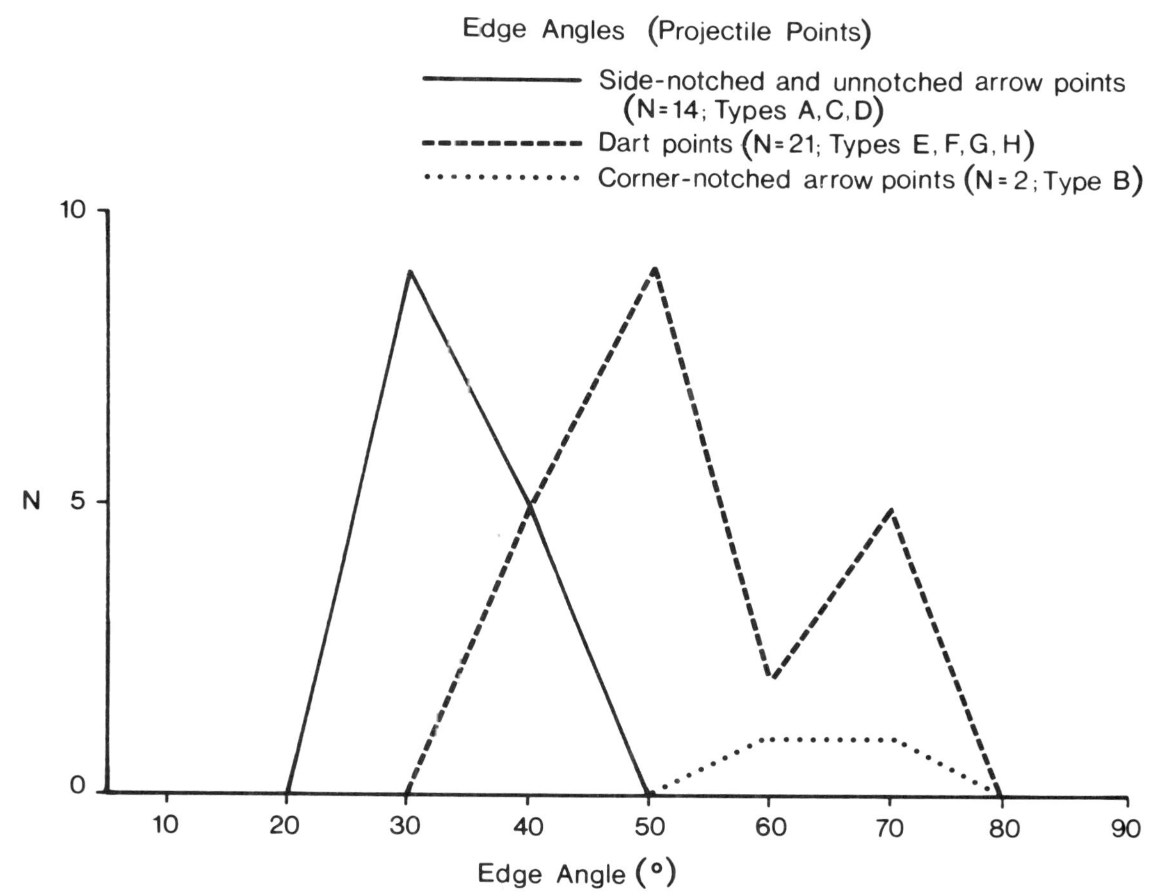

Fig. 34. Edge-angle distribution of projectile points from Garnsey Spring campsite.

weapon points. Thus, the differences between "dart points" and "arrow points" cannot be attributed solely to chronology, but instead may be due at least in part to their use in different tasks.

Other Tools

In addition to projectile points, 282 other retouched tools or tool fragments were recovered from excavations at the Garnsey Spring campsite. These included 75 bifaces, 58 scrapers, and 149 retouched flake tools. The bifaces were all highly fragmentary, and appear to represent a range of both finished tools as well as unfinished preforms for projectile points and other tools. Tools classified as scrapers had steep, continuous unifacial retouch along a major portion of their edges, yielding a regular outline shape, although the specific shapes of the tools and position of retouch were highly variable. As with other implements, most specimens were fragmentary. Retouched flake tools were flakes with unifacial or bifacial retouch along a portion of their edges, but retouch was restricted to the edges and did not alter the overall shape of the flake. This group of implements was highly variable in form; many specimens were represented only by tiny fragments. Representative tools are illustrated in Figs. 35 and 36a-f; additional data are presented in Appendix C.

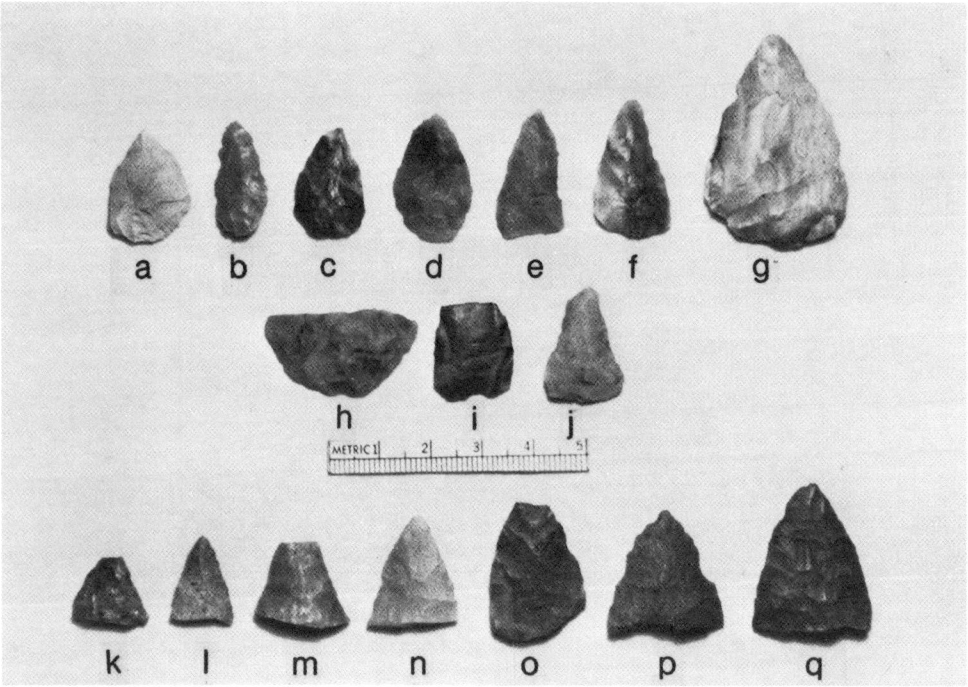

Fig. 35. Bifaces and biface fragments from Garnsey Spring campsite in amateur's collection, Roswell, New Mexico.

A number of flakes and fragments were utilized as tools without prior retouch. Evidence of utilization (in the form of macroscopic edge damage) was observed on 143 unretouched specimens. The vast majority of

Fig. 36. Representative tools from Garnsey Spring campsite in Michigan collection. a, combination end- and side-scraper; b, denticulated core-scraper; c, steep denticulated side-scraper; d, utilized flake; e, biface fragment (burned); f, unfinished biface fragment; g, core; h, core.

excavated flakes, however, exhibited no obvious edge damage. The 7581 unused or unmodified flakes were highly variable in size and form, and included core fragments, decortication flakes, biface thinning flakes, and other debitage from tool manufacture, as well as many small retouch flakes and undiagnostic pieces of shatter. Two hammerstones (Fig. 37a) and 72 cores (Fig. 36g-h) also provided evidence of tool manufacture in the excavated areas.

It is worth noting that all of these cores were imported to the site from elsewhere, because there are no suitable lithic raw materials, gravels included, within a radius of several kilometers of the site. The local bedrock is highly friable gypsum which is useless for the manufacture of tools.

Site Function

Detailed morphological and functional analyses of the stone tools were not undertaken. It was felt that such analyses would be of limited value, owing to the badly disturbed and mixed nature of the deposits that prevented separation of the various chronological components and occupations. In addition, most specimens are fragmentary, and many are burned or patinated, which renders technological analysis difficult and precludes detailed analysis of microscopic use-wear (Keeley 1980). For these reasons, analysis of the stone tools has been limited, and directed toward a comparison of the excavated collection as a whole (ignoring chronological variability) with the small assemblage recovered from the neighboring bison kill. It is assumed that the campsite has been the scene of repeated occupations, during which a wide range of habitation, processing, maintenance, and manufacturing activities occurred. The bison kill, on the other hand, is interpreted as an extractive site where a very limited range of activities related to the procurement and processing of bison was carried out (Speth and Parry 1980; Speth 1983). It was anticipated that these general differences in site function would be reflected by variations in the lithic assemblages from the two sites.

The two sites were compared through analysis of the typological composition of their assemblages, frequencies of different edge forms of tools, and distributions of edge angles. As anticipated, each of these traits varied between the two sites, reflecting the different mix of activities at each site.

The proportions of generalized categories of artifacts are presented in Table 10. As this table indicates, the campsite differs from the bison kill in having a lower proportion of tools and a higher proportion of debitage (cores and unmodified flakes). This difference is even more pronounced than the proportions suggest, as the waste flakes from the bison kill are mostly retouch and resharpening flakes (the byproducts of tool use), while the campsite assemblage includes a significant percentage of primary manufacturing debitage, reflecting on-site tool manufacture. It appears that tool manufacturing occurred with much greater frequency at the campsite than at the bison kill. The

Fig. 37. Miscellaneous artifacts from Garnsey Spring campsite in Michigan collection. a, chert hammerstone; b, sandstone metate fragment (burned); c, igneous one-handed mano fragment.

Table 10
Proportions of chipped stone artifacts from Garnsey Bison Kill and Garnsey Spring campsite (excavated specimens only)

Artifact	Bison Kill (N=544) (%)	Campsite (N=8140) (%)
Retouched tools	7.9	4.2
Utilized flakes	7.4	1.8
Cores	0.4	0.9
Unmodified flakes	84.4	93.1

proportions of different types of retouched tools are generally similar at the two sites (Table 11), although the proportion of unretouched utilized flakes is much greater at the bison kill (Table 10).

Table 11
Proportions of retouched tools from Garnsey Bison Kill and Garnsey Spring campsite (excavated specimens only)

Artifact	Bison Kill (N=43) (%)	Campsite (N=344) (%)
Points	23.3	18.0
Bifaces	18.6	21.8
Scrapers	16.3	16.9
Retouched flakes	41.9	43.3

Although the proportion of tools is lower at the campsite, the absolute density of tools is much higher. With the exception of bones (which were poorly preserved), the density of every class of artifact is higher in excavated areas at the campsite than at the bison kill (Table 12). This reflects the frequent reoccupation of the former, and suggests much more intensive utilization of that location in general.

Comparison of the shapes of the working edges of chipped stone tools from the two sites reveals some interesting differences. Virtually all stone tools from the bison kill have simple edge shapes: tool edges are straight, or slightly concave or convex. Excluding projectile points, there is only one specimen that has a denticulated edge. In contrast, complex edge shapes are relatively common at the campsite. Although simple edges predominate, there are a substantial number of tools with denticulated edges (Table 13). A common tool form at the campsite is a steep-edged denticulate scraper, flaked by hard-

Table 12
Artifact density at Garnsey Bison Kill and Garnsey Spring campsite

Artifact	Density (no./m^2)	
	Bison Kill	Campsite
Retouched tools	0.15	6.62
Utilized flakes	0.14	2.75
Cores	0.01	1.38
Unmodified flakes	1.65	145.79
Ceramic sherds	0.06	17.29
Identifiable bones	12.76	0.81
Total bone fragments	24.47	18.87

hammer percussion to create a jagged working edge (Fig. 36b-c). These tools, possibly used for processing tough plant fibers, are relatively abundant at the campsite and are entirely absent from the bison kill.

Table 13
Proportion of different edge shapes of chipped stone tools (excluding projectile points) from Garnsey Bison Kill and Garnsey Spring campsite (excavated specimens only)

Edge Shape	Bison Kill (N=85) (%)	Campsite (N=501) (%)
Straight	40.0	33.7
Convex	47.1	37.3
Concave	11.8	13.0
Denticulate	1.2	12.6
Other	0.0	3.4

Finally, the distribution of tool edge angles differs between the two sites. As noted above, edge angle is closely related to function, because the angle affects the durability of the working edge, influencing its suitability for different tasks (Parry 1980). In general, tools with very acute edges are most effective for slicing and cutting soft materials such as meat, hides, and various plant materials. Somewhat steeper edges are better suited to whittling, while the steepest edges are appropriate for scraping, planing, or shredding a variety of hard materials, including bone and hard wood (Wilmsen 1968). Therefore, it seems likely that tools used in extractive tasks, such as plant gathering or bison butchering, would tend to have relatively acute edges, while tools with steep edges were more likely to have served in maintenance tasks such as woodworking. Thus, if our assumption is correct that a wide range of maintenance and manufacturing activities occurred at the campsite, then steep-edged tools should be more abundant there than at the bison kill.

Although the distributions of edge angles from the two sites overlap substantially, tools with steep edges are, as anticipated, proportionately more common at the campsite, while tools with acute edges are proportionately more abundant at the bison kill (Fig. 38). In Figure 39 the bison kill assemblage has been subdivided into samples from butchering and processing areas (see Speth and Parry 1980 for a discussion of activity areas at the kill site). The distributions of edge angles are similar for the two areas of the bison kill, but tools from the processing areas tend to have slightly steeper edges than tools from the butchering areas, possibly reflecting the greater importance of maintenance activities in the processing areas (e.g., hide-scraping or rehafting projectile points). Tools from the campsite tend to have even steeper edges (Fig. 39). As shown in Figure 38, this pattern holds for both unifacial retouched tools and unretouched utilized flakes; both tool classes are represented by proportionately more steep-edged examples and fewer acute-edged examples at the campsite than at the kill.

While it is true that some variations in the lithic assemblages between these two neighboring sites may be attributed to chronological differences, the dissimilarities discussed above are probably largely the result of different mixes of activities carried out at the two loci. The Garnsey Spring campsite was repeatedly occupied over a long period of time, resulting in a much higher density of lithic artifacts. A higher frequency of debitage resulted from tool manufacturing on the site, while the presence of a broader range of tool forms (including denticulates) and a higher proportion of steep-edged tools reflects the performance of a broader range of maintenance and manufacturing activities. The Garnsey Bison Kill was an extractive site where a more limited range of tasks was performed on infrequent occasions.

Finally, in the discussion of site function it is noteworthy that no manos, metates, mortars or other ground stone tools traditionally associated with the processing of maize, seeds, and other plant foods were recovered in the excavations at the campsite, and only one burned fragment of a shallow sandstone metate (Fig. 37b) and a fragment of a one-handed mano of an unidentified igneous material (Fig. 37c) were found on the surface. As noted earlier, their virtual absence on the surface of the site can easily be attributed to recent collecting activity. Their absence in the midden deposits, however, may be a real reflection of the restricted nature of subsistence activities carried on at the campsite.

Obsidian Sourcing and Hydration

Twenty obsidian flakes were selected for sourcing and hydration dating. Nineteen of the specimens were from the campsite (out of a total of 51 obsidian specimens recovered, or 37.3%); and 1 was from the Garnsey Bison Kill (out of 4 obsidian specimens recovered, or 25.0%).

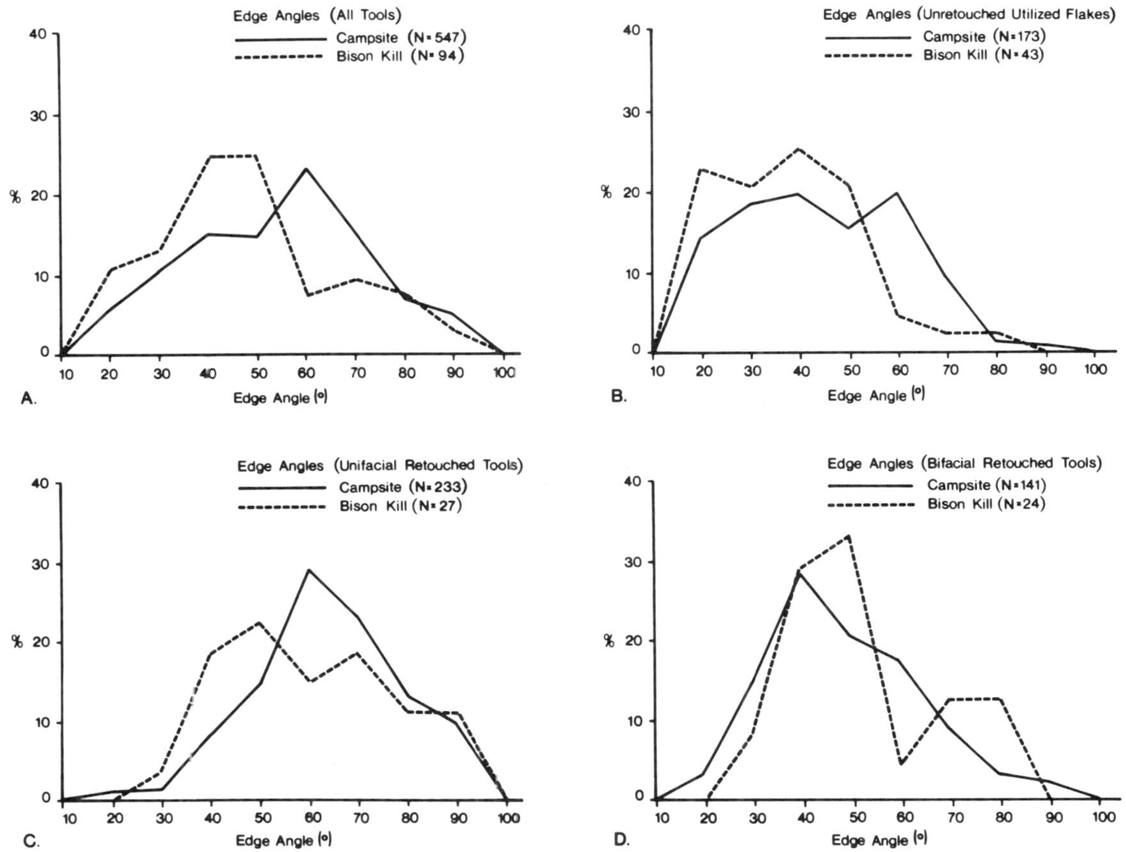

Fig. 38. Edge-angle distributions of different classes of tools from Garnsey Spring campsite and Garnsey Bison Kill.

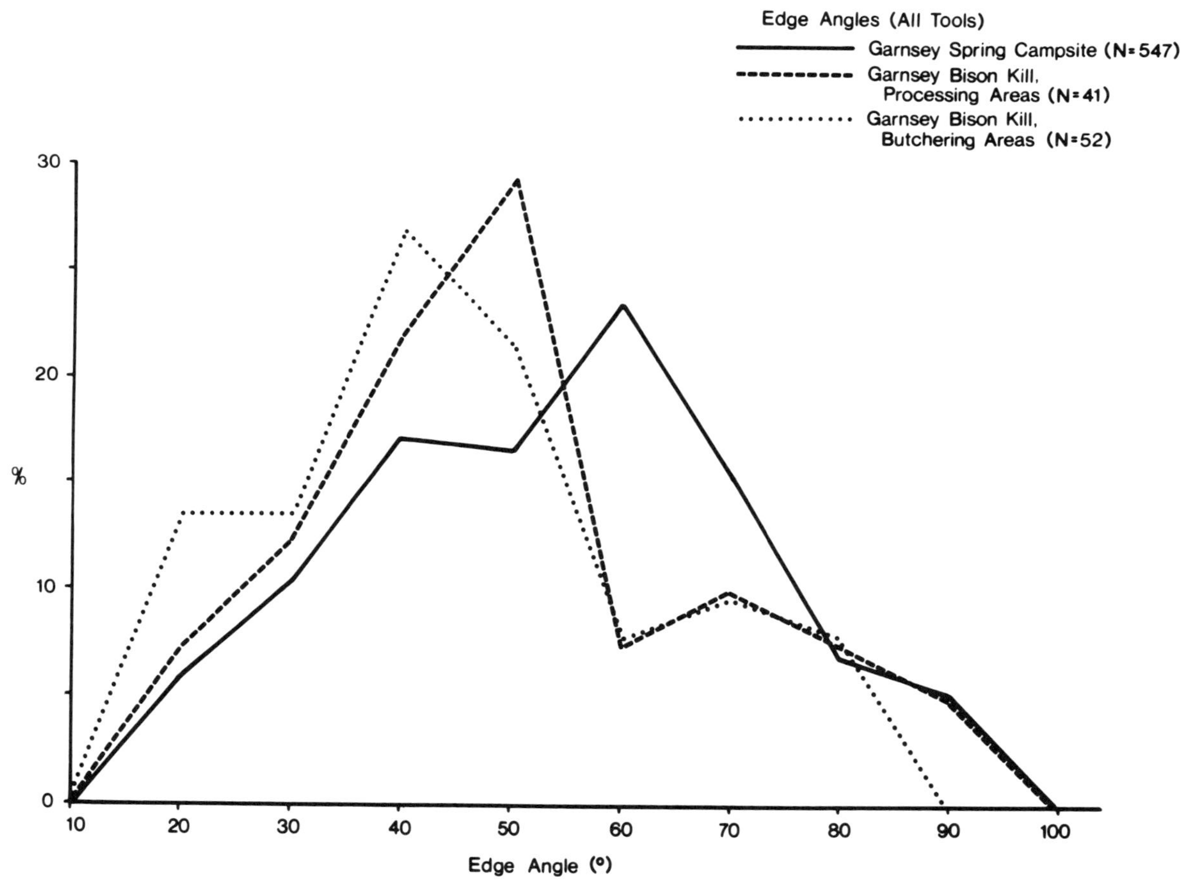

Fig. 39. Edge-angle distributions of tools (all classes combined) from Garnsey Spring campsite and butchering and processing areas at Garnsey Bison Kill.

Only below-surface items were analyzed. The campsite specimens were chosen by laying out all of the subsurface obsidian by stratigraphic level and selecting at least one specimen (usually the largest) from each level. The total number of samples chosen was dictated by budget limitations.

The weight of each specimen (after removal of a sample for hydration dating) is given in Table 14. The specimens are obviously very tiny (mean weight 0.39 g). Nineteen of the specimens were large enough to be dated; only 15 were large enough to be sourced (samples 8, 9, 10, 15, and 17 were too small).

Table 14
Weight of obsidian specimens analyzed for source[1]

Mich. Sample No.	Provenience[2]	Weight (g)	Site
1	514S468W/6	1.25	Bison Kill
2	499N504W/5-10	0.25	Campsite
3	499N515W/5-10	0.32	Campsite
4	499N505W/5-10	0.90	Campsite
5	499N516W/10-15	0.13	Campsite
6	500N512W/10-15	1.25	Campsite
7	503N515W/10-15	0.38	Campsite
8	500N516W/15-20	0.05	Campsite
9	500N500W/15-20	0.11	Campsite
10	500N515W/15-20	0.08	Campsite
11	500N514W/20-25	0.58	Campsite
12	500N516W/20-25	0.50	Campsite
13	500N505W/20-25	0.55	Campsite
14	500N504W/20-25	0.30	Campsite
15	499N506W/20-25	0.05	Campsite
16	512N515W/25-30	0.38	Campsite
17	500N513W/25-30	0.08	Campsite
18	499N506W/30-35	0.30	Campsite
19	499N512W/30-35	0.18	Campsite
20	499N512W/35-40	0.25	Campsite

[1]Weight of specimen available for source analysis after removal of sample for hydration dating (see Appendix C3 for weight of specimen prior to hydration sampling).
[2]Figures following slash are sequential item number (bison kill) or stratigraphic level in cm below surface (campsite).

Sourcing

The chemical composition of 15 obsidian specimens was determined using wavelength-dispersive X-ray fluorescence spectrometry of powdered samples. The analyses were carried out by Fred W. Nelson at A & G Analyses in Provo, Utah (see Nelson and Holmes 1979 for a description of instrumentation and laboratory procedures). The results of these analyses, extracted from Nelson's report, are summarized in Table 15. The composition of the archaeological specimens was compared to geologic source samples using SPSS subprogram DISCRIMINANT (Nelson and Holmes 1979:68; Nie et al. 1975:434-467) and three-coordinate triangular graphs. Two of these graphs are shown in Figures 40 and 41. The solid circles and ellipses in these graphs represent the range of values for the sources, and the points represent the archaeological specimens. Group A represents an unknown source which, according to Nelson (personal communication), shows up very commonly in collections of Southwestern obsidian artifacts. The known range for Source A, based on previous artifact analyses by Nelson, is indicated by a dashed circle or ellipse. This source is similar to others in the Jemez area and may derive from the same general region of New Mexico. Another place of origin is by no means precluded, however.[1]

The results shown in Table 15 indicate that three sources of obsidian are represented at the campsite. Of the 14 campsite specimens, 9 (64%) come from Obsidian Ridge, New Mexico (Source 82); 4 (29%) come from unknown Source A; and 1 (7%) comes from Polvadera Peak, New Mexico (Source 85). The single specimen analyzed from the Garnsey Bison Kill comes from unknown Source A.

Hydration Dating

Prior to sourcing, the obsidian specimens were dated by obsidian hydration; nineteen of the specimens yielded results. These analyses were performed by Clement W. Meighan and Brian Picken at the Obsidian Hydration Laboratory, University of California at Los Angeles. Their results are included in Table 15. Although no calibration scheme has as yet been developed for hydration dating in southeastern New Mexico, our reasons for having the determinations made were the following: (1) to provide an independent check on the degree of stratigraphic disturbance of the campsite midden deposits; and (2) should a reasonable degree of stratigraphic integrity remain in the deposits, to determine whether there were any significant shifts through time in the principal source

---

[1]Note: Just as the final camera-ready manuscript went to press, Fred W. Nelson (personal communication) established the location for Source A. This obsidian derives from Cerro del Medio, Jemez Mountains, Sandoval County, New Mexico (see USGS Valle Toledo, New Mexico 7.5 minute quadrangle, 1977).

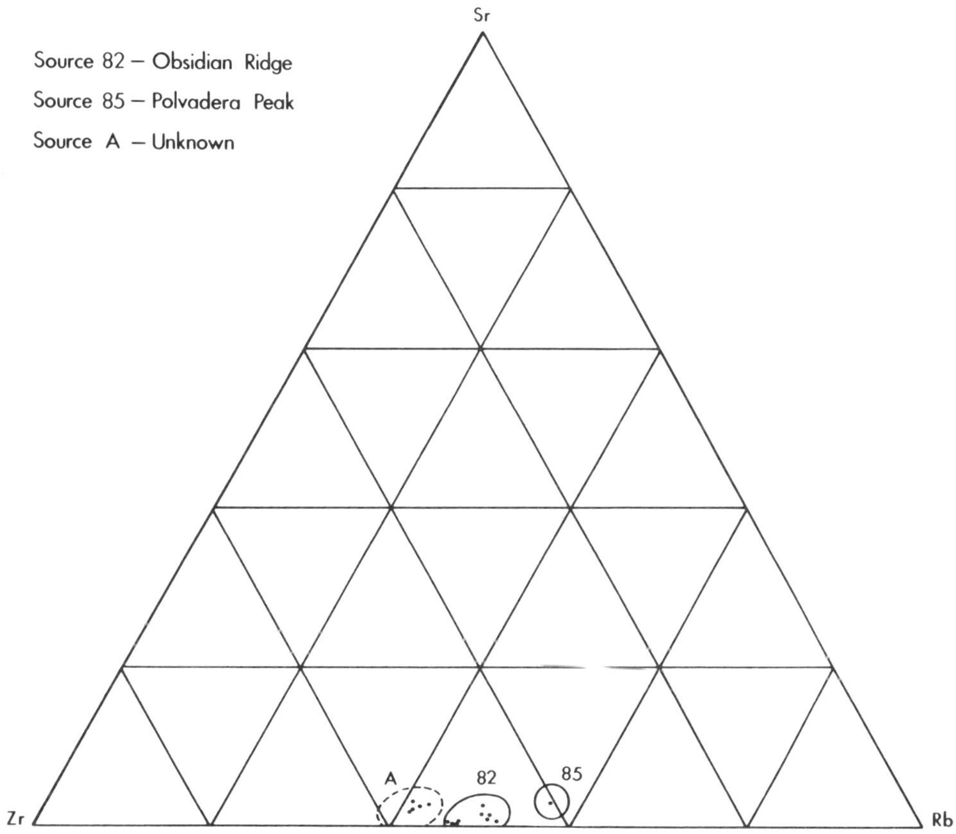

Fig. 40. Rb, Sr, and Zr composition of obsidian from Garnsey Spring campsite and Garnsey Bison Kill compared to composition of Sources 82 (Obsidian Ridge, New Mexico), 85 (Polvadera Peak, New Mexico), and A (unknown). Points denote values for archaeological specimens; solid circle and ellipse represent range of source values; dashed ellipse represents known range for Source A based on previous artifact analyses.

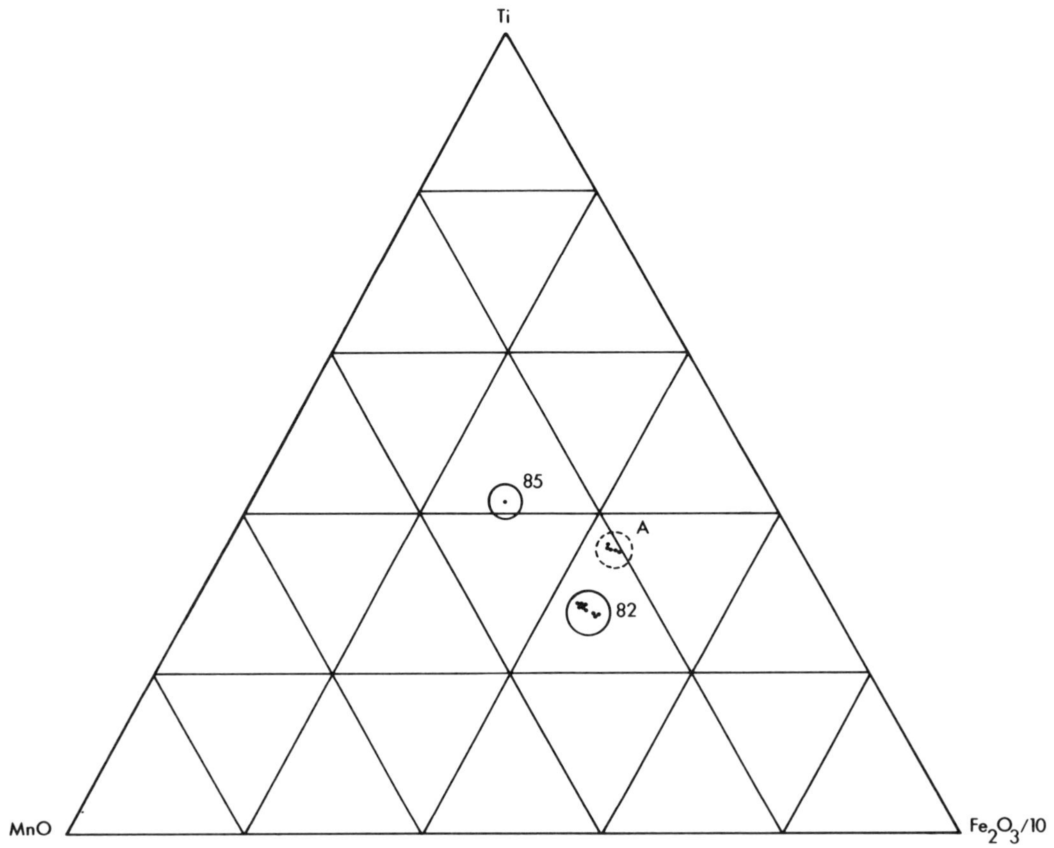

Fig. 41. Fe, Ti, and Mn composition of obsidian from Garnsey Spring campsite and Garnsey Bison Kill compared to composition of Sources 82 (Obsidian Ridge, New Mexico), 85 (Polvadera Peak, New Mexico), and A (unknown). Points denote values for archaeological specimens; solid circles represent range of source values; dashed circle represents known range for Source A based on previous artifact analyses.

Table 15

Chemical composition and hydration layer thickness of obsidian samples from Garnsey Bison Kill and Garnsey Spring campsite

Mich. Sample No.	Provenience[1]	OHL[2] No.	Hydration (microns)	A & G[3] No.	Rb (ppm)	Sr (ppm)	Y (ppm)	Zr (ppm)	Nb (ppm)	MnO (%)	Fe_2O_3 (%)	TiO_2 (%)	Ba (ppm)	Na_2O (%)	Source[4]
1	514S468W/6	10143	2.6	1378	157.4	7.4	55.7	215.2	70.4	.060	1.22	.101	34.8	4.22	A
2	499N504W/5-10	10144	6.5	1379[5]	211.5	6.0	54.4	202.0	92.8	.083	1.44	.085	6.2	4.43	82
3	499N515W/5-10	10145	3.1	1380[5]	204.3	3.9	52.0	197.5	97.6	.083	1.35	.084	4.9	4.43	82
4	499N505W/5-10	10146	4.0/4.5	1381	202.0	3.3	72.6	222.7	111.9	.083	1.27	.084	8.1	4.34	82
5	499N516W/10-15	10147	4.5	1382[5]	163.7	9.4	32.8	117.1	65.3	.064	0.62	.089	15.0	4.23	85
6	500N512W/10-15	10148	6.5	1383	200.4	0.5	79.0	225.2	112.6	.083	1.27	.084	7.0	4.40	82
7	503N515W/10-15	10149	4.4	1384[5]	164.5	10.5	59.5	215.2	72.1	.061	1.31	.104	31.8	4.32	A
8	500N516W/15-20	10150	8.2	----	-----	----	----	-----	-----	----	----	----	----	----	--
9	500N500W/15-20	10151	5.8	----	-----	----	----	-----	-----	----	----	----	----	----	--
10	500N515W/15-20	10152	2.2	----	-----	----	----	-----	-----	----	----	----	----	----	--
11	500N514W/20-25	10153	3.6	1385	203.0	1.0	74.8	224.6	113.9	.083	1.29	.084	6.1	4.36	82
12	500N516W/20-25	10154	4.1/4.4	1386	155.6	7.6	55.7	210.3	72.0	.061	1.24	.104	34.8	4.21	A
13	500N505W/20-25	10155	4.4	1387	194.6	1.8	80.5	224.2	113.3	.083	1.31	.084	6.8	4.38	82
14	500N504W/20-25	10156	6.0/6.4	1388[5]	155.1	12.2	56.5	211.0	73.0	.061	1.27	.103	30.5	4.39	A
15	499N506W/20-25	10157	6.2/5.5	----	-----	----	----	-----	-----	----	----	----	----	----	--
16	512N515W/25-30	10158	2.8	1389[5]	196.8	3.3	52.8	180.6	99.4	.083	1.39	.084	3.5	4.51	82
17	500N513W/25-30	10159	4.4	----	-----	----	----	-----	-----	----	----	----	----	----	--
18	499N506W/30-35	10160	---	1390[5]	217.0	12.8	65.2	214.1	95.5	.081	1.38	.082	4.6	3.54	82
19	499N512W/30-35	10161	4.9	1391[5]	168.7	11.4	54.4	212.4	67.4	.061	1.33	.105	30.1	4.36	A
20	499N512W/35-40	10162	5.2	1392[5]	209.4	7.1	54.0	206.3	88.5	.083	1.32	.085	3.2	4.53	82

[1] First entry is from Garnsey Bison Kill; remainder are from Garnsey Spring campsite. Figures following slash are sequential item number (bison kill) or stratigraphic level in cm below surface (campsite).

[2] OHL, Obsidian Hydration Laboratory sample number. University of California at Los Angeles.

[3] A & G, Archaeological and Geological Analyses sample number, Provo, Utah.

[4] Source 82, Obsidian Ridge, New Mexico; Source 85, Polvadera Peak, New Mexico; Source A, location unknown, perhaps Jemez area, New Mexico.

[5] Because of small sample size, values for Rb, Sr, Y, Zr, Nb were extrapolated to what they probably would have been if 0.50 g of sample had been available.

area(s) for obsidian coming into the Roswell area. The dates for such shifts, if present, would obviously have to remain relative until a calibration scheme was worked out for the area.

Plots (not shown) of hydration layer thickness (in microns) against stratigraphic level for Sources 82 and A display no obvious relationship between relative age of specimen and depth, confirming our suspicions about the extent of midden disturbance. Given this high degree of mixing, any shift through time that might have occurred in source area will be effectively masked.

8. CERAMICS FROM THE GARNSEY SPRING CAMPSITE

by

Regge N. Wiseman
Museum of New Mexico
Santa Fe, New Mexico 87503

Introduction

Nearly 900 pottery fragments representing at least 15 pottery types were recovered from the surface and the excavations at the Garnsey Spring campsite (Table 16). Most were identified on the basis of long-established type descriptions and can be considered fairly typical. Exceptions include the locally made incised ware (here termed Playas Incised, Sierra Blanca var.) and brown wares named by Jelinek (1967), including Roswell Brown, South Pecos Brown, and McKenzie Brown. The sherds classified as Jelinek's types were identified principally on the basis of tempering materials, largely because so many of the surface characteristics were destroyed by weathering. The sherds, as might be expected from a shallow site, are small and battered; most are the size of a quarter dollar or smaller. Pertinent notes for a number of the types follow. Examinations of sherd pastes were made under a 30-power binocular microscope.

Notes on Pottery Types

Painted Wares

Chupadero Black-on-White: All sherds in the Garnsey campsite collection that possess the general characteristics of this pottery type were so classified. Closely related types such as Crosby Black-on-Gray, Middle Pecos Black-on-White, and Casa Colorado Black-on-White, as well as some recognized but not formally described types (such as Elmendorf Black-on-White), are undoubtedly present in the collection, but for a variety of reasons, no attempt was made to segregate them. Therefore, as might be expected, a large variety in various attributes was noted. For instance, most sherds have gray slips; some have thin, streaky white slips; others have thick white slips. Paint ranges from a carbon-based variety on a few sherds to brownish-black and black mineral-based paints on the rest. Several have sub-glazed or slightly glazed pigments.

Examination of all sherds under the microscope revealed that virtually every one contained crushed sherd and crushed aplite in varying quantities as tempering materials (Table 18). The aplite is characterized by clear to white grains of feldspar and quartz, and is apparently the material described by J. H. Kelley (1979:123) as "leucocratic grit." Accessory minerals in varying combinations in some

Table 16
Pottery tabulations by provenience group for Garnsey Spring campsite

Pottery Type	Group[1] 1	Group 2	Group 3	Group 4	Group 5	Group 6	Group 7	Group 8	Group 9	Site Total
Chupadero B/W	25	74	5	8	12	1	1	-	20	146
San Andres R/T	1	10	-	1	-	-	-	-	-	12
Three Rivers R/T	-	8	-	4	-	-	-	-	-	12
Three Rivers Ware	2	11	1	4	2	-	-	-	-	20
Lincoln B/R	1	1	-	-	-	-	-	-	-	2
Redwashed Brown	1	1	-	1	2	-	-	-	-	5
Playas Incised, Sierra Blanca var.	-	5	-	-	1	-	-	-	-	6
Jornada Brown	35	98	12	19	18	-	1	5	12	200
Roswell Brown	14	36	4	5	6	-	-	2	5	72
South Pecos Brown	16	138	16	40	14	-	-	5	16	245
McKenzie Brown	9	70	21	3	6	-	-	1	2	112
El Paso Brown	6	18	3	-	1	-	-	1	1	30
Corona (?) Corrugated	-	1	-	-	-	-	-	-	-	1
Mangas/Mimbres B/W	-	4	1	-	9	-	-	-	-	14
Red Mesa B/W	-	2	-	-	-	-	-	-	-	2
Galisteo B/W	-	2	-	-	-	-	-	-	-	2
St. Johns Polychrome	-	4	-	-	-	-	-	-	-	4
Unidentified Painted	-	2	-	-	1	-	-	-	1	4
Unidentified Brown	-	4	1	1	2	-	1	1	-	10
TOTALS	110	489	64	86	74	1	3	15	57	899

[1] Figures are raw counts by provenience group; see Table 17 for definition of groups.

Table 17
Definition of provenience groups for ceramic tabulations

Ceramic Group	Trench[1]	Provenience[1]
1	A	499-500N500-506W
2	B	499-500N512-518W
3	TT1	TT1
4	C	503-506N515W
5	D	510-512N514-516W
6	TT2	TT2
7	E	503-504N568-569W
8	F	495N519W
9	-	Surface

[1]See Fig. 42 for location of provenience groups.

of the sherds include golden biotite, various mafic minerals common to some aplites, and crushed yellowish caliche or similar carbonate material. In a number of examples, crushed sherd and/or crushed aplite are the accessories. An uncommon tempering constituent is a type of burned, bubbly appearing crushed sherd called "clinker" (J. H. Kelley 1979:32-33) because of its resemblance to the ash produced by coal-burning power plants and locomotives.

Only two vessel forms--bowl (28 rim sherds) and jar (113 rim sherds)--were recognized in the sherds, with 6 sherds being unclassifiable. Roughly guessing, the "average" Chupadero jar, when broken, will produce two to three times as many sherds as the "average" Chupadero bowl. Thus, the jar-to-bowl ratio at the site is conservatively estimated to be 1:1 or 2:1. The original number of whole vessels represented by the sherds could not be ascertained.

El Paso Polychrome: Although no obvious sherds of this type are present in the campsite collection, it is entirely possible that some or all of those typed as El Paso Brown are actually from polychrome vessels (see remarks under that type).

Galisteo Black-on-White: The 2 sherds of this type are from the same bowl.

Lincoln Black-on-Red: It could not be determined with certainty whether 1 or 2 bowls are represented by the 2 sherds of this type.

Mangas/Mimbres Black-on-White: Fourteen sherds belong to one or the other of the types Mangas Black-on-White and Mimbres Black-on-White. Only 2 could be definitely assigned to the latter type; the rest are too weathered. The number of vessels is unknown, but judging by the distribution of the sherds, 2 bowls are postulated.

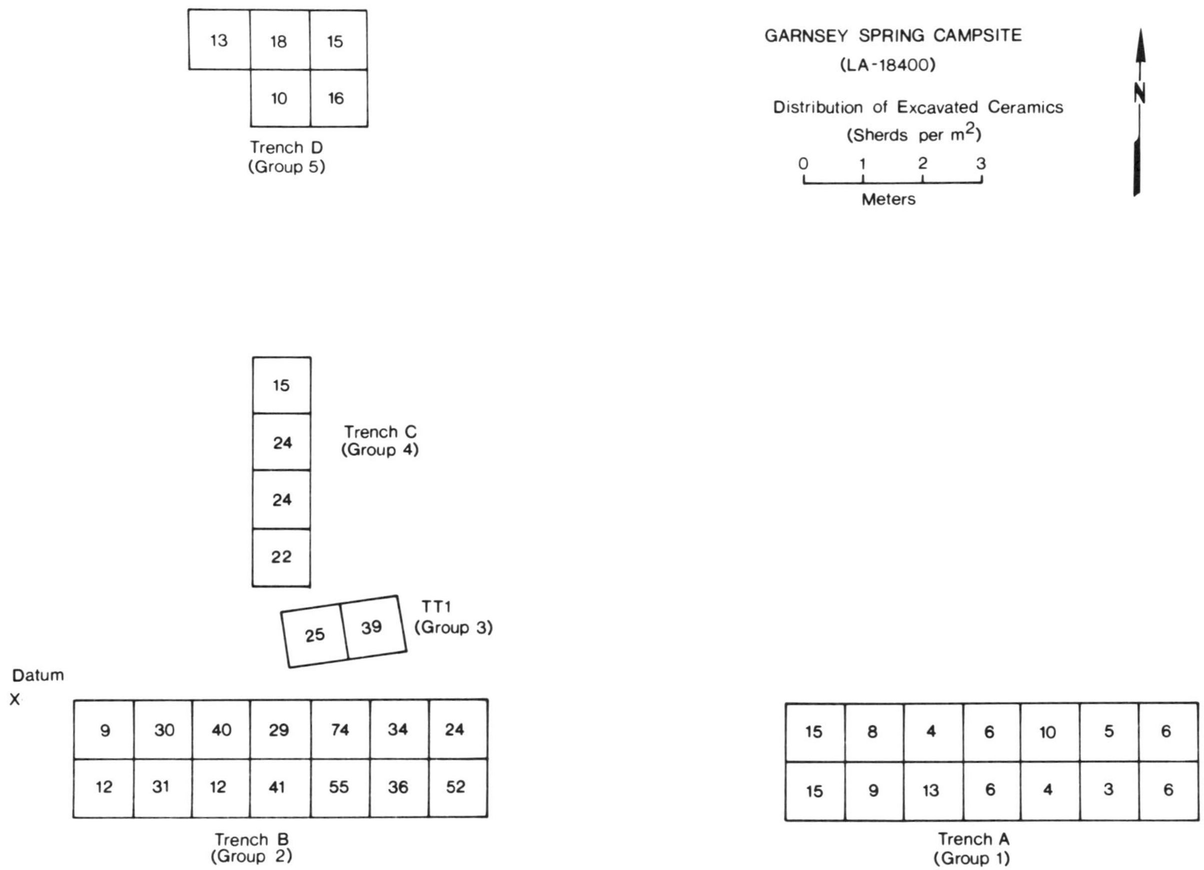

Fig. 42. Distribution by provenience group of excavated ceramics (sherds per m^2) from Garnsey Spring campsite (see Table 17 for definition of provenience groups).

Table 18
Major component temper classes of Chupadero Black-on-White from Garnsey Spring campsite

Tempering Material	%[1]
Sherd and aplite	64
Sherd	18
Aplite	8
Sherd, aplite, and caliche	8
Caliche	1
Aplite and caliche	0.5
Aplite and "clinker"	0.5

[1]Percentages are of total Chupadero B/W sample (N=147). Temper components occurring as accessory materials are not reflected in this table.

Playas Incised, Sierra Blanca var.: These 6 sherds possess the outward characteristics of Playas Red Incised and the gray feldspar temper common to the Sierra Blanca region 100 km (60 mi) west of the Garnsey Spring campsite. This same tempering material is also characteristic of South Pecos Brown, a type common at the campsite. One or 2 vessels are represented.

Red Mesa Black-on-White: The 2 sherds of this type derive from the same jar.

Redwashed Brown Ware: All 5 bowl sherds in this group have the gray feldspar typical of the tempering material of the Sierra Blanca region. Three vessels appear to be represented on the basis of sherd distributions.

San Andres Red-on-Terracotta: The characteristics of the sherds and their distributions indicate that 2 or possibly 3 vessels (1 jar and 1 or 2 bowls) are represented.

St. Johns Polychrome: Probably only 1 bowl is represented by the 4 sherds.

Three Rivers Red-on-Terracotta: At least 3 or 4 bowls are represented by the 12 sherds of this type.

Three Rivers Ware: The sherds in this category are from unpainted body portions of San Andres and/or Three Rivers Red-on-Terracotta vessels.

Utility Wares

Corona Corrugated (?): The 1 indented sherd has the paste and temper characteristics of McKenzie Brown (Jelinek 1967:51ff.). The indentations are sloppily executed (partially obliterated) and strongly resemble some of the sherds recovered from LA-2112 and attributed to Corona Corrugated (Wiseman 1976).

El Paso Brown: All but 1 or 2 of the sherds recorded as this type have a black core sandwiched between reddish interior and exterior vessel surfaces. The temper is composed primarily of crushed whitish feldspar and rounded quartz grains (not aplite); the particles tend to be quite large relative to the very thin walls of the vessels. On the whole, these sherds contrast with those of Jornada Brown in paste color, and the fact that the latter tends to have relatively fine temper and somewhat thicker sherds. While the finer temper particles in the El Paso sherds are in the same size range as the temper particles in the Jornada sherds, the larger particles in the former are noticeably larger than those in Jornada. In general, the attributes of these sherds (El Paso Brown) are reminiscent of those of the unpainted portions of El Paso Polychrome vessels; the striated appearance produced by the smoothing tool is particularly characteristic. It is considered likely that these sherds are from polychrome vessels, though no polychrome sherds as such were recovered from the campsite. The one or two exceptions noted above have brown paste colors and probably belong to the true plain brown type.

Jornada Brown: As noted in the introductory comments, most of the brown ware sherds are too small and weathered for the consistent use of surface finish criteria in typing the pottery. Jelinek's descriptions (particularly temper) of Jornada Brown and related types (see below) were used in this analysis. Sherds tabulated in this category possessed a fairly wide range of surface finish (where determinations are reliable) from well polished to only slightly polished. No attempt was made to determine vessel forms or numbers because of small sherd sizes. Only 4 rim sherds of this type were found, and only 3 are large enough for description. Two are slightly tapered with rounded lips, and 1 has a curved exterior with a rounded lip which ends fairly abruptly at the interior edge. One of both types are bowl sherds, and the remaining 1 is presumably a jar sherd.

McKenzie Brown: This type, named and described by Jelinek (1967), was recognized by its characteristic black paste and predominantly crushed quartz temper. A large number of sherds lacked more than an occasional fleck of mica, a fact which is at variance with the original description. Only 1 rim sherd is present, and that is tapered with a rounded lip.

Roswell Brown: This type, also named and described by Jelinek (1967), differs from Jornada Brown primarily by the presence of reddish temper fragments. Problems encountered in segregating unweathered sherds of Roswell from Jornada in regional collections raise doubts about the validity of Roswell as a separate type. No rims attributable to this type are present in the campsite collection.

South Pecos Brown: The temper hallmark of this, another Jelinek (1967) type, is the gray feldspar which derives from certain rocks of the Sierra Blanca region (A. H. Warren, personal communication; Burns 1977:229ff.). Temper particles are fairly large and sparse (compared to Jornada and Roswell Brown). The paste in almost all examples is somewhat blocky or platy, resulting in an irregular fracture. This contrasts with the grainy, more regular fracture of Jornada and Roswell Brown. The 4 rim sherds of South Pecos Brown are: tapered with a flat lip; tapered with a rounded lip (jar sherd); direct with a squarish lip (bowl sherd); and direct with a rounded lip.

Ceramic Distribution

An assessment of ceramic distributions was made by tabulating the ceramics in groups according to contiguous excavation units (Table 16). No discrimination was made between vertical excavation units (levels) because of the shallowness of the deposits and evidence for severe rodent disturbance (Chapter 4). All surface collections were combined into a single lot because only one 20 x 20 m square, that in the area of the major excavations, produced more than a few sherds. Chupadero Black-on-White and occasional brown ware sherds occurred in the remaining squares which suggests that no major definable differences in the ceramics exist from one part of the site surface to another.

The situation is little better with regard to the excavated collections. In several instances, localizations of a type or types were noted and are discussed below. However, it appears that the entire area of the site saw use throughout the occupation span and that there are no concrete ceramic data to indicate that one part of the site was used only during one period, another during a later period, and so on.

Five pottery types--Chupadero Black-on-White, Jornada Brown, Roswell Brown, South Pecos Brown, and McKenzie Brown--occurred in almost all surface collected and excavated squares. All other types occurred rather sporadically, but like the major types, all seemed to center on the excavation units herein referred to as Group 2. This group is located in the south-central part of the site area and in the southwest part of the major excavations. Although over half of the sherds came from this group of squares, it is still noticeable that most of the low frequency types of pottery (e.g., Red Mesa Black-on-White, Galisteo Black-on-White, St. Johns Polychrome, etc.) were restricted to these same squares. Given the range of dates represented by these types (Table 19 below), it seems likely that this area saw the full range and most intense occupations which took place at the site.

An inspection of Table 16 reveals several aspects of interest. For instance, all Mangas/Mimbres Black-on-White sherds came from excavation Groups 2, 3, and 5, the central portion of the excavated area and that with the deepest cultural fill. South Pecos Brown, which Jelinek (1967:67) considers to have been one of the earlier dominant types in the Middle Pecos region (greatest popularity A.D. 900-1100), was abundant in excavation Groups 2, 3, and 5; however, it was most abundant percentage-wise in the Group 4 squares where no Mangas/Mimbres Black-on-

White occurred at all. By way of contrast, McKenzie Brown, a type Jelinek (1967:65, his Fig. 9) considers to have been one of the later popular types, is best represented percentage-wise in excavation Groups 2 and 3. At least one factor contributing to the high Group 3 percentage of McKenzie Brown is the large number of sherds found in two adjacent levels of one square, a distribution strongly suggesting that they all derive from a single vessel. It is suspected that similar situations exist elsewhere in the site.

Dating the Occupations

As indicated in the above discussion of pottery distributions at the campsite, no temporal/spatial correlates can be made on the basis of the ceramics. We are left with only the all-inclusive dates derived from an evaluation of the dated pottery types listed in Table 19. Accuracy in the dating is necessarily suspect because of the poorly dated nature of most of the pottery types involved. The problem is particularly acute at the early end. The dates used for the brown wares are those suggested by Jelinek (1967:65, his Fig. 9) who seems to have based his estimates on those of Lehmer (1948) for Jornada Mogollon brown wares in general. More recent work by Whalen (1981) indicates that brown wares in the El Paso region date as early as the first one or two centuries A.D., hence the possibility of similarly early dates for those of the Roswell and Sierra Blanca regions. The proposed terminal date fares only slightly better and is based in part on pottery types which are absent from the Garnsey Spring campsite and data for the general period of abandonment of prehistoric settlements in southeastern New Mexico.

Table 19
Posited dates of various pottery types from Garnsey Spring campsite

Pottery Type	Date (A.D.)	Reference
Chupadero B/W	1150-1400+	Breterzitz (1966)
Galisteo B/W	1300-1400+	Breterzitz (1966)
Jornada Brown	pre 900-1300	Jelinek (1967)
Lincoln B/R	14th cent.	Breternitz (1966)
Mangas B/W	775- 923+	Breternitz (1966)
McKenzie Brown	1100-1300+	Jelinek (1967)
Mimbres B/W	1100-1250+	Breternitz (1966)
Red Mesa B/W	900-1200	Jelinek (1967)
Roswell Brown	900-1250	Jelinek (1967)
South Pecos Brown	pre 900-1300+ best 900-1100	Jelinek (1967)
St. Johns Polychrome	1175-1300	Breternitz (1966)
Three Rivers R/T	1150-1300	Breternitz (1966)

The tempering materials of almost all of the major pottery types at the campsite indicate that most of the ceramics were made in the general Sierra Blanca-Capitan Mountain region or in their eastern drainages. As J. H. Kelley (1966) and others have reported, numerous villages of the appropriate time period and ceramic content occur in that region and some (such as Bloom Mound, Rocky Arroyo, and Henderson Pueblo) are found at the west edge of the Pecos Valley only about 30-35 km (20 mi) west of the campsite (Fig. 1). The abandonment of these sites appears to have taken place about A.D. 1400 even though certain of the pottery types (such as Chupadero Black-on-White) were apparently produced past that time in their "home" regions.

The suggested end date of A.D. 1400 is based on the presence of Rio Grande Glaze A Red (or Agua Fria Glaze-on-Red and related types) in some quantity in the Sierra Blanca-Capitan Mountain pueblos of the late Glencoe and Lincoln Phases. Successor types in the Glaze B and later groups are absent; Glaze B ceramics were manufactured starting about A.D. 1400. Judging by the number of Glaze A sherds in the mountain pueblos (as well as at Bloom Mound and Henderson Pueblo near Roswell), it seems reasonable to assume that an important trade network connected the Rio Grande inhabitants with those in southeastern New Mexico and that this network was interrupted prior to the inception of Glaze B. Since Glaze B and later types have occasionally been found in sites east of the Pecos River (Collins 1971:88-89; Spielmann 1982), it is clear that some peoples were present in southeastern New Mexico at these later dates. However, the absence of Glaze B and later pottery types in both the mountain pueblos and in the Pecos Valley pueblos indicates that they were abandoned, presumably by about A.D. 1400.

Before proceeding, three observations should be noted with respect to the discussion just given. First, Rio Grande Glaze A Red is absent from the Garnsey Spring campsite. However, the presence of Lincoln B/R demonstrates a 14th-century use of the site. Second, recent investigations in the Socorro region (the most likely source of glazes in the Sierra Blanca and Roswell regions) have yielded data which indicate Rio Grande Glaze A Red may have been made as late as A.D. 1500 in that region (Cordell and Earls 1982). This, plus the third observation that Rio Grande Glaze B may have been areally restricted in its manufacture and distribution, opens the possibility that the village sites in the Sierra Blanca and Roswell regions may have been occupied later than herein suggested. The absence of Rio Grande Glaze A Red at the Garnsey Spring campsite, however, weakens any contention that this site was occupied very late, and the A.D. 1400 end-date appears to be reasonable, if not too liberal.

In summary, the inclusive dates for the Garnsey Spring campsite occupation, on the basis of ceramic evidence, are A.D. 900 or earlier to A.D. 1400. Judging by the length of this span, the shallowness of the midden, and the apparent absence of architecture, several different occupations are postulated.

Trade Contacts

All of the pottery types recovered from the Garnsey Spring campsite have been recorded from other sites in the surrounding region. While the major types found at the campsite may have been made in the mountainous region to the west (Sierra Blanca and Capitan Mountains), or employed tempering materials derived from the west, for the purposes of the present discussion they are considered to be essentially of local manufacture. Types traded into the area from substantially greater distances include:

1. Galisteo Black-on-White, a type from the middle Rio Grande region (Albuquerque-Santa Fe), 280 km (175 mi) northwest of the campsite.

2. Red Mesa Black-on-White, a type common in Pueblo II sites in northwestern New Mexico, ca. 400 km (250 mi) northwest of the campsite.

3. St. Johns Polychrome, a widely traded ceramic type made in the Zuni region of west-central New Mexico and east-central Arizona, ca. 440 km (275 mi) northwest of the campsite.

4. Mangas and Mimbres Black-on-White, two types common to southwestern New Mexico, 320 km (200 mi) west of the campsite.

The mechanisms and reasons behind the trade network are mostly speculative at this time. J. H. Kelley (1966:207) produced evidence and implied motivation for a trade route between the El Paso region and Bloom Mound. She suggested that Bloom Mound was a trade center between Plains-dwelling groups and the pueblo-inhabiting groups to the west, much in the same way Pecos Pueblo was during late prehistoric and early historic times. Other trade routes remain to be elucidated.

Summary and Conclusions

The ceramics recovered from the Garnsey Spring campsite are those typically found on other sites in this part of the Jornada Branch of the Mogollon Culture. The major, locally made types include Chupadero Black-on-White, Jornada Brown, Roswell Brown, South Pecos Brown, and McKenzie Brown. Locally made types occurring in smaller quantities include San Andres Red-on-Terracotta, Three Rivers Red-on-Terracotta, Lincoln Black-on-Red, and Playas Incised (Sierra Blanca var.), among others. The types traded into the region include Red Mesa Black-on-White, Mangas and/or Mimbres Black-on-White, Galisteo Black-on-White, and St. Johns Polychrome. The last group indicates some form of trade network linking southeastern New Mexico with areas in a radius of 320 km to 480 km (200-300 mi) to the northwest and west of the campsite. The intensity of that network was low, if intensity can be measured by the relative numbers of non-local sherds found in a site whose role within a larger settlement system is unclear. A similar low intensity of interchange is generally posited for most other sites of the Jornada Branch.

The distributions of the types throughout the Garnsey Spring campsite show no clear spatial or chronological clustering. The largest number and greatest typological variety of sherds occurred in the area of greatest midden accumulation and presumably the most intensely occupied part of the site. Types from the peripheral areas of the site are those best represented throughout the site. Since they are also some of the longest-lived types, they afford no temporal discrimination. Consequently, only the beginning and ending dates for the ceramic period occupations can be estimated, and those are A.D. 900 and A.D. 1400 respectively.

9. POLLEN ANALYSIS OF THE GARNSEY BISON KILL SITE, SOUTHEASTERN NEW MEXICO

by

Stephen A. Hall
Department of Geography
North Texas State University
Denton, Texas 76203

Introduction

The Garnsey Bison Kill site (LA-18399) is located east of Roswell, in Chaves County, southeastern New Mexico, in an upland draw about 1 km from the east escarpment of the Pecos River. The site is a series of nearly contemporaneous kills of over 35 bison by hunters using triangular side-notched projectile points. The series of kills is dated between A.D. 1450 and 1500 (Speth and Parry 1978, 1980; Speth 1983). Pollen samples were collected from an alluvial section adjacent to the site excavations. Analysis of the samples indicates that a major late prehistoric drought occurred in the southwestern Plains, affecting vegetation, bison, and man. This report presents the pollen analyses from which the new paleoenvironmental information is derived.

Stratigraphy

The sediments exposed in the arroyo and Garnsey Bison Kill site excavations have been differentiated into four units, A through D, top to bottom (Speth and Parry 1980). The section from which the pollen samples were collected is about 40 m upstream from the main excavations (Trenches 77-1 and 78-1) and about 10 m upstream from a gypsum bedrock ledge exposed in the channel floor (see Figs. 6, 43). The pollen section lies in square 499S466W of the Garnsey Bison Kill site grid system (Speth and Parry 1980:21). The identity of units A and B at the pollen site has been clearly determined. However, the lower boundary of unit B and the presence of unit C are not certain owing to rapid lateral changes in stratigraphic position and the discontinuity of gravel, sand, and clay beds. Unit D, restricted to a deeper scoured area of the wash (Speth and Parry 1980:27), is not present at the pollen section.

Where measured at the pollen section, unit A is a 170-cm-thick brown sandy clay with some gravel (Figs. 44 and 45). An interval of hard clay at a depth of 60 to 70 cm yielded carbonized remains of grasses, possibly originating from a range fire, that have been radiocarbon-dated 455±100 years B.P. (Beta-1925; ^{13}C fractionation-corrected; Speth 1983:46-47). The top of unit A is undated. Sediments may have been accumulating in the small valley up until the time of channel trenching initiated by nearby highway construction in the 1950s.

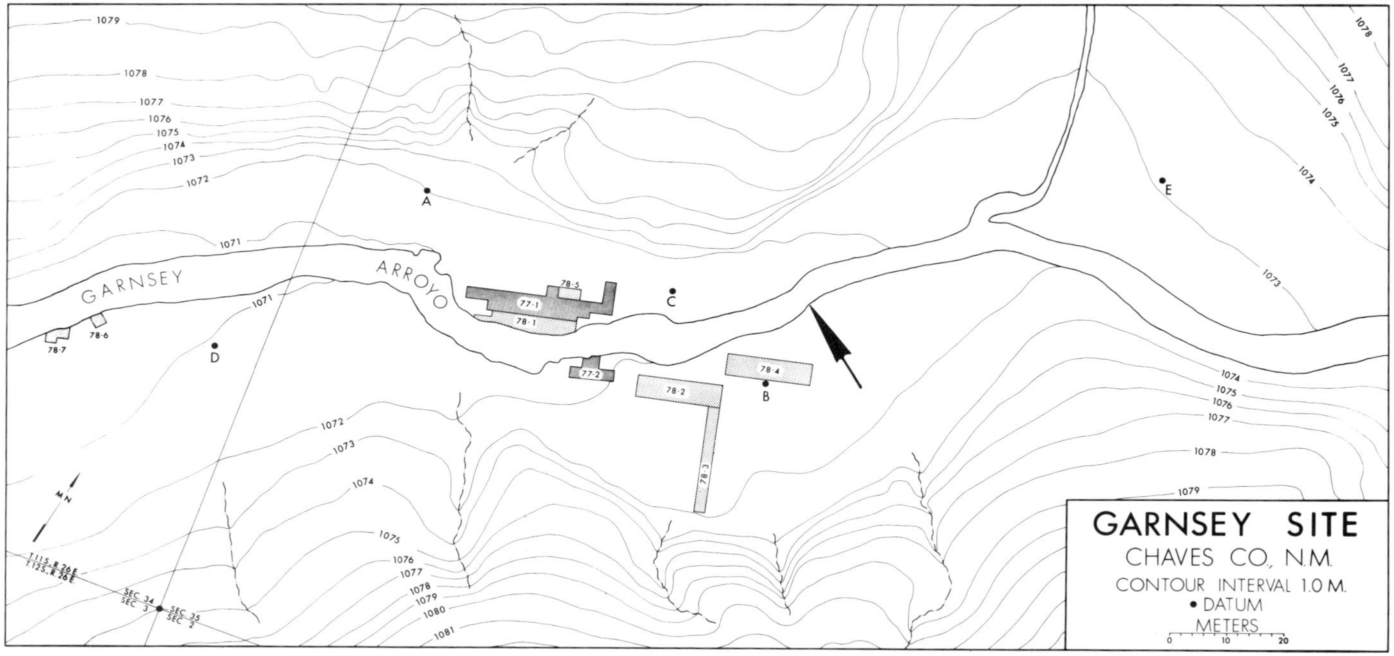

Fig. 43. Map of Garnsey Bison Kill site showing location of pollen section (arrow).

If so, the top of unit A could have been deposited in the early 20th century. Neither geological nor archaeological work at Garnsey provides information on the antiquity of the upper part of unit A.

Unit B is characterized by light red gravels and greenish-gray sandy clays. The red color of the gravels is derived from local red Permian shale and sandstone bedrock (Artesia Group; V. Kelley 1971). The unit accumulated in the small valley during episodes of torrential discharge that partly scoured out previously deposited beds, leaving behind thin layers of pollen-bearing sandy gravels. The greenish-gray sandy clays are wet-meadow or cienega deposits that probably represent moister conditions. Whether the moist cienega environment was restricted to the local area or was a regional phenomenon cannot be determined from the sediments alone. However, the pollen data (discussed below) indicate that the climate was becoming drier and/or warmer during the cienega stage. After cienega clay deposition ended and during the time interval required for an additional 80 cm of gravels and sandy clays to be deposited, the dry period was at its extreme.

Most of the bison remains were excavated from the upper part of unit B above the cienega clays, corresponding to the 235 to 170 cm interval at the pollen section (Fig. 45). Speth (1983:21, 49) reports that 90% of the bison remains, representing a series of nearly contemporaneous kill events, were recovered from that stratigraphic interval (B3). Fourteen bone samples (charcoal was not recovered from the archaeological excavations) were radiocarbon-dated; the ages of the bison bone cluster between 450 and 500 years B.P. (Speth 1983:45-48).

The 4-m alluvial sequence at the Garnsey site represents a brief period of time. The major portion of the sequence dates from about 600 to 400 years B.P., deposition taking place over a period of only 200 years or less. The uppermost 50 cm of unit A may have accumulated slowly during the past 400 years with deposition extending up to the time of mid-20th century arroyo cutting.

Pollen Analysis

Field and Laboratory Methods. Pollen samples were collected from a 4-m arroyo face where the stratigraphy was easily correlated to the Garnsey Bison Kill site excavations about 40 m downstream. After the stratigraphic section was measured, samples were collected at 10 cm intervals, except at lithologic boundaries where separate samples were collected below and above the contacts. The pollen samples were chopped from the outcrop with a rock hammer. Each sample represents a stratigraphic thickness of about 5 cm.

In the laboratory, the samples were processed by methods developed over the years to deal with alluvium and coarse-grained sediments. Each sample was oven-dried, weighed, and washed in hydrochloric acid. Lycopodium spore tablets were added to each sample to facilitate the determination of pollen grain concentration (per gram oven-dry weight of sediment processed). The samples were then washed in hydrofluoric acid followed by a second hydrochloric acid wash, heavy liquid separation

Fig. 44. Garnsey Bison Kill site pollen section. Short section from which lower 3 samples were collected visible at left. Photographed July 1981.

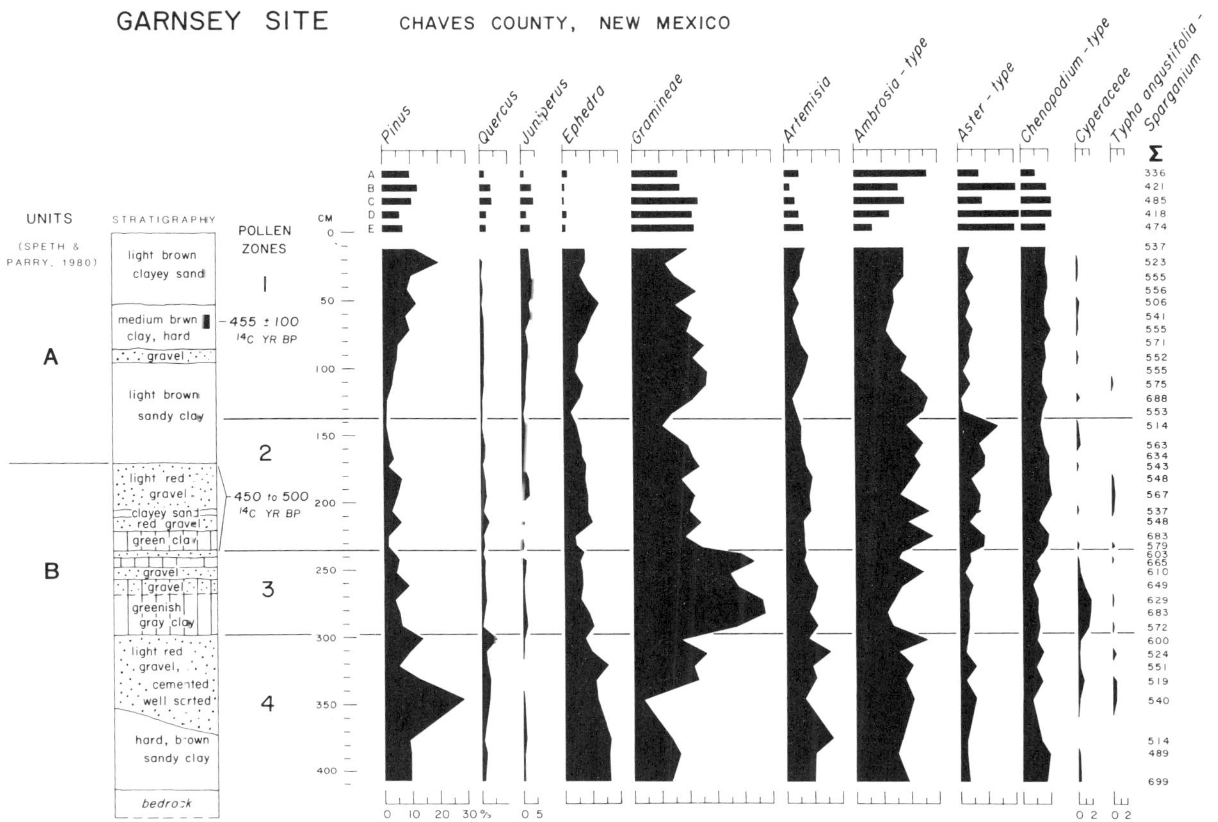

Fig. 45. Relative frequency pollen diagram from Garnsey Bison Kill site (LA-18399), Chaves County, southeastern New Mexico. Lower 3 spectra collected from short section off-set about 1.5 m from main section (see Fig. 44). Localities of surface samples A-E shown in Fig. 46; pollen data given in Tables 20-27. Percentage scale of Cyperaceae and <u>Typha angustifolia</u>/<u>Sparganium</u> expanded (neither were tabulated in surface samples). Pollen sums on right.

(zinc chloride, specific gravity 1.955), and acetolysis solution. If fine quartz particles were present after heavy liquid separation, a second hydrofluoric acid wash was applied prior to acetolysis. After acetolysis, the organic residue was washed in 10% ammonium hydroxide, stained with safranin O, and mounted on glass slides with a medium of glycerine jelly, glycerol, and water. At least 500 pollen grains (excluding lycopodium spike grains) were tabulated from each residue. Pollen counts are given in Tables 20-27.

Pollen Preservation and Concentration. The condition of pollen in the alluvium at Garnsey is judged fair or stage 2 preservation class (Hall 1981). About 20 to 60% of the grains are deteriorated, mostly degraded or corroded (Cushing 1967), although the assemblages are not altered to the degree that would greatly affect grain counts. When pollen grains were not identifiable, they were counted as indeterminable. The abundance of indeterminable grains in the alluvial pollen spectra ranges from 5 to 25% of the pollen sum.

Pollen concentrations in the Garnsey alluvium range from 350 to 97,000 grains per gram of processed sediment (see Tables 23-27). Higher concentrations occur in unit A than in unit B, probably due to less rapid rates of deposition and to a smaller component of gravels than is characteristic of unit B.

Surface Samples. Surficial sediment was collected at five localities in the Garnsey drainage basin (Fig. 46). Pollen assemblages in these samples show the relationship between present-day influx and the modern vegetation. The surface samples were collected by the pinch method, each an aggregate of 20 pinches collected over a 20 m^2 area. The surface pollen spectra, labelled A through E, are shown at the top of the pollen diagram (Fig. 45).

Pollen preservation in the surface samples is moderate, the grains showing definite effects of deterioration with 15% indeterminable. Concentrations of pollen in the five surface samples averaged 48,000 grains per gram of sediment processed. Only one alluvial sample contained a greater amount of pollen.

Analyses show a difference between the relative pollen frequencies of the surface material and the recent upper alluvium. While frequencies of *Pinus*, *Juniperus*, Gramineae, *Artemisia*, *Ambrosia*-type, and *Chenopodium*-type in the upper alluvium are similar to those in the surficial materials, frequencies of *Quercus*, *Ephedra*, and *Aster*-type are quite different. *Quercus* and *Aster* percentages are significantly higher in the surface samples than in the upper alluvium. *Ephedra*, on the other hand, makes up less than 2% of the surface pollen assemblages; in the upper alluvium *Ephedra* percentages are generally greater than 5%.

The differences between alluvial and surface pollen assemblages indicate that *Ephedra* has been dramatically reduced in the present-day Garnsey rangeland and that a yet undetermined member of the Compositae family with long-spined pollen grains has recently become abundant. In 1980, when surface samples were collected, the writer observed only an

Table 20

Pollen counts for surface samples and pollen zone 1 shown in pollen diagram (Fig. 45).

Ref. No.	Pollen Types	Surface Samples					(top)					Pollen Zone 1							
		A	B	C	D	E	10-15	20-25	30-35	40-45	50-55	60-65	70-75	80-85	90-95	100-105	110-115	120-125	130-135
1	Pinus undiff.	33	53	50	25	34	62	104	55	47	60	41	52	32	30	22	18	13	7
2	Quercus	4	16	20	9	10	--	5	2	6	4	7	8	6	8	5	6	5	2
3	Juniperus	3	15	21	8	14	13	15	17	25	13	15	8	13	11	7	6	9	3
4	Ephedra undiff.	6	2	2	5	4	44	42	35	51	64	55	46	30	28	24	40	40	15
5	Gramineae	56	73	116	89	105	106	63	82	128	77	116	109	147	120	149	150	150	76
6	Artemisia	17	8	19	21	31	37	30	28	15	25	13	19	29	44	37	28	16	18
7	Ambrosia type	88	65	88	52	60	94	92	99	78	72	66	62	78	103	91	127	184	137
8	Aster type	25	85	41	91	95	18	13	28	11	16	11	27	17	17	6	20	5	7
9	Chenopodium type	17	40	53	47	43	46	42	52	51	42	46	58	47	49	41	42	64	41
10	Cyperaceae	--	--	--	--	--	--	1	1	--	2	1	1	--	1	1	--	3	--
11	Typha angustifolia/ Sparganium	--	--	--	--	--	--	--	--	--	--	--	--	--	--	--	1	--	--
12	Pollen sum (Tables 20-27; all grains)	336	421	485	418	474	537	523	555	556	506	541	555	571	552	555	575	688	553

Table 21
Pollen counts for pollen zones 2 and 3 shown in pollen diagram (Fig. 45).

Ref. No.	Pollen Types	(top)			Pollen Zone 2							(top)			Pollen Zone 3			
		140-145	155-160	165-168	172-175	180-185	192-197	205-208	213-218	223-227	230-235	238-240	242-245	250-255	260-265	270-275	280-285	290-295
1	Pinus undiff.	5	13	21	10	38	29	15	38	15	9	25	37	27	53	27	41	39
2	Quercus	2	8	9	3	8	12	6	15	8	8	6	10	10	9	13	11	2
3	Juniperus	5	7	1	1	13	14	--	1	--	1	--	7	5	1	3	7	10
4	Ephedra undiff.	24	39	43	42	41	49	45	55	28	24	44	40	38	42	36	58	59
5	Gramineae	53	112	136	129	95	126	111	135	129	143	232	287	211	244	293	325	213
6	Artemisia	29	30	42	38	50	45	44	32	41	40	43	45	47	69	63	54	63
7	Ambrosia type	94	135	138	127	114	89	144	106	190	138	101	103	151	113	91	81	76
8	Aster type	70	38	52	22	41	36	18	50	58	25	29	24	13	31	20	23	19
9	Chenopodium type	36	44	62	53	53	60	40	33	64	51	47	36	42	21	34	37	35
10	Cyperaceae	1	2	--	1	--	--	1	--	--	1	--	1	2	6	12	12	9
11	Typha angustifolia/ Sparganium	--	--	--	--	1	2	1	--	--	2	--	1	--	--	1	--	1
12	Pollen sum (Tables 20-27; all grains)	514	563	634	543	548	567	537	548	683	579	603	665	610	649	629	683	572

Table 22
Pollen counts for pollen zone 4 shown in pollen diagram (Fig. 45).

Ref. No.	Pollen Types	Pollen Zone 4							
		(top)					(top)	Short Section	
		300-305	310-315	320-325	330-335	345-350	25-30	34-40	55-60
1	Pinus undiff.	99	46	28	65	154	45	46	64
2	Quercus	31	7	12	15	14	3	9	7
3	Juniperus	5	3	--	--	1	4	2	1
4	Ephedra undiff.	44	52	83	60	63	85	76	111
5	Gramineae	100	141	122	121	18	73	81	97
6	Artemisia	46	82	51	55	37	84	51	69
7	Ambrosia type	146	82	112	67	113	87	75	131
8	Aster type	15	5	30	40	31	13	12	22
9	Chenopodium type	32	38	28	38	17	32	48	59
10	Cyperaceae	2	1	1	4	1	--	1	2
11	Typha angustifolia/ Sparganium	--	2	--	2	2	--	--	--
12	Pollen sum (Tables 20-27; all grains)	600	524	551	519	540	514	489	699

Table 23
Pollen counts for surface samples not shown in pollen diagram (Fig. 45).

Ref. No.	Pollen Types	Surface Samples				
		A	B	C	D	E
13	Abies	--	--	--	--	--
14	Picea	--	--	1	--	--
15	Pseudotsuga	--	--	--	--	--
16	Juglans	1	4	1	--	--
17	Carya	--	--	1	--	2
18	Celtis	--	--	--	--	--
19	Ulmus	--	1	--	--	--
20	Populus	--	--	--	--	--
21	Salix	3	4	5	10	6
22	cf. Fraxinus	--	--	--	--	2
23	Alnus	--	--	--	--	--
24	cf. Prosopis	--	--	--	--	--
25	Yucca	--	--	--	--	--
26	Eriogonum	3	3	2	6	2
27	Polygonaceae	--	--	--	--	--
28	Sphaeralcea	--	--	--	--	--
29	Malvaceae	--	--	--	--	--
30	Liguliflora	--	--	--	--	--
31	Tidestromia	2	--	--	--	--
32	Sarcobatus	--	--	--	--	--
33	Cruciferae	--	--	--	--	--
34	Onagraceae	1	--	1	--	4
35	Umbelliferae	--	--	--	--	--
36	Fern spores, undiff.	--	--	--	--	1
37	Unknown	14	18	5	8	3
38	Indeterminable	63	34	55	47	58
39	Lycopodium spores, spike	120	320	181	146	95
40	Concentration/gram (x1000)	60.87	26.30	36.20	49.40	69.30
41	Degraded grains	43	13	68	109	146
42	Corroded grains	52	41	89	41	44

Table 24
Pollen counts for pollen zone 1 not shown in pollen diagram (Fig. 45).

Ref. No.	Pollen Types	(top) 10-15	20-25	30-35	40-45	50-55	60-65	70-75	80-85	90-95	100-105	110-115	120-125	130-135
		Pollen Zone 1												
13	Abies	--	--	--	--	--	--	--	--	1	--	--	--	--
14	Picea	1	--	--	--	--	--	--	--	--	--	--	--	--
15	Pseudotsuga	--	1	1	1	--	1	--	--	--	--	--	1	2
16	Juglans	--	--	--	--	--	--	--	--	--	--	--	--	--
17	Carya	--	--	--	--	--	1	--	--	--	--	--	--	--
18	Celtis	--	--	--	--	--	--	--	--	--	--	--	--	--
19	Ulmus	--	1	--	--	--	--	--	--	--	--	--	--	--
20	Populus	1	--	--	--	--	--	--	1	1	--	--	--	1
21	Salix	--	--	--	1	--	--	1	2	--	2	1	1	--
22	cf. Fraxinus	6	4	3	15	20	6	4	4	9	9	5	3	--
23	Alnus	1	--	--	--	--	--	--	--	--	--	--	--	--
24	cf. Prosopis	--	--	--	--	--	1	--	--	--	--	2	--	--
25	Yucca	--	--	--	--	--	--	--	--	--	--	--	--	--
26	Eriogonum	4	2	3	5	4	4	1	2	6	3	8	7	2
27	Polygonaceae	--	--	1	--	--	1	1	3	--	--	1	3	--
28	Sphaeralcea	--	--	--	--	--	--	--	--	--	--	--	1	--
29	Malvaceae	--	1	1	--	--	--	--	--	--	--	--	1	--
30	Liguliflora	--	--	1	--	--	--	--	--	--	--	--	1	--
31	Tidestromia	--	1	1	1	3	1	1	3	3	5	6	1	4
32	Sarcobatus	3	--	--	2	--	--	--	--	--	1	--	2	--
33	Cruciferae	1	--	--	--	3	1	--	1	3	--	1	1	--
34	Onagraceae	--	--	1	1	1	1	1	--	--	--	--	4	1
35	Umbelliferae	--	--	--	1	--	--	--	--	--	--	--	--	--
36	Fern spores, undiff.	--	3	2	--	--	--	--	1	3	1	--	1	1
37	Unknown	3	9	12	9	7	4	4	6	0	4	6	10	5
38	Indeterminable	97	94	130	108	93	149	152	149	115	147	107	162	228
39	Lycopodium, spike	75	72	55	19	24	12	18	7	15	23	46	123	66
40	Concen./g (x1000)	8.65	8.62	9.98	30.83	21.40	37.80	34.84	97.28	35.77	23.10	12.67	5.44	8.23
41	Degraded grains	196	178	248	178	177	231	261	262	279	264	247	333	357
42	Corroded grains	117	129	115	99	94	137	104	93	107	122	125	129	106

Table 25
Pollen counts for pollen zone 2 not shown in pollen diagram (Fig. 45).

Ref. No.	Pollen Types	(top) 140-145	155-160	165-168	172-175	180-185	192-197	205-208	213-218	223-227	230-235
		Pollen Zone 2									
13	Abies	--	--	--	--	--	--	--	--	--	--
14	Picea	--	--	--	--	--	1	--	--	--	--
15	Pseudotsuga	1	--	--	--	--	--	--	--	--	1
16	Juglans	--	--	--	1	--	--	--	--	--	--
17	Carya	--	--	--	--	--	--	--	--	--	--
18	Celtis	--	--	--	--	2	--	--	--	--	--
19	Ulmus	--	--	--	--	--	--	--	--	--	--
20	Populus	1	--	--	--	4	--	--	--	--	--
21	Salix	1	1	1	2	--	--	--	2	--	--
22	cf. Fraxinus	3	6	6	9	6	3	5	1	11	6
23	Alnus	--	--	--	--	--	--	--	--	--	1
24	cf. Prosopis	--	--	--	--	--	--	--	--	--	--
25	Yucca	--	1	--	--	--	--	--	--	--	--
26	Eriogonum	5	6	6	6	9	7	8	14	6	8
27	Polygonaceae	5	3	2	3	1	1	--	2	4	--
28	Sphaeralcea	--	--	--	1	--	--	--	--	--	--
29	Malvaceae	--	--	--	--	--	--	--	--	--	--
30	Liguliflora	--	--	--	--	--	2	--	--	--	--
31	Tidestromia	2	5	6	1	--	--	2	--	4	2
32	Sarcobatus	--	--	--	--	--	--	--	--	--	--
33	Cruciferae	--	--	--	--	--	--	--	--	--	--
34	Onagraceae	--	--	2	--	--	1	1	1	--	--
35	Umbelliferae	--	--	--	--	--	--	--	--	--	--
36	Fern spores, undiff.	4	--	--	3	--	--	--	--	--	--
37	Unknown	7	16	5	11	22	18	4	20	13	10
38	Indeterminable	166	97	102	80	50	72	92	42	112	109
39	Lycopodium, spike	90	77	37	168	344	297	173	677	345	376
40	Concen./g (x1000)	6.28	5.46	14.18	1.68	0.64	0.80	2.35	0.483	1.16	1.006
41	Degraded grains	326	249	335	246	215	189	301	97	375	276
42	Corroded grains	92	98	88	92	45	75	41	51	62	85

Table 26
Pollen counts for pollen zone 3 not shown in pollen diagram (Fig. 45).

Ref. No.	Pollen Types	(top)	Pollen Zone 3					
		238-240	242-245	250-255	260-265	270-275	280-285	290-295
13	Abies	--	--	--	--	--	--	--
14	Picea	--	--	--	--	--	1	--
15	Pseudotsuga	1	--	--	--	--	--	1
16	Juglans	--	--	--	--	--	--	1
17	Carya	--	--	--	--	--	--	--
18	Celtis	--	--	--	--	--	--	--
19	Ulmus	--	--	--	--	--	--	--
20	Populus	--	--	--	--	--	--	--
21	Salix	3	--	4	1	--	5	4
22	cf. Fraxinus	6	6	--	4	4	--	--
23	Alnus	--	--	--	--	--	--	--
24	cf. Prosopis	--	--	--	--	--	--	--
25	Yucca	--	--	1	--	--	--	--
26	Eriogonum	2	--	--	--	--	--	--
27	Polygonaceae	2	--	2	3	1	--	--
28	Sphaeralcea	1	1	--	4	2	--	1
29	Malvaceae	--	--	--	--	--	--	1
30	Liguliflora	--	--	--	2	--	--	--
31	Tidestromia	4	6	3	1	5	2	1
32	Sarcobatus	--	--	--	--	--	--	--
33	Cruciferae	--	--	--	--	--	--	--
34	Onagraceae	1	1	2	1	4	1	5
35	Umbelliferae	--	--	--	--	--	--	--
36	Fern spores, undiff.	1	--	--	--	--	--	--
37	Unknown	19	10	11	11	0	1	1
38	Indeterminable	36	50	41	33	20	24	31
39	Lycopodium spores, spike	173	101	142	278	53	27	101
40	Concentration/gram (x1000)	2.56	4.95	3.095	1.69	8.31	15.30	3.78
41	Degraded grains	161	136	173	159	131	123	128
42	Corroded grains	64	74	56	51	53	69	73

Table 27
Pollen counts for pollen zone 4 not shown in pollen diagram (Fig. 45).

Ref. No.	Pollen Types	Pollen Zone 4							
		(top)					(top)	Short Section	
		300-305	310-315	320-325	330-335	345-350	25-30	34-40	55-60
13	Abies	--	--	--	--	--	--	--	--
14	Picea	--	--	--	--	--	--	--	--
15	Pseudotsuga	2	--	--	--	--	--	--	--
16	Juglans	1	1	--	--	1	--	--	--
17	Carya	--	--	--	--	--	--	--	--
18	Celtis	5	--	--	--	2	--	--	--
19	Ulmus	--	--	--	--	--	--	--	--
20	Populus	--	1	--	--	2	--	--	5
21	Salix	9	1	1	--	1	3	3	1
22	cf. Fraxinus	--	1	1	--	--	--	--	9
23	Alnus	--	--	--	--	--	--	--	--
24	cf. Prosopis	--	2	--	--	--	--	--	--
25	Yucca	--	--	--	--	--	--	--	--
26	Eriogonum	2	3	1	2	1	--	--	12
27	Polygonaceae	--	1	--	--	4	--	1	1
28	Sphaeralcea	--	1	--	--	5	--	--	1
29	Malvaceae	--	--	--	3	--	--	--	--
30	Liguliflora	--	--	--	--	--	1	--	--
31	Tidestromia	--	2	--	--	--	--	1	--
32	Sarcobatus	--	--	--	--	--	--	--	--
33	Cruciferae	--	--	--	--	--	--	--	--
34	Onagraceae	1	5	--	--	3	1	2	1
35	Umbelliferae	--	--	--	--	--	--	--	--
36	Fern spores, undiff.	--	--	--	--	--	--	1	1
37	Unknown	7	13	14	10	6	9	6	8
38	Indeterminable	50	33	67	37	63	74	74	97
39	Lycopodium spores, spike	735	57	917	1,265	316	37	73	37
40	Concentration/gram (x1000)	0.56	8.18	0.37	0.29	1.34	9.21	5.80	10.60
41	Degraded grains	118	179	209	128	160	214	187	299
42	Corroded grains	61	88	63	112	51	119	101	65

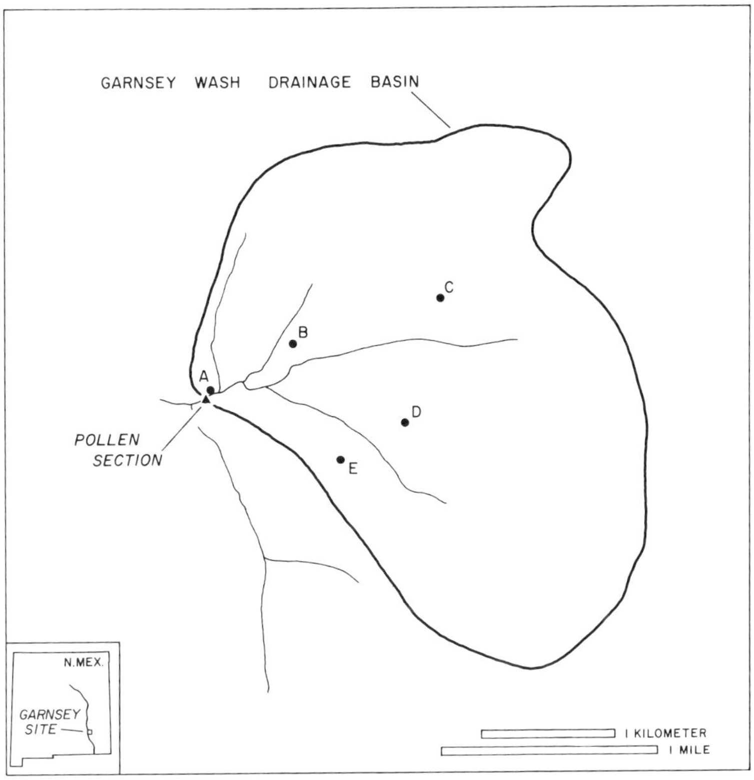

Fig. 46. Map of Garnsey drainage basin showing sampling points for modern surficial pollen samples A-E (drawn from USGS Bottomless Lakes 7.5 minute quadrangle, topographic series, 1950, photorevised 1975).

occasional small clump of *Ephedra*. The decimation of the *Ephedra* population and the appearance of *Aster*-type plants may be a result of recent intense cattle grazing.

In four of the five surface samples, *Quercus* pollen frequencies are greater at the 0.95 confidence limit than those of the upper alluvium.

Pollen Zones. The Garnsey site pollen diagram is divided into four zones (Fig. 45). The zones are delineated at major changes in frequencies of some pollen types and are regarded as zones of convenience facilitating discussion; they should not be construed as formal biostratigraphic or paleoclimatic zones.

Zone 4 at the base of the 4-m section is characterized by comparatively high frequencies of *Ephedra* (10 to 15%), *Pinus* (10%), *Artemisia* (10%), and *Quercus* (5%). Gramineae pollen frequencies (15 to

25%) and Juniperus frequencies (less than 1%) are low when compared with the rest of the pollen diagram. Chenopodium-type abundance decreases by about 2% in the lower part of zone 4.

Zone 3 is distinguished by a marked increase in Gramineae percentages (35 to 45%) and the presence of sedge (Cyperaceae) (2%). Pinus and Ephedra frequencies are lower than in zone 4. The lithology is a greenish-gray sandy clay, representing cienega or wet-meadow conditions. Pollen preservation in zone 3 is best of the entire sequence; indeterminable grains average 5% of the pollen sum and degraded-corroded pollen grains total 30% compared with 60% elsewhere in the section.

Zone 2 is defined by an increase in Aster-type frequencies. The identity of the long-spined pollen type(s) belonging to the Compositae is unknown. The zone is also characterized by a slight increase in Chenopodium-type frequencies and a continuing trend of decreased Pinus pollen abundance. The upper part of the zone contains the lowest Pinus pollen frequencies observed in the study.

The lower part of zone 1 contains the same small amounts of Pinus pollen that characterize the uppermost part of zone 2. From base to top of zone 1, however, Pinus percentages gradually increase as do those of Juniperus and Ephedra. Aster-type frequencies decrease sharply at the boundary of zone 2 and zone 1.

Alluvial Palynology

Pollen Origins. The processes by which pollen grains are incorporated in fluvial sediments are inadequately known. It has been established, however, that a vast proportion of the mineral sediment deposited as alluvium in semiarid regions originates from hillslopes, transported to flowing streams by overland flow (Leopold, Emmett, and Myrick 1966). Pollen grains can be regarded as sedimentary particles (ranging in size from medium silt to very fine sand; Folk 1968), a view applied to Chaco Canyon where it was proposed that pollen in the canyon fill originated by sheet wash of surficial materials (Hall 1977). It follows that pollen assemblages in alluvium would represent a mixture of plant communities in an entire watershed. In that respect, the Garnsey site is an excellent locality for alluvial pollen analytical studies; the drainage basin is less than 10 km^2 in area, encompassing a single, moderately uniform vegetation type. The alluvial pollen assemblages at Garnsey are thus mixtures of pollen grains from plants in three different situations: (1) the hillslopes and uplands of the Garnsey drainage basin, (2) the floors of the narrow drainages, and (3) distant localities from which pollen grains have been carried by long-distance atmospheric transport to the Garnsey watershed. Distant sources of pollen include the wide floodplain of the Pecos River as well as the surrounding grasslands of the region and the Sacramento Mountains 100 km to the west.

Today at Garnsey, pollen grains from extra-local plants (pine, oak, juniper, and sage) are 20% of the total pollen accumulation in surficial materials. This is a minimum value for long-distance transported pollen because it is impossible to distinguish between the pollen of grasses, ambrosia, asters, chenopods, and *Ephedra* of local origin and the pollen grains of these plants that have been transported from distant populations. It is not unlikely that as much as 30% of the surface pollen assemblages at Garnsey have originated from localities outside the drainage basin. As a result, the pollen sequence at Garnsey reflects not only local vegetational events but serves as well as an index to vegetational history of both the regional grasslands and the forest communities in the Sacramento Mountains.

Resolution of Vegetational Events Using Pollen Analysis. The potential of an alluvial pollen record to show small changes in vegetation is limited by two variables that cannot be manipulated by the investigator: (1) the sedimentation rate of the pollen-bearing deposit, and (2) the number of years of pollen influx mixed together in the surficial materials. Surface pollen samples are analyzed to provide information on pollen assemblages produced by the plant community at the site of surface pollen collection. The general uniformity of pollen frequencies from similar plant communities sampled at different times of the year and the large number of pollen grains in the surface materials have led to the general conclusion that the surface pollen assemblages represent a mixture of many years of pollen influx. If surface pollen flushed into a flowing stream represents, for example, 20 years of atmospheric influx and mixing, the resulting pollen-bearing alluvium may not fully depict vegetational changes of less than 20 years duration.

Differences in sedimentation rates and the discontinuous nature of alluviation also limit the resolving power of vegetational events. Deposition occurs in increments of millimeters to decimeters in a single flood episode. Thus, even though a thick alluvial sequence may be viewed as having accumulated at an average rate in centimeters per year, an individual bed within the sequence may have been deposited in one day, yet contain a pollen assemblage that is an amalgam of 20 years of influx and mixing.

At the Garnsey site, two zones in the alluvium are radiocarbon-dated, indicating that much of the 4-m section accumulated rapidly, perhaps in 200 years. The pollen record is unusual in that it is from a long stratigraphic section representing a short period of time, resulting in a potential resolution of changes in plant populations that have occurred within one century, a resolution seldom obtainable from lacustrine deposits that exhibit slow rates of sedimentation.

Present-Day Vegetation (1980)

The character of the present-day plant communities in the drainage basin has probably been altered in historic time by cattle grazing. The vegetation type is a semiarid grassland (annual rainfall, 295 mm) dominated by black grama (*Bouteloua eriopoda*) and tobosa (*Hilaria mutica*). Prickly pear (*Opuntia*), yucca (*Yucca*), and *Ephedra* occur infrequently on hillslopes, and scattered individuals of honey mesquite (_Prosopis juliflora_) are present in the upper portion of the drainage basin as well as on the floor of Garnsey Wash. The valley floor vegetation has probably changed since the 1950s owing to the channel trenching that has occurred since then. A thick growth of sacaton (_Sporobolus airoides_) is present today in the wash near the spring upstream from the pollen section. Salt cedar (_Tamarix pentandra_; historical introduction), broom snakeweed (_Gutierrezia sarothrae_), Apache plume (_Fallugia paradoxa_), four-wing saltbush (_Atriplex canescens_), and javelina bush (_Condalia ericoides_) also occur sporadically in the Garnsey drainage (Speth 1983:12-13).

A map of potential natural vegetation of New Mexico (U.S. Department of Agriculture 1978) depicts the area including the Garnsey watershed as a northern outlier of desert shrub in a broader grassland vegetation of the Chihuahuan region. The vegetation is classed as a creosote bush/bush muhly association with the description: "At one time these were predominantly grasslands with scattered creosotebush. Principal grasses were black grama, bush muhly, scattered tobosa in rills, and creosotebush." Creosote bush does not occur in the Garnsey drainage today.

Nineteenth century field notes of the Territorial Survey provide a record of the general vegetation and the presence of specific plant species. These field notes have been analyzed by Gross and Dick-Peddie (1979), Gardner (1951), York and Dick-Peddie (1969), and Buffington and Herbel (1965) and indicate that the Garnsey area was a grassland lacking mesquite, although numerous individuals of mesquite were recorded to the east and northwest.

Past Vegetation: Pollen Evidence

The Garnsey site pollen succession indicates a local grassland vegetation and a regional vegetation that includes components of pine, oak, juniper, and sage. Even though the complete pollen sequence points to the persistence of grassland vegetation, changes occurred in plant populations within the grassland.

As discussed in the section on "Surface Samples," as much as 30% of the modern pollen grain influx in the Garnsey watershed may originate from plants outside the drainage basin. If this were true in the past, some of the fluctuations in relative pollen frequencies in the alluvial record may be in response to changes in the extra-local vegetation.

Pinus. The clearest trend of regional vegetational and climatic significance is exhibited by the _Pinus_ frequency curve. _Pinus_ frequencies decrease steadily from a high of 10% in zone 4 to a low of 1% in the uppermost sample of zone 2. _Pinus_ then increases to about 10% in the upper levels of the pollen section and in the modern surface samples. Today, as in the 19th century, the nearest pine stand is a small outlier of pinyon (_Pinus edulis_) about 60 km west of the Garnsey site (Gross and Dick-Peddie 1979). The outlier is 25 km from the margin of the pine woodland and forest of the Sacramento Mountains. The pine populations in the Sacramentos 90 to 100 km west of Garnsey are the nearest major sources for the pine pollen influx that today makes up 10% of the surface pollen spectra.

Diminished pine pollen frequencies, reaching lowest values about 450 years B.P., indicate a decrease in pine populations in the Sacramento Mountains. Montane forest vegetation is generally restricted at high elevations by low temperatures and, at low elevations where trees border the grasslands, by low precipitation and high temperatures. During the onset of a drier and/or warmer climate, trees at the lower elevational limits of forest growth would die or fail to reproduce, resulting in an eventual upslope migration of vegetation zones, the ranges of tree populations becoming spatially more narrow with an accompanying reduction in numbers of individuals.

Pollen evidence at Garnsey for a decrease in montane pine forests at about 450 years B.P. has not been previously reported from the Sacramento Mountain region or from other regions in the Southwest. The lack of supporting pollen evidence can be explained by the fact that the vegetation change documented at Garnsey occurred over a comparatively brief time interval. Few geological situations have been investigated where a well-dated stratigraphically thick sequence of pollen-bearing alluvium has been deposited rapidly. Also, very few pollen records are available for the past 600 years.

<u>Quercus</u>. From base to top of the pollen diagram, oak frequencies gradually diminish. Oak today is absent from the area although it is present in the Sacramento Mountains to the west and in the sandy plains to the east, where low shrubs of shinnery oak (<u>Quercus</u> <u>havardii</u>) were observed in the last century (Gross and Dick-Peddie 1979). York and Dick-Peddie (1969), using Territorial Survey field notes, mapped the 19th century distribution of shinnery oak in southeastern New Mexico. Upon comparison with mid-20th century distributions, they found that shinnery oak has recently expanded its range, possibly in response to decreased incidence of range fires. The higher percentages of <u>Quercus</u> pollen in the surface samples compared to the upper alluvium at Garnsey probably reflect the recently expanded distribution of shinnery oak. Higher percentages of <u>Quercus</u> pollen have also been reported from modern surface samples in the El Paso area (Horowitz, Gerald, and Chaiffetz 1981).

<u>Juniperus</u>. The increase in juniper pollen frequencies through time is a clear trend. A slight increase occurs in the zone from which most of the bison remains were recovered, and a subsequent short-term decrease coincides with the lowest pine percentages. Juniper frequencies then increase along with pine; surface samples contain amounts of juniper similar to those found in the upper alluvium. Today junipers are scattered sparsely along the west bluff of the Pecos River within 2 km of the Garnsey site. It is doubtful that pollen from these few scattered trees can account for 4% of the modern pollen assemblages found in surface samples at Garnsey. It is likely that some of the surficial <u>Juniperus</u> pollen is being transported long-distance from

juniper populations in the Sacramento Mountains. The recent trend toward greater frequencies in the alluvium probably represents an increase in juniper populations in the mountains.

Ephedra. In Southwestern pollen analysis, grains of Mormon tea are generally differentiated into two morphological groups referable to E. nevadensis-type and E. torreyana-type. Other morphological types can be recognized when grain preservation is good. Ephedra pollen grains are not well preserved at Garnsey. Most of the tabulated grains fall into the E. torreyana-type category. Others were observed in the lower half of the pollen sequence, including E. nevadensis-type, although these never exceeded 1% of the pollen sum. Today only E. torreyana-type occurs in the surface samples at Garnsey. The low Ephedra percentages in surface samples indicate Ephedra has been greatly reduced by recent grazing. The frequency curve of Ephedra in the alluvium generally parallels that of Pinus. The Ephedra pollen record reflects both local and regional abundances of the shrub.

Gramineae. Grass pollen dominates the pollen diagram. Increased Gramineae frequencies in zone 3 occur in cienega clays and probably represent a thick growth of wet-meadow grasses. Sedges (Cyperaceae) also occur in the same stratigraphic interval. The sharp decrease in grass at the boundary of zones 1 and 2 is probably explained by the corresponding marked increase in indeterminable grain frequencies in those two specific samples (see pollen data in Tables 20-27).

The culms of carbonized grasses in stratigraphic unit A (pollen zone 1) that were radiocarbon-dated 455±100 years B.P. (discussed above) are similar in size to sacaton, the dominant grass on the floor of Garnsey Wash today. Sacaton, however, is a warm-season (C_4) species, whereas the ^{13}C fractionation value of the unit A grass culms (-24.2 per mil) is typical of cool-season (C_3) forms (Speth 1983:46, 140, and references therein). It is possible, therefore, that the species of grasses growing on the valley floor 400 to 600 years B.P. were different from those growing there today.

Artemisia. Artemisia frequencies decrease from bottom to top, indicating a possible diminished regional abundance of sagebrush. However, deterioration of pollen grains is greater in stratigraphic unit A than in unit B. The tectate structure of the Artemisia exine fuses during deterioration, resulting in a degraded grain that often cannot be recognized or distinguished from degraded pollen grains of other plants that also exhibit a tectate structure such as species in the mustard family (Cruciferae). The decrease in Artemisia percentages may therefore be related in part to an increase in deterioration of the pollen assemblages.

Ambrosia. The Ambrosia-type pollen category corresponds to the "low-spine Compositae" of Martin (1963) and includes species of Franseria, Xanthium, Iva, and Hymenoclea in which the spines of the grains are less than 3.0 μm in length. The relative frequencies of Ambrosia-type pollen are generally constant with decreases in the cienega deposits of zone 3 and in the upper half of zone 1. Modern surface pollen assemblages show a wide range of variability with the largest percentage (26%) obtained from the present-day valley floor above the arroyo.

Martin (1963) observed high abundances of Ambrosia-type pollen on the floor of modern Empire Cienega in southeastern Arizona and concluded that fossil pollen records from alluvium containing high percentages of Ambrosia-type pollen represent undissected cienegas. The Garnsey site pollen data indicate that Martin's observations do not apply to southeastern New Mexico.

Aster. The Aster-type category is equivalent to Martin's (1963) "high-spine Compositae" with spines 3.0 μm and greater in length. The high percentages of Aster-type pollen in modern surface samples indicate the local abundance of long-spine Compositae (species and genera undetermined), perhaps a result of present-day overgrazing. Pollen zone 2 is characterized by comparatively high Aster-type frequencies that may also represent a period of disturbed or intensely grazed rangeland, similar to present-day conditions.

Chenopodium. The Chenopodium-type category includes all members of the Chenopodiaceae as well as Amaranthus of the Amaranthaceae. Martin (1963) referred to this pollen type as "cheno-ams," including the commonly occurring genera Chenopodium, Atriplex, and Amaranthus. The chenopod pollen curve is comparatively unchanging; surface samples contain chenopod percentages similar to those found in the alluvium. The cienega zone, however, has slightly lower frequencies, probably reflecting decreased abundance of a local unidentified species.

Cienega Environment

The greenish-gray clay beds of unit B at Garnsey represent sediment deposited in a reducing environment such as associated with a wet meadow or cienega. A present-day active spring in Garnsey Wash creates a pocket of standing water at the spring itself as well as a band of moist soil extending 20 to 30 m downstream along the valley floor. Near the spring the moist floor of the wash is overgrown with dense bunches of sacaton. Downstream, where channel trenching since the 1950s has produced a 1.5-m deep arroyo, sacaton is still present although the surface is high above the local spring-fed water table. Farther downstream, where the arroyo is 4 m deep, sacaton is absent.

A present-day analog to past cienega environments at Garnsey Wash can be seen 6 km north at Comanche Wash (Fig. 47). The wash floor is undissected by an arroyo but has a system of two low, connected channels, each about 0.2 to 0.7 m below the general level of the wash, through which infrequent runoff is discharged. Low places in these channels become ephemeral ponds restricted to the channel, seldom exceeding 2 m in width and 5 m in length. Sediment in the wash is highly alkaline; gypsum crystals are precipitated in situ. Where not shaded by dense bunches of sacaton, an algal mat has formed, binding sediment and probably contributing to the reducing conditions that result in the development of greenish-gray clay. This is speculative, however, and suffers from the general absence of studies of modern cienega soils and their geomorphology.

Fig. 47. Undissected Comanche Wash, 6 km north of Garnsey. Garnsey Wash may have looked like this A.D. 1450-1500. Photographed August 1977.

The greenish-gray clay exposed in Garnsey arroyo indicates a downstream spread and prominence of the spring-fed cienega about 500 years B.P. The high frequencies of Gramineae pollen that coincide with the lower two green clays probably represent a moist habitat grass, possibly sacaton, although as discussed above an unknown cool-season species is suggested by the ^{13}C fractionation value obtained on charred grass remains from pollen zone 1. Sedge (Cyperaceae) pollen is present throughout the alluvial sequence, indicating the continual presence of moist ground and in turn the permanence of the spring. The small percentages (less than 0.5%) of narrow-leaved cattail (*Typha angustifolia*) in the lower half of the pollen section suggest that spring flow was sufficiently great on occasions for standing water to accumulate and cattails to become established and flower.

Cienega, Climate, and Bison

The spring-fed cienega at Garnsey was active at the time of a regional climatic drying and/or warming trend. The local cienega environment may have been sustained by exceptionally heavy winter snowfall or several prolonged spring rain storms, either of which could have been a water source maintaining spring flow independent of the increasingly arid climate. Bison and their hunters would be drawn to the Garnsey cienega during the drying episode. Increased grazing pressure by congregating bison would result in damage to the already drought-injured rangeland. The decline of *Ephedra* and the marked rise in *Aster*-type pollen frequencies may reflect that intense grazing. The present-day rangeland is heavily grazed and surface sample pollen assemblages have low *Ephedra* and high *Aster*-type percentages.

At the time of maximum drought about 450 years B.P., the cienega at Garnsey was greatly reduced from its former length although a local moist habitat was not completely eliminated as indicated by sedge pollen in unit A. The increase in pine pollen in zone 1 marks the change toward a regional increase in moisture availability. At that time, local rangelands improved at the expense of *Aster*-type annuals, and *Ephedra* began to recover in abundance.

The drought probably lasted no longer than 50 to 100 years. The increase in pine tree abundance in the Sacramento Mountains to pre-drought levels probably took 100 or more years.

On a larger time scale, the drought was an episode of extreme aridity within a period of generally dry climate. Compilation of paleoenvironmental information from several localities in the Southern Plains has led to the general conclusion that the last 1000 years was drier than the preceding millennium (Hall 1982). At present, however, well-documented archaeological or non-archaeological records from which paleoclimatic inferences can be made are few.

Other Pollen Studies. The pollen analytical study geographically closest to the Garnsey site is the alluvial pollen record from Wolf Ranch Canyon on the Penasco River southwest of Roswell. Carbonized plant remains at a depth of 2.9 m were radiocarbon-dated 2850±100 years B.P. (Hafsten 1961:67). Fluctuations in *Pinus* pollen and a decrease in *Artemisia* frequencies in the upper part of the section may parallel the trends documented at Garnsey. Only one date has been obtained from the Wolf Ranch Canyon locality, however, and it cannot be determined whether or not the upper section correlates with Garnsey.

Pollen was recovered from archaeological middens dated A.D. 900 to 1250 at localities along the Pecos River south of Fort Sumner. Although only 7 samples were analyzed, it was found that the abundance of chenopod pollen was related to sherd counts; matrix containing large numbers of sherds also had pollen assemblages with high frequencies of chenopod pollen (greater than 40%), indicating increased weed growth as a response to increased disturbance of the area by prehistoric man. Adjusted pollen frequencies (Jelinek 1966; Martin 1967) show a decline in sagebrush and composites with a net increase in grasses. While these trends are interpreted by Jelinek as a shift toward more moist conditions at a time of increased local reliance on bison, the data are too scanty for strong conclusions. Also, the sites pre-date Garnsey.

The Salt Cedar site at Andrews Lake, Andrews County, Texas, is a pollen-bearing archaeological midden radiocarbon-dated A.D. 1540±100 and 1780±200 near the base and A.D. 1530±100 at the top (dates not corrected for possible ^{13}C fractionation). The 0.5-ft sampling interval and 200-grain counts are coarse methods for documenting small fluctuations in pollen influx. However, one clear trend is an increase in percentages of chenopod pollen through time (from 6 to 35%); a surface sample spectrum at the site contains 31% chenopods. This probably represents an increase in local abundance of chenopod plants that may be related to the drying of Andrews Lake. The investigator (Collins 1968) interprets the midden sediments to be eolian in origin, perhaps indicating the same drying conditions as were found at Garnsey.

To the south, in the vicinity of El Paso, two separate pollen studies conclude that the early historic-prehistoric vegetation was a dry grassland, very different from the creosote bush and mesquite dominated vegetation of today (Horowitz, Gerald, and Chaiffetz 1981; O'Laughlin 1980). Nineteenth century Territorial Survey field notes also indicate the region was characterized by a grassland vegetation (York and Dick-Peddie 1969; Gardner 1951). However, the time period of the Garnsey site is either not represented or is unrecognized in the El Paso area pollen sequences.

Summary

The Garnsey Bison Kill site pollen record depicts an important drought event and fills a small but important time gap in the paleoenvironmental history of the southwestern Plains.

1. The main portion of the 4-m pollen section was deposited in no more than 200 years during the period 400 to 600 years B.P.

2. A fluctuation in *Pinus* pollen frequencies reflects reduced pine populations in the Sacramento Mountains, evidence for a regional 50- to 100-year drought that is dated about 450 to 500 years B.P. (A.D. 1450 to 1500).

3. A cienega environment prevailed at Garnsey during the early stage of the regional drought, attracting late prehistoric bison and bison hunters.

4. The concentration of bison in the area may have increased grazing pressure on dry rangeland as indicated by high *Aster*-type and low *Ephedra* pollen frequencies. Present-day intensely grazed rangeland has similar high *Aster*-type and low *Ephedra* pollen percentages.

Acknowledgments

I thank John D. Speth for field assistance and for helpful discussions of the results. Gil J. Stein assisted in collecting modern surface pollen samples in the Garnsey drainage basin. Funding for the analysis was provided by National Science Foundation Grant BNS-7806875.

10. CONCLUSIONS

Work at the Garnsey Spring campsite was originally undertaken because we felt that it might represent a specialized processing locus associated with the nearby Garnsey Bison Kill. A full understanding of the events and activities carried out at the latter necessitated investigation of the former. However, subsequent work at the campsite demonstrated that it was functionally unrelated to the kill, and in fact may not have been occupied during the latter half of the 15th century when bison were being hunted in the Garnsey Wash. We nevertheless proceeded with limited excavations at the campsite in order to gain further insights into the nature of late prehistoric subsistence-settlement systems in this part of southeastern New Mexico.

Artifactual evidence, supported by radiocarbon dates, indicates that the campsite locality had been repeatedly used for nearly a millennium, beginning sometime prior to about A.D. 800-900 and continuing at least intermittently into the protohistoric and historic periods. Unfortunately, the deposits proved to be poorly preserved and badly disturbed, precluding definitive statements about the seasonality of the site, its overall function, or its placement within a regional settlement framework. Despite these shortcomings, we felt an obligation to report the results of our excavations as fully as possible. We hope that as research progresses in the region these data can be reassessed and incorporated into a more comprehensible picture of evolving prehistoric adaptations in southeastern New Mexico.

The chronology of the campsite remains elusive. Two radiocarbon dates from the lower part of the midden indicate that extensive use of the locality may have begun in the 8th or 9th century A.D. This is consistent with the ceramics. However, earlier occupation may have occurred in areas of the midden not sampled, or may simply be obscured by the tremendous amount of mixing that the midden has undergone. The lack of clear stratigraphy made it impossible to pin down the age of specific projectile point forms, an important job that remains to be done in southeastern New Mexico. We had especially hoped to be able to establish dates for the Carlsbad and Ellis-like points, the two most common types at the campsite. An 8th- or 9th-century placement for these types is plausible, but this dating must be regarded as speculative until it can be verified by materials recovered in more secure contexts. We did succeed in dating the youngest point type on the site, the Garza, confirming its protohistoric to early historic placement.

The absence of triple-notched Harrell points and Glaze B or later ceramic types at the campsite point to non-use of the locality during the latter half of the 15th and early 16th century. Harrell points, however, are present only a few hundred meters away at the Garnsey Bison Kill, indicating that people were in the area at least seasonally during the spring or early summer to hunt bison. Abandonment of the campsite during this period may be due to deterioration of local resources and perhaps also the nearby spring. Pollen analyses of the Garnsey Wash alluvium, as well as a variety of other evidence from the kill site, point to sharply increasing aridity in southeastern New Mexico in the mid- to late 15th century (Hall, this volume; Speth 1983). While the details of this climatic event remain to be worked out, its impact on late prehistoric adaptations in the region are likely to have been substantial.

The proximity of the campsite to the spring, one of the few along the east side of the Pecos Valley in the Roswell area, suggests that the availability of fresh water was indeed an important factor in the placement of the site. The location also provided easy access to a diversity of habitats which offered a variety of potential plant and animal resources. The extensive riverine and riparian habitats of the Pecos Valley were within a short distance of the site, and would have provided aquatic resources such as fish and waterfowl, as well as deer and numerous edible plant species in their appropriate seasons. The gently dissected, grass-covered plains surrounding the site offered additional edible plant species including yucca, prickly pear, mesquite, and many others. In addition, rabbits, antelope, mule deer, and bison would have been available on the grassy uplands or in the more heavily vegetated bottoms of the many washes that crisscross the area. Small stands of wild walnut and hackberry occur today just upstream from the campsite in one of the deeper stretches of the Garnsey Wash; similar stands may have occurred there in the past. Less than 30 km east of the campsite begin the vast expanses of low dunes that extend eastward over the Mescalero Pediment to the caprock escarpment of the Llano Estacado. The dunes would have offered a variety of small shrubs, herbs, and dense growths of mesquite and shinnery oak (*Quercus havardii*). The acorns of the shinnery oak are large and sweet, and would have required relatively little preparation to render them edible.

Unfortunately, given the poor preservation of subsistence remains at the campsite, we can do very little at present to specify which of the area's many potential resources were actually being exploited. Flotation yielded no evidence of plant foods, either cultivated or wild. The faunal remains, while somewhat more informative, are far from ideal. Rabbits and ungulates, including bison, were being hunted, but in what numbers or in which seasons we can only speculate. The scanty remains point to winter and/or spring as the most probable seasons of occupation at the campsite, but other seasons are by no means precluded.

Other aspects of the data also provide clues to the nature of subsistence activities at the site, but their full significance remains to be elucidated. For example, fire-cracked rock was scattered throughout the midden, and two small concentrations may represent disturbed remnants of small earth ovens. However, they in no way resemble the huge concentrations of ash and fire-cracked rock, thought to represent mescal roasting pits, found to the south in the Guadalupe Mountain area. What was being cooked or roasted at the campsite is unknown. While ash and charcoal were abundant throughout the campsite midden, fire-cracked rock was not, suggesting that the earth oven was not the principal mode of food preparation.

Notably absent from the campsite were manos, metates, stone mortars or pestles, anvils, nutting stones or other groundstone artifacts traditionally associated with plant-food processing. Steep, denticulated scrapers or core-scrapers, however, were common. Similar tools are often thought to have been used for extracting and processing fibers from plants such as agave, mescal, or yucca (Hester and Heizer 1972). There is no direct evidence, however, that these plants were exploited for food or fiber at the campsite. In general, the chipped stone tools from the site appear to have been used for a variety of processing, manufacturing, and maintenance tasks, and provide little secure information on subsistence activities.

The duration of occupations at the campsite is presently unknown. We found no evidence of permanent structures (i.e., pit rooms; slab, jacal, or adobe above-ground structures). Postmolds left by more ephemeral types of structures were not encountered but would have been extremely difficult, if not impossible, to detect in the midden. The artifactual data point to repeated occupations, but not necessarily extended ones.

The vast majority of artifacts from the site point to its use by local groups. Most of the ceramics are types that are common throughout southeastern New Mexico during the late prehistoric period. The occurrence in some of the ceramic wares of tempering materials that derive from sources in the Sacramento Mountains could reflect the annual range of mobility of the campsite's inhabitants. However, it could also reflect infrequent long-distance treks to obtain the temper, or exchange relations between neighboring groups that involved whole pots or just tempering material. The obsidian from the campsite reflects longer-distance interaction, since most, and perhaps all, of the obsidian appears to have come from sources in the Jemez area of north-central New Mexico. In addition, a small number of sherds derive from ceramic vessels manufactured in western New Mexico or eastern Arizona, up to 400 km from the campsite. In both cases, however, the small amounts involved point to low-intensity interaction.

The information that we can presently extract from the campsite data concerning local late prehistoric subsistence-settlement systems is obviously limited. Despite these limitations, we have attempted to present the data in as complete and detailed a manner as possible. In addition to the insights already gained from the analysis of these materials, we hope that future research in the area will be able to reassess these data and incorporate them into a fuller understanding of late prehistoric adaptations in the region.

APPENDIX A.

FAUNAL REMAINS

Table A1
Identified bones from Garnsey Spring campsite

I. LARGE MAMMAL BONE

1. METATARSAL
   Provenience: 500N512W(Item 1)/22.0
   Portion: distal; left condyle damaged; weathered
   Butchering: shaft broken immediately above distal epiphysis, shaft splintered (fragments associated but not restorable).
   Fusion: distal epiphysis fused
   Side: left
   Identification: Bison
   Measurements:
      Bd (von den Driesch 1976): (5.48)
      WCm (Payne 1969): (2.54)
      WTm (Payne 1969): (2.10)
      WCl (Payne 1969): (2.36)
      WTl (Payne 1969): [2.13]

2. PROXIMAL SESAMOID
   Provenience: TT1-W(Item 2)/12.0
   Portion: complete; weathered
   Butchering: none evident
   Side: peripheral, right side of foot; side of animal unknown
   Identification: Bison
   Measurements:
      GB: (1.41)
      GL: (2.04)
      GD: (1.81)

3. VERTEBRA
   Provenience: 511N514W/2-5
   Portion: caudal pad only; weathered and damaged
   Butchering: none evident
   Fusion: caudal pad unfused
   Identification: large mammal; size comparable to Bison vertebrae from Garnsey Bison Kill
   Measurements:
      BFcd (von den Driesch 1976): [3.69]
      HFcd (von den Driesch 1976): [3.12]

4. VERTEBRA
   Provenience: 511N514W/5-10
   Portion: cranial pad only; weathered and damaged
   Butchering: none evident
   Fusion: cranial pad unfused
   Identification: large mammal; size comparable to Bison vertebrae from Garnsey Bison Kill
   Measurements:
      BFcr (von den Driesch 1976): [2.57]
      HFcr (von den Driesch 1976): (3.14)

5. RIB
   Provenience: 500N504W(Item 1)/26.0
   Portion: blade midsection; highly weathered
   Butchering: probable
   Fusion: unknown
   Side: unknown
   Identification: large mammal; size comparable to _Bison_ ribs from Garnsey Bison Kill
   Measurements:
      GL: [14.60]
      Max. width of blade: [2.99]

6. COSTAL CARTILAGE
   Provenience: 499N516W/15-20
   Portion: blade midsection
   Butchering: none evident
   Side: unknown
   Identification: large mammal; size comparable to _Bison_ costal cartilage from Garnsey Bison Kill
   Measurements:
      Max. width of blade: (2.15)

II. MEDIUM MAMMAL BONE

1. RIB
   Provenience: 500N512W/20-25
   Portion: blade midsection, near vertebral end
   Butchering: tubercle, head, and neck butchered off; sternal end of blade butchered off
   Fusion: unknown
   Side: left
   Identification: medium mammal; size, curvature, and morphology identical to canid ribs from Garnsey Bison Kill
   Measurements:
      GL: [9.39]
      Max. width of blade: (0.75)

2. METAPODIAL
   Provenience: 499N518W/2-5
   Portion: fragment of distal condyle only; burned
   Butchering: probable
   Fusion: unknown
   Side: unknown
   Identification: _Odocoileus_ (deer) or _Antilocapra_ (antelope)
   Measurements: --

3. PATELLA
   Provenience: 512N516W/2-5
   Portion: complete
   Butchering: none
   Side: right
   Identification: cf. _Antilocapra_ (antelope)
   Measurements:

GB (von den Driesch 1976): 1.82
GL (von den Driesch 1976): 2.41

4. VERTEBRA
Provenience: 500N514W/20-25
Portion: cranial pad only
Butchering: none evident
Fusion: cranial pad unfused
Identification: medium(?) mammal
Measurements:
BFcr (von den Driesch 1976): (1.81)
HFcr (von den Driesch 1976): (1.50)

III. SMALL MAMMAL BONE

1. CRANIUM
Provenience: 500N517W/10-15
Portion: right malar bone only
Identification: Sylvilagus (cottontail rabbit)
Measurements: --

2. SCAPULA
Provenience: TT1-W/1-5
Portion: fragment of glenoid process, neck, and proximal blade only
Side: right
Identification: Sylvilagus
Measurements:
SLC (von den Driesch 1976): 0.33

3. HUMERUS
Provenience: TT1-E/5-10
Portion: distal; burned
Fusion: distal epiphysis fused
Side: right
Identification: Sylvilagus
Measurements:
Bd (von den Driesch 1976): 0.61

4. HUMERUS
Provenience: 499N515W/15-20
Portion: distal
Fusion: distal epiphysis fused
Side: right
Identification: Sylvilagus
Measurements:
SD (von den Driesch 1976): (0.33)
Bd (von den Driesch 1976): 0.58

5. ULNA
Provenience: 500N515W/20-25
Portion: trochlear notch and adjacent portion of proximal shaft only

Fusion: unknown
Side: right
Identification: Sylvilagus
Measurements:
BPC (von den Driesch 1976): (0.52)

6. INNOMINATE
Provenience: 499N513W/30-35
Portion: fragment of acetabulum and adjacent shafts of ischium and pubis
Fusion: ischium and pubis fused
Side: right
Identification: Sylvilagus
Measurements: --

7. INNOMINATE
Provenience: 500N512W/30-35
Portion: fragment of acetabulum and adjacent shaft of ischium
Fusion: unknown
Side: right
Identification: Sylvilagus
Measurements: --

8. CALCANEUS
Provenience: 500N514W/10-15
Portion: complete; burned
Fusion: fused
Side: right
Identification: Sylvilagus
Measurements:
GL (von den Driesch 1976): 1.73
GB (von den Driesch 1976): 0.50

9. SECOND PHALANX
Provenience: 500N504W/30-37, Feature 2 (flotation sample)
Portion: complete; burned
Fusion: fused
Identification: Sylvilagus
Measurements:
GL (von den Driesch 1976): 0.37
Bp (von den Driesch 1976): 0.19
SD (von den Driesch 1976): 0.15
Bd (von den Driesch 1976): 0.15

10. CRANIUM
Provenience: 499N512W/40-45
Portion: left malar bone only
Identification: Lepus (jackrabbit)
Measurements: --

11. MANDIBLE
Provenience: 500N503W/1-5
Portion: fragment of molar row only; teeth missing
Side: right(?)

Identification: <u>Lepus</u>
Measurements: --

12. SCAPULA
Provenience: 499N513W/30-35
Portion: proximal part of spine and adjacent blade only
Side: left (?)
Identification: <u>Lepus</u>
Measurements: --

13. HUMERUS
Provenience: TT1-W/5-10
Portion: distal epiphysis; burned
Fusion: distal epiphysis fused(?)
Side: right
Identification: <u>Lepus</u>
Measurements:
Bd (von den Driesch 1976): 1.03

14. HUMERUS
Provenience: 499N512W/30-35
Portion: distal shaft only; both epiphyses missing
Fusion: unknown
Side: right
Identification: <u>Lepus</u>
Measurements:
SD (von den Driesch 1976): (0.49)

15. HUMERUS
Provenience: 499N512W/35-40
Portion: distal epiphysis; burned
Fusion: distal epiphysis fused (?)
Side: left
Identification: <u>Lepus</u>
Measurements:
Bd (von den Driesch 1976): 1.08

16. HUMERUS
Provenience: 499N516W/15-20
Portion: distal
Fusion: distal epiphysis fused
Side: right
Identification: <u>Lepus</u>
Measurements:
Bd (von den Driesch 1976): (0.97)

17. RADIUS
Provenience: TT1-E/0-5
Portion: proximal; burned
Fusion: proximal epiphysis fused
Side: right
Identification: <u>Lepus</u>
Measurements:
Bp (von den Driesch 1976): 0.74

18. RADIUS
    Provenience: 499N516W/10-15
    Portion: midsection of shaft only; burned
    Fusion: unknown
    Side: unknown
    Identification: Lepus(?)
    Measurements: --

19. ULNA
    Provenience: 500N513W/25-30
    Portion: proximal; olecranon missing, distal shaft missing; weathered
    Fusion: unknown
    Side: right
    Identification: Lepus
    Measurements:
        DPA (von den Driesch 1976): (0.93)
        BPC (von den Driesch 1976): 0.63

20. INNOMINATE
    Provenience: 500N518W/10-15
    Portion: fragment of ischium adjacent to obturator foramen
    Fusion: unknown
    Side: unknown
    Identification: Lepus(?)
    Measurements: --

21. TIBIA
    Provenience: 499N504W/20-25
    Portion: midsection of shaft near distal end; burned
    Fusion: unknown
    Side: unknown
    Identification: Lepus
    Measurements: --

22. CALCANEUS
    Provenience: 500N515W/5-10
    Portion: complete; weathered
    Fusion: fused(?)
    Side: right
    Identification: Lepus
    Measurements:
        GL (von den Driesch 1976): (2.70)
        GB (von den Driesch 1976): (0.87)

23. ASTRAGALUS
    Provenience: 500N513W/15-20
    Portion: proximal; burned
    Side: left
    Identification: Lepus
    Measurements: --

24. ASTRAGALUS
    Provenience: 500N514W/20-25

Portion: proximal; burned
Side: left
Identification: <u>Lepus</u>
Measurements: --

25. METATARSAL I
    Provenience: 499N512W/40-45
    Portion: proximal; burned
    Fusion: unknown
    Side: right
    Identification: <u>Lepus</u>
    Measurements: --

26. HUMERUS
    Provenience: 499N503W/15-20
    Portion: shaft only; both epiphyses missing
    Fusion: unknown
    Side: left
    Identification: rodent
    Measurements:
        SD (von den Driesch 1976): (0.35)

27. HUMERUS
    Provenience: 500N514W/10-15
    Portion: shaft only; both epiphyses missing
    Fusion: unknown
    Side: left
    Identification: rodent
    Measurements:
        SD (von den Driesch 1976): (0.33)

---

[1]Measurements presented are comparable to those reported in Speth and Parry (1978, 1980). Measurements enclosed in parentheses represent approximations of real value; measurements enclosed in brackets apply to broken, damaged, or incomplete specimens and do not reflect real values for complete specimens.

Table A2
Mollusc shells

Provenience	Hinge Fragments	Unidentified Fragments	Weight (g)
499N501W/5-10	1	-	0.36
499N506W/5-10	-	1	0.16
499N513W/25-30	1	10+	3.50
500N504W/10-15	-	1	0.12
500N505W/10-15	-	1	0.06
500N517W/15-20	-	1	0.07

Table A3
Distribution of faunal remains (bones and teeth)
All fragments (identified and unidentified)
from screened samples included

Provenience	Fragments (N)	Weight (g)
TT1-E/0-5	81	18.85
TT1-E/5-10	16	2.54
TT1-E/10-25	9	2.76
TT1-E/15-30	5	0.60
TT1-E/30-45	1	0.14
TT1-W/0-5	51	18.94
TT1-W/5-10	25	4.48
TT1-W/10-25	14	5.08
TT1-W/15-30	1	0.09
TT1-W/30-45	1	1.10
495N519W/0-5	4	1.24
495N519W/5-10	1	0.20
495N519W/10-15	4	0.93
495N519W/15-20	2	0.92
495N519W/20-25	1	0.21
499N500W/10-15	1	0.16
499N500W/20-25	1	0.30
499N501W/5-10	1	0.22
499N501W/20-25	3	0.76
499N501W/25-30	1	0.16
499N502W/5-10	1	0.11
499N502W/20-25	1	1.30
499N502W/25-30	2	0.18
499N503W/10-15	2	0.10
499N503W/15-20	4	0.88
499N504W/10-15	1	0.19
499N504W/20-25	3	1.01
499N505W/20-25	1	2.58
499N505W/25-30	2	0.42
499N506W/15-20	4	0.87
499N512W/0-5	2	0.91
499N512W/5-10	1	0.21
499N512W/10-15	6	1.43
499N512W/15-20	5	1.33
499N512W/20-25	3	0.70
499N512W/25-30	4	1.01
499N512W/30-35	1	0.94
499N512W/35-40	5	1.17
499N512W/40-45	5	0.98
499N513W/0-5	2	0.92
499N513W/5-10	7	2.16
499N513W/15-20	4	6.05
499N513W/20-25	4	0.97

Table A3. (continued)

Provenience	Fragments (N)	Weight (g)
499N513W/25-30	8	0.72
499N513W/30-35	5	1.02
499N513W/35-40	3	1.06
499N513W/40-45	1	0.10
499N514W/0-5	4	1.27
499N514W/5-10	1	0.25
499N514W/10-15	2	0.36
499N514W/15-20	7	1.67
499N514W/20-25	1	0.21
499N514W/25-30	2	0.24
499N515W/0-5	36	16.07
499N515W/5-10	13	4.62
499N515W/10-15	2	2.05
499N515W/15-20	3	0.37
499N515W/20-25	5	3.35
499N516W/0-5	10	1.91
499N516W/10-15	13	3.41
499N516W/15-20	10	4.97
499N516W/20-25	4	0.60
499N517W/0-5	19	5.99
499N517W/5-10	8	2.00
499N517W/10-15	13	2.23
499N517W/15-20	4	1.01
499N517W/20-25	3	0.78
499N518W/0-5	10	3.58
499N518W/5-10	8	2.35
499N518W/10-15	5	1.06
499N518W/15-20	3	0.44
499N518W/20-25	2	0.28
500N500W/0-5	2	0.28
500N500W/15-20	1	0.15
500N501W/10-15	7	9.40
500N502W/0-5	1	0.39
500N502W/10-15	1	0.30
500N502W/20-25	2	1.30
500N503W/0-5	3	0.45
500N504W/10-15	2	0.72
500N504W/15-20	2	0.42
500N504W/20-25	1	0.18
500N504W/25-30	19	48.59
500N505W/5-10	1	0.21
500N505W/15-20	7	5.72
500N505W/20-25	12	2.37
500N505W/25-30	2	0.33
500N505W/30-35	2	1.57
500N506W/5-10	3	0.95
500N506W/15-20	9	1.25

Table A3. (continued)

Provenience	Fragments (N)	Weight (g)
500N506W/20-25	1	0.10
500N506W/30-35	1	0.03
500N512W/0-5	3	0.79
500N512W/5-10	8	2.26
500N512W/10-15	7	1.81
500N512W/15-20	4	3.19
500N512W/20-25	13	50.67
500N512W/25-30	1	0.10
500N512W/30-35	2	0.36
500N513W/0-5	4	2.44
500N513W/5-10	5	1.66
500N513W/10-15	5	1.18
500N513W/15-20	8	1.90
500N513W/20-25	5	1.12
500N513W/25-30	1	0.29
500N513W/30-35	2	0.53
500N514W/0-5	8	2.51
500N514W/5-10	7	1.84
500N514W/10-15	14	2.16
500N514W/15-20	6	2.17
500N514W/20-25	9	2.16
500N514W/25-30	2	0.16
500N515W/0-5	17	4.77
500N515W/5-10	5	2.50
500N515W/10-15	8	2.31
500N515W/15-20	6	0.94
500N515W/20-25	3	0.50
500N516W/0-5	10	2.79
500N516W/5-10	2	0.71
500N516W/10-15	4	1.22
500N516W/15-20	5	0.73
500N516W/20-25	2	1.19
500N516W/25-30	1	0.01
500N517W/0-5	4	1.28
500N517W/5-10	2	0.60
500N517W/10-15	14	4.32
500N517W/15-20	7	2.18
500N517W/20-25	6	1.46
500N517W/25-30	3	0.77
500N518W/0-5	1	0.30
500N518W/5-10	2	0.47
500N518W/10-15	2	0.51
503N515W/0-5	1	0.46
503N515W/5-10	3	0.77
503N515W/10-15	3	1.23
503N515W/15-20	8	4.12
503N515W/20-25	2	0.29

Table A3. (continued)

Provenience	Fragments (N)	Weight (g)
503N515W/25-30	8	2.00
504N515W/0-10	6	1.51
504N515W/10-15	1	0.25
504N515W/15-20	6	1.09
504N515W/20-25	5	1.47
504N515W/25-30	1	0.22
505N515W/0-5	3	0.60
505N515W/10-15	2	0.68
505N515W/15-20	7	1.62
505N515W/20-25	3	0.82
505N515W/25-30	3	0.72
506N515W/0-5	3	0.40
506N515W/5-10	2	0.80
506N515W/10-15	10	2.02
506N515W/15-20	10	1.78
506N515W/20-25	2	0.49
506N515W/25-30	2	0.80
511N514W/0-5	2	4.04
511N514W/5-10	1	2.51
511N514W/10-15	1	0.21
511N514W/15-20	7	1.47
511N514W/20-25	2	1.13
511N514W/25-30	1	0.73
511N514W/30-35	1	0.14
511N515W/0-5	2	0.44
511N515W/5-10	1	0.13
511N515W/10-15	3	0.76
511N515W/15-20	2	0.53
511N515W/20-25	7	0.68
511N515W/30-35	8	2.85
512N514W/10-15	2	0.24
512N514W/15-20	1	0.44
512N514W/20-25	1	0.25
512N514W/25-30	1	0.29
512N514W/30-35	3	0.75
512N515W/0-5	2	0.34
512N515W/10-15	2	0.48
512N515W/15-20	4	1.14
512N515W/20-25	1	0.10
512N515W/25-30	5	0.96
512N516W/0-5	4	3.02
512N516W/10-15	6	1.42
512N516W/15-20	7	2.11
512N516W/20-25	2	0.40
512N516W/25-30	10	1.67

APPENDIX B.

CHARCOAL FROM THE GARNSEY SPRING CAMPSITE

(Report No. 525 of the Ethnobotanical Laboratory of the University of Michigan Museum of Anthropology)

by

Virginia Popper
Museum of Anthropology
University of Michigan
Ann Arbor, Mich. 48109

The analysis of botanical remains from the Garnsey Spring campsite revealed the use of several species of wood, mainly Atriplex (saltbush), Prosopis (mesquite) and Forestiera (New Mexico olive). Juniperus (juniper) was found in one sample and small amounts of Ephedra and Rhamnus (buckthorn) were tentatively identified in others. No charred plant remains other than charcoal were present. The few uncarbonized seeds found were considered modern.

All specimens were identified to the generic level when possible by examining a cross section under a 7-30x binocular microscope, and if necessary under a 80-400x research microscope. Most identifications were verified by comparing the specimens with modern wood samples collected by Richard I. Ford, Curator of Ethnobotany at the University of Michigan, from the vicinity of the site. Sampling procedures varied according to the type of sample, and as the analysis progressed. First, a few screened samples were completely analyzed to determine the full range of wood types present at the site. Then, 20 pieces from each subsequent screened sample were examined in accordance with general sampling procedures practiced at the Ethnobotanical Laboratory of the University of Michigan (Minnis and Ford n.d.:4-5). The light fractions of the flotation samples were split to obtain subsamples of approximately 10 g. Both the light fraction subsample and the heavy fraction were examined under the binocular microscope for evidence of botanical remains, followed by the identification of 20 pieces of charcoal, if possible. Inventories of all identified botanical remains are presented in this appendix.

Table B1
Identification of charcoal samples from Garnsey Spring campsite (Part 1)

Provenience[1]	*Atriplex*		*Prosopis*		Unknown (cf. *Prosopis*)		*Forestiera*		*Juniperus*	
	N[2]	g	N	g	N	g	N	g	N	g
499N512W/15-20/S	4	0.27	1	0.15	1	0.04	1	0.08	-	-
499N512W/20-25/S	14	2.64	5	0.48	-	-	1	0.07	-	-
499N512W/25-30/S	18	1.61	2	0.12	-	-	-	-	-	-
499N512W/30-35/S	9	0.65	-	-	-	-	1	0.11	-	-
499N512W/40-45/S	2	0.12	5	0.36	-	-	1	0.06	-	-
499N512W/45-50/S	6	0.61	-	-	-	-	-	-	-	-
499N513W/15-20/S	6	0.66	-	-	-	-	1	0.22	-	-
499N513W/20-25/S	19	1.82	2	0.20	-	-	1	0.06	-	-
499N513W/25-30/S	16	1.29	3	0.24	-	-	-	-	-	-
499N513W/30-35/S	2	0.18	1	0.11	-	-	-	-	-	-
499N513W/35-40/S	7	0.58	2	0.33	-	-	-	-	-	-
499N513W/40-45/S	7	0.84	2	0.04	-	-	-	-	-	-
499N515W/15-20/S	71	6.67	5	0.37	-	-	-	-	-	-
499N515W/25-30/S	47	4.41	5	0.51	-	-	4	0.64	-	-
500N502W/5-9,F1/FL	-	-	-	-	-	-	-	-	5	0.03
500N502W/5-9,F1/FH	-	-	-	-	-	-	-	-	-	-
500N504W/10-15/FL	3	0.02	-	-	-	-	-	-	-	-
500N504W/30-37,F2/FL	3	0.02	1	0.01	-	-	2	0.01	-	-
500N504W/30-37,F2/FH	17	0.24	-	-	-	-	-	-	-	-
505N515W/20-25/S	32	2.86	5	0.33	2	0.46	-	-	-	-
511N514W/17-28,F3/FL	13	0.37	-	-	-	-	4	0.14	-	-
511N514W/17-28,F3/FH	19	0.23	1	0.02	-	-	-	-	-	-
511N515W/17-28,F3/FL	16	0.60	3	0.11	-	-	1	0.05	-	-
511N515W/17-28,F3/FH	19	0.23	1	0.02	-	-	-	-	-	-
512N515W/10-15/S	1	0.13	-	-	-	-	-	-	-	-

Table B1. (continued)

Provenience[1]	*Atriplex*		*Prosopis*		Unknown (cf. *Prosopis*)		*Forestiera*		*Juniperus*	
	N[2]	g	N	g	N	g	N	g	N	g
512N515W/15-20/S	10	1.00	10	0.89	-	-	-	-	-	-
512N515W/20-25/S	13	1.75	7	0.72	-	-	-	-	-	-
512N515W/25-30/S	14	1.86	6	0.45	-	-	-	-	-	-
512N515W/30-35/S	9	1.06	1	0.06	-	-	-	-	-	-
512N515W/35.0/S	17	4.41	4	1.29	-	-	-	-	-	-
512N515W/35-40,F4/FL	15	0.81	4	0.11	-	-	-	-	-	-
512N516W/30-42,F4/FL	16	1.22	5	1.17	-	-	-	-	-	-
512N516W/30-42,F4/FH	16	0.26	4	0.09	-	-	-	-	-	-

[1]F1=Feature 1, F2=Feature 2, etc.; S=screened sample, 1/4 inch mesh; FL=light fraction of flotation sample, screened through 1/32 inch mesh; FH=heavy fraction of flotation sample, screened through 1/16 inch mesh.

[2]N=number of fragments; g=weight in grams.

Table B2
Identification of charcoal samples from Garnsey Spring campsite (Part 2)

Provenience[1]	Unknown (cf. *Ephedra*)		Unknown (cf. *Rhamnus*)		Unknown		Knot		Diseased Wood	
	N[2]	g	N	g	N	g	N	g	N	g
499N512W/15-20/S	-	-	-	-	-	-	-	-	-	-
499N512W/20-25/S	-	-	-	-	-	-	-	-	-	-
499N512W/25-30/S	-	-	-	-	-	-	-	-	-	-
499N512W/30-35/S	2	0.09	-	-	-	-	-	-	-	-
499N512W/40-45/S	-	-	-	-	-	-	-	-	-	-
499N512W/45-50/S	1	0.09	-	-	-	-	-	-	-	-
499N513W/15-20/S	-	-	-	-	-	-	1	0.06	-	-
499N513W/20-25/S	-	-	-	-	-	-	-	-	1	0.07
499N513W/25-30/S	-	-	-	-	-	-	1	0.07	-	-
499N513W/30-35/S	-	-	-	-	-	-	-	-	-	-
499N513W/35-40/S	1	0.07	-	-	-	-	-	-	-	-
499N513W/40-45/S	-	-	-	-	-	-	-	-	-	-
499N515W/15-20/S	1	0.10	-	-	-	-	1	0.04	-	-
499N515W/25-30/S	1	0.04	-	-	2	0.12	-	-	1	0.07
500N502W/5-9,F1/FL	-	-	-	-	-	-	-	-	1	0.07
500N502W/5-9,F1/FH	-	-	-	-	-	-	-	-	-	-
500N504W/10-15/FL	-	-	-	-	-	-	-	-	-	-
500N504W/30-37,F2/FL	-	-	-	-	-	-	1	0.01	1	0.01
500N504W/30-37,F2/FH	-	-	-	-	-	-	-	-	-	-
505N515W/20-25/S	1	0.36	2	0.78	1	0.05	2	0.30	-	-
511N514W/17-28,F3/FL	-	-	-	-	-	-	1	0.04	2	0.05
511N514W/17-28,F3/FH	-	-	-	-	-	-	-	-	-	-
511N515W/17-28,F3/FL	-	-	-	-	-	-	-	-	-	-
511N515W/17-28,F3/FH	-	-	-	-	-	-	-	-	-	-
512N515W/10-15/S	-	-	-	-	-	-	-	-	-	-

Table B2. (continued)

Provenience[1]	Unknown (cf. *Ephedra*)		Unknown (cf. *Rhamnus*)		Unknown		Knot		Diseased Wood	
	N[2]	g	N	g	N	g	N	g	N	g
512N515W/15-20/S	-	-	-	-	-	-	-	-	-	-
512N515W/20-25/S	-	-	-	-	-	-	-	-	-	-
512N515W/25-30/S	-	-	-	-	-	-	-	-	-	-
512N515W/30-35/S	-	-	-	-	-	-	-	-	-	-
512N515W/35.0/S	-	-	-	-	-	-	1	0.06	-	-
512N515W/35-40,F4/FL	-	-	-	-	-	-	1	0.04	-	-
512N516W/30-42,F4/FL	-	-	-	-	-	-	-	-	-	-
512N516W/30-42,F4/FH	-	-	-	-	-	-	-	-	-	-

[1] F1=Feature 1, F2=Feature 2, etc.; S=screened sample, 1/4 inch mesh; FL=light fraction of flotation sample, screened through 1/32 inch mesh; FH=heavy fraction of flotation sample, screened through 1/16 inch mesh.

[2] N=number of fragments; g=weight in grams.

APPENDIX C.

LITHIC ARTIFACTS

Key to Tables C1 and C2 (projectile points)

Form (generalized outline form of projectile):
- A = unnotched triangular arrow point with bifurcated base (Garza)
- B = corner-notched triangular arrow point
- C = side-notched triangular arrow point (Washita)
- D = unnotched triangular arrow point (Fresno) or preform
- E = small broadly side-notched dart point
- F = broad-bladed, barbed corner-notched dart point
- G = corner-notched dart point
- H = stemmed dart point ("Carlsbad")
- I = corner-notched dart point with bifurcated base
- J = unclassified stemmed or notched dart point

Port. (portion):
- C = nearly complete
- D = distal (tip)
- F = small fragment only
- L = lateral (edge)
- M = medial (midsection)
- P = proximal (base)

Mat. (lithic material):
- C = chert or chalcedony
- I = fine-grained igneous
- M = misc. highly weathered or patinated materials
- O = obsidian
- Q = quartzite

Axial Length, Blade Length, Notch Length, Tang Length, Base Width, Tang Width, Shoulder Width, Max. Thickness:

Linear measurements, in centimeters, as defined in Figure 43. Measurements enclosed in brackets apply to broken, damaged, or incomplete specimens and do not reflect values for complete specimens; measurements enclosed in parentheses represent reasonable estimates of the values for complete specimens

Edge Angle (average lateral edge angle, in degrees):

Weight (weight of fragment, in grams):

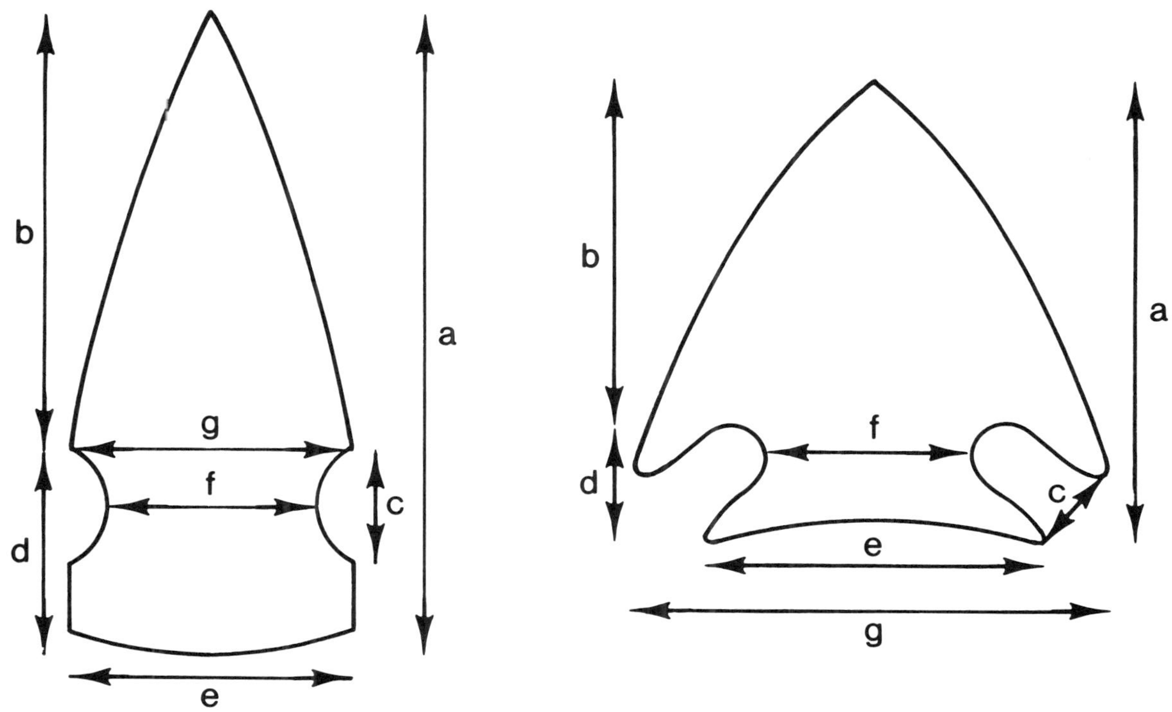

Fig. 48. Linear measurements recorded in Tables C1 and C2 for projectile points.

Table C1
Projectile points (Part 1)

Provenience	Fig.	Form	Port.	Mat.	Axial Length	Blade Length	Notch Length	Tang Length
TT1-E/0-5	---	-	M	C	-	-	-	-
TT1-E/0-5	31g	F	F	C	-	-	-	-
TT1-E/5-10	33a	G/H	P	C	-	-	-	-
TT1-E/10-25	---	F	L	C	-	[1.46]	-	-
TT1-W/5-10	29a	D	P	C	[1.72]	[1.72]	0.00	0.00
TT1-W/15-30	---	-	D	C	-	[1.40]	-	-
TT2-N/0-1	---	-	D	C	-	[2.21]	-	-
TT2-S/0-1	---	-	M	C	-	[1.44]	-	-
499N500W/0-10	29j	B	D	C	-	1.57	-	[0.11]
499N501W/20-25	33b	G/H	P	C	-	-	-	[0.89]
499N503W/0-5	---	-	M	C	-	[2.02]	-	-
499N503W/10-15	---	-	D	Q	-	[1.85]	-	-
499N504W/15-20	---	-	D	C	-	[1.90]	-	-
499N504W/25-30	33c	G/H	P	C	-	-	-	[0.99]
499N505W/5.0	291	C	P	O	[1.36]	[0.72]	[0.26]	[0.69]
499N505W/7.0	33d	G/H	P	O	-	-	-	[0.97]
499N512W/5-10	---	J	D	C	-	(2.70)	-	-
499N512W/10-15	29b	D	P	C	[1.76]	[1.76]	0.00	0.00
499N512W/10-15	31h	F	L	C	-	[1.35]	-	[0.34]
499N512W/15-20	---	-	D	C	-	[1.29]	-	-
499N512W/15-20	---	-	M	C	-	[1.21]	-	-
499N513W/5-10	29m	C	(C)	C	[2.08]	[1.43]	0.43	0.74
499N513W/20-25	29k	B	C	C	(2.03)	(1.49)	0.27	0.63
499N513W/20-25	31d	I?	F	C	-	-	-	[0.82]
499N515W/0-5	31b	I	(C)	C	[3.55]	[2.81]	(0.40)	0.71
499N515W/0-5	---	-	D	C	-	[1.07]	-	-
499N515W/10-15	---	-	D	C	-	[2.34]	-	-

Table Cl. (continued)

Provenience	Fig.	Form	Port.	Mat.	Axial Length	Blade Length	Notch Length	Tang Length
499N517W/5-10	29c	D	P	C	[2.30]	[2.30]	0.00	0.00
499N518W/5-10	33e	G/H	P	C	-	-	-	[1.13]
500N460W/0-1	29d	D	L	C	[2.20]	[2.20]	0.00	0.00
500N501W/0-5	---	-	D	C	-	[1.09]	-	-
500N501W/6.5	32a	H	P	C	[2.61]	[1.48]	0.89	1.05
500N501W/15-20	32b	H	P	Q	-	-	(0.57)	(1.26)
500N502W/5-10	32c	H	P	C	-	-	0.52	0.98
500N504W/0-5	29n	C	(C)	C	1.86	1.19	(0.25)	0.67
500N504W/0-5	---	-	M	C	-	[1.06]	-	-
500N504W/5-10	31e	F	P	C	[2.26]	[1.50]	[0.60]	0.80
500N504W/5-10	29e	D	P	C	[1.68]	[1.68]	0.00	0.00
500N505W/0-5	30a	E	(C)	C	(2.36)	(1.22)	0.74	(1.03)
500N505W/10-15	---	-	D	C	-	[1.43]	-	-
500N512W/10-15	29f	D	P	C	[1.15]	[1.15]	0.00	0.00
500N512W/30-35	33f	G/H	P	C	-	-	-	[0.83]
500N513W/10-15	---	-	D	C	-	[1.22]	-	-
500N514W/10-15	31i	F	L	C	[1.39]	[1.11]	-	-
500N514W/15-20	33g	G/H	P	C	-	-	-	(1.00)
500N515W/0-5	---	-	M	C	-	[1.60]	-	-
500N515W/0-5	---	-	D	C	-	[1.07]	-	-
500N515W/0-5	31j	F	M	C	[1.74]	[1.30]	-	-
500N515W/5-10	---	-	D	C	-	[1.12]	-	-
500N517W/0-5	---	-	D	C	-	[1.34]	-	-
500N518W/5-10	31a	J	C	C	3.21	2.07	0.93	1.14
500N518W/5-10	33h	G/H	P	C	-	-	-	[0.79]
504N515W/15-20	---	J	F	C	-	-	-	-
504N568W/10-15	29g	D	P	C	[1.31]	[1.31]	0.00	0.00
505N515W/10-15	33i	G/H	P	C	-	-	-	(1.02)
505N515W/15-20	32d	H	C	C	3.87	2.18	1.28	1.70

Table C1. (continued)

Provenience	Fig.	Form	Port.	Mat.	Axial Length	Blade Length	Notch Length	Tang Length
505N515W/15-20	32e	H	L	C	[2.95]	[1.67]	0.96	1.31
511N514W/5-10	---	-	M	C	-	[1.00]	-	-
511N514W/10-15	---	-	M	C	-	[1.42]	-	-
511N514W/25-30	30b	E	C	Q	2.76	1.71	0.43	1.13
511N515W/15-20	33j	G/H	P	C	-	-	-	[1.08]
512N514W/5-10	29o	C	P	C	-	-	-	0.90
surface	30e	E	C	C	[2.43]	[1.61]	0.67	0.78
surface	33l	G/H	P	C	-	-	(0.65)	(0.75)
surface	30f	E	C	C	2.08	0.83	0.89	1.12
surface	31k	G	L	C	[2.02]	[1.41]	(0.50)	(0.60)
surface	32j	H	P	C	[2.88]	[1.35]	(1.12)	(1.53)
surface	32i	H	C	C	2.75	1.64	(0.74)	1.12
surface	32k	H	P	C	-	-	(0.85)	(1.18)
surface	30c	E	C	C	(2.10)	1.32	0.55	(0.72)
surface	---	-	L	I	-	[1.30]	-	-
surface	---	D?	L	C	-	-	-	[0.86]
surface	29h	A	C	C	(1.56)	(1.56)	0.00	0.00
surface	---	G	L	C	-	[1.37]	-	-
surface	---	-	L	O	-	[0.95]	-	-
surface	29p	C	C	C	1.62	0.95	0.22	0.67
surface	29q	C	C	C	1.85	1.10	0.26	0.73
surface	---	-	M	C	-	[1.28]	-	-
surface	32f	H	C	C	3.80	2.27	(1.15)	1.39
surface	---	-	M	C	-	[1.00]	-	-
surface	---	J	M	C	-	[1.66]	-	-
surface	29r	C	L	C	[1.65]	[1.18]	0.13	[0.50]
surface	---	-	D	C	-	[1.78]	-	-
surface	30d	E	P	C	[1.62]	[0.77]	0.57	1.02
surface	33k	G/H	P	C	-	-	-	[0.80]

Table C1. (continued)

Provenience	Fig.	Form	Port.	Mat.	Axial Length	Blade Length	Notch Length	Tang Length
surface	31f	G	D	C	(2.35)	(1.74)	0.60	(0.85)
surface	---	-	D	C	-	[2.15]	-	-
surface	31c	I	L	C	[2.20]	[1.11]	(0.70)	1.07
surface	32g	H	C	C	[2.72]	[1.71]	0.74	0.96
surface	---	J	D	C	-	2.30	-	-
surface	32h	H	C	C	(4.05)	(3.09)	(0.71)	0.80
surface	---	-	D	C	-	[1.76]	-	-
surface	---	D?	L	C	-	-	-	-
surface	---	-	D	C	-	[0.90]	-	-

Table C2
Projectile points (Part 2)

Provenience	Fig.	Base Width	Tang Width	Should. Width	Max. Thick.	Edge Angle	Weight
TT1-E/0-5	---	-	-	[2.53]	(0.60)	40	2.5
TT1-E/0-5	31g	-	-	-	-	-	0.3
TT1-E/5-10	33a	1.32	-	-	[0.33]	-	0.3
TT1-E/10-25	---	-	-	[1.35]	[0.34]	40	0.7
TT1-W/5-10	29a	1.42	1.42	1.42	0.44	25	0.9
TT1-W/15-30	---	-	-	[1.26]	[0.45]	50	0.5
TT2-N/0-1	---	-	-	[1.50]	0.39	20	1.1
TT2-S/0-1	---	-	-	[1.14]	[0.24]	25	0.3
499N500W/0-10	29j	-	(0.55)	(1.30)	0.36	70	0.7
499M501W/20-25	33b	(1.50)	-	-	[0.36]	-	0.6
499N503W/0-5	---	-	-	[1.05]	0.50	55	0.9
499N503W/10-15	---	-	-	[2.09]	[0.53]	55	1.9
499N504W/15-20	---	-	-	[1.20]	[0.40]	55	0.5
499N504W/25-30	33c	1.82	-	-	[0.45]	-	0.7
499N505W/5.0	291	[0.86]	0.63	0.92	0.33	35	0.4
499N505W/7.0	33d	(1.92)	-	-	[0.39]	-	0.8
499N512W/5-10	---	-	-	[2.04]	0.55	55	2.7
499N512W/10-15	29b	(1.16)	(1.16)	(1.16)	0.40	35	0.8
499N512W/10-15	31h	-	-	[1.43]	0.45	40	0.5
499N512W/15-20	---	-	-	[1.36]	[0.35]	35	0.4
499N512W/15-20	---	-	-	[1.55]	[0.47]	45	0.7
499N513W/5-10	29m	[0.99]	0.59	1.25	0.37	40	0.9
499N513W/20-25	29k	[0.98]	0.71	(1.43)	0.35	60	0.9
499N513W/20-25	31d	[1.10]	[1.10]	-	[0.25]	-	0.3
499N515W/0-5	31b	1.70	1.28	(2.29)	0.42	45	3.2
499N515W/0-5	---	-	-	[1.23]	[0.26]	30	0.3
499N515W/10-15	---	-	-	[1.50]	(0.36)	35	0.9

Table C2. (continued)

Provenience	Fig.	Base Width	Tang Width	Should. Width	Max. Thick.	Edge Angle	Weight
499N517W/5-10	29c	1.38	1.38	1.38	0.35	35	1.3
499N518W/5-10	33e	1.59	-	-	[0.42]	-	0.7
500N460W/0-1	29d	[1.28]	[1.28]	[1.28]	[0.38]	30	1.1
500N501W/0-5	---	-	-	[1.35]	[0.41]	40	0.4
500N501W/6.5	32a	1.65	1.57	2.38	0.67	45	4.0
500N501W/15-20	32b	1.44	1.20	-	[0.50]	-	1.0
500N502W/5-10	32c	1.44	1.24	(1.59)	[0.50]	-	1.4
500N504W/0-5	29n	[0.85]	0.81	1.14	0.31	35	0.6
500N504W/0-5	---	-	-	[1.31]	[0.23]	20	0.3
500N504W/5-10	31e	1.11	1.05	[2.70]	(0.54)	70	3.0
500N504W/5-10	29e	1.37	1.37	1.37	0.30	30	0.7
500N505W/0-5	30a	(1.40)	(1.32)	(1.87)	(0.58)	40	2.1
500N505W/10-15	---	-	-	[1.35]	[0.32]	35	0.5
500N512W/10-15	29f	1.66	1.66	1.66	(0.26)	30	0.5
500N512W/30-35	33f	1.98	-	-	[0.38]	-	0.6
500N513W/10-15	---	-	-	[1.18]	[0.46]	45	0.4
500N514W/10-15	31i	-	[1.07]	[1.66]	[0.49]	40	0.8
500N514W/15-20	33g	1.80	(1.45)	-	[0.48]	-	0.8
500N515W/0-5	---	-	-	[1.95]	[0.62]	65	2.2
500N515W/0-5	---	-	-	[0.97]	0.24	30	0.2
500N515W/0-5	31j	-	-	[2.50]	0.55	50	2.6
500N515W/5-10	---	-	-	[0.73]	[0.28]	40	0.2
500N517W/0-5	---	-	-	[0.83]	[0.30]	45	0.3
500N518W/5-10	31a	1.09	1.08	1.50	0.57	55	2.8
500N518W/5-10	33h	[1.32]	-	-	[0.38]	-	0.3
504N515W/15-20	---	-	-	-	-	45	0.4
504N568W/10-15	29g	1.51	1.51	1.51	0.40	30	0.7
505N515W/10-15	33i	1.55	(1.19)	-	[0.41]	-	0.5
505N515W/15-20	32d	1.80	1.41	2.11	0.70	60	4.7

Table C2. (continued)

Provenience	Fig.	Base Width	Tang Width	Should. Width	Max. Thick.	Edge Angle	Weight
505N515W/15-20	32e	1.41	0.98	-	0.47	50	1.7
511N514W/5-10	---	-	-	[1.08]	[0.23]	25	0.2
511N514W/10-15	---	-	-	[1.71]	[0.38]	40	0.7
511N514W/25-30	30b	1.75	1.50	1.57	0.72	60	3.2
511N515W/15-20	33j	1.76	(1.40)	-	[0.45]	-	0.9
512N514W/5-10	29o	1.42	(0.75)	-	[0.25]	-	-
surface	30e	(1.57)	1.34	1.93	0.53	45	2.3
surface	33l	1.82	(1.58)	-	[0.38]	-	1.0
surface	30f	1.58	1.32	(1.57)	0.61	70	2.2
surface	31k	[0.92]	[0.92]	[1.44]	[0.60]	50	1.3
surface	32j	(1.50)	1.23	[2.17]	0.62	-	3.4
surface	32i	1.30	1.07	(2.14)	0.48	50	2.2
surface	32k	(1.52)	1.18	-	[0.68]	-	1.7
surface	30c	(1.50)	1.12	[1.59]	0.50	70	1.8
surface	---	-	-	[1.14]	[0.48]	40	0.5
surface	---	[1.29]	-	-	[0.34]	-	0.2
surface	29h	1.24	1.24	1.24	0.23	30	0.3
surface	---	-	[0.80]	[1.10]	[0.47]	40	0.9
surface	---	-	-	[0.99]	[0.29]	40	0.2
surface	29p	1.28	0.67	1.03	0.30	30	0.5
surface	29q	1.31	0.72	1.03	0.31	30	0.6
surface	---	-	-	[1.11]	[0.60]	70	1.0
surface	32f	[1.60]	1.28	(2.46)	0.60	50	4.4
surface	---	-	-	[2.01]	[0.37]	35	0.8
surface	---	-	-	[1.75]	[0.77]	45	2.1
surface	29r	[1.19]	(0.91)	[1.10]	0.32	30	0.6
surface	---	-	-	[1.38]	[0.52]	60	0.8
surface	30d	2.06	1.53	[2.06]	[0.56]	45	2.2
surface	33k	[1.39]	(1.22)	-	[0.36]	-	0.7

Table C2. (continued)

Provenience	Fig.	Base Width	Tang Width	Should. Width	Max. Thick.	Edge Angle	Weight
surface	31f	-	-	(1.92)	0.42	50	1.7
surface	---	-	-	[2.15]	0.54	45	2.3
surface	31c	[0.80]	[0.87]	[1.38]	[0.36]	80	1.0
surface	32g	1.39	(1.37)	[1.70]	0.58	70	3.0
surface	---	-	(0.85)	1.86	(0.60)	40	2.7
surface	32h	1.40	1.29	2.68	0.84	65	8.2
surface	---	-	-	[1.27]	[0.44]	45	0.8
surface	---	[0.95]	-	-	[0.20]	-	0.2
surface	---	-	-	[0.76]	[0.24]	40	0.1

<u>Key to Table C3 (excavated lithic artifacts excluding projectile points)</u>

N (total number of specimens):

Wt. (total weight of specimens, in grams):

Mat. (lithic material):

- C = chert or chalcedony
- I = fine-grained igneous
- M = misc. coarse, highly weathered, or patinated materials
- O = obsidian
- Q = quartzite
- V = vein quartz

Utilized Edges: some specimens have more than one utilized edge; in those cases, each edge is described individually

- Type:
  - BR = bifacially retouched edge
  - UR = unifacially retouched edge
  - Ut = unretouched utilized edge
- Shape (of utilized edge):
  - 1 = point
  - 2 = straight
  - 3 = convex
  - 4 = concave
  - 5 = notched
  - 6 = nosed
  - 7 = denticulated
  - 8 = sinusoidal
  - 9 = irregular or misc.
- Angle (mean angle of working edge, in degrees):

Table C3
Inventory of excavated lithic artifacts (excluding projectile points)

Provenience	N	Wt.	Mat.	Description	Utilized Edges Type	Shape	Angle
TT1-E/0-5	1	6.8	C	crude biface (preform)			
TT1-E/0-5	1	2.1	C	scraper frag.	BR	3	55
					UR	3	65
TT1-E/0-5	1	1.8	C	retouched flake frag.	UR	3	45
					UR	5	60
TT1-E/0-5	1	0.4	C	biface frag.	BR	2	40
TT1-E/0-5	1	2.1	Q	utilized flake	Ut	5	60
TT1-E/0-5	1	31.0	C	core			
TT1-E/0-5	84	36.3	C	unmodified flakes			
TT1-E/0-5	11	10.8	Q	unmodified flakes			
TT1-E/0-5	2	0.6	I	unmodified flakes			
TT1-E/0-5	10	15.8	M	unmodified flakes			
TT1-E/5-10	1	2.2	C	scraper frag.	UR	2	90
TT1-E/5-10	1	1.4	C	utilized flake	Ut	2	50
					Ut	2	30
					Ut	4	50
TT1-E/5-10	1	0.6	C	utilized flake frag.	Ut	2	30
TT1-E/5-10	1	0.3	C	utilized flake frag.	Ut	2	45
TT1-E/5-10	1	0.4	C	utilized flake frag.	Ut	3	20
TT1-E/5-10	59	44.5	C	unmodified flakes			
TT1-E/5-10	5	1.7	Q	unmodified flakes			
TT1-E/5-10	2	0.4	O	unmodified flakes			
TT1-E/5-10	1	0.8	I	unmodified flake			
TT1-E/5-10	3	0.8	M	unmodified flakes			
TT1-E/10-25	1	0.6	C	retouched flake frag.	UR	2	60
TT1-E/10-25	32	13.4	C	unmodified flakes			

Table C3. (continued)

Provenience	N	Wt.	Mat.	Description	Utilized Edges Type	Shape	Angle
TT1-E/10-25	2	1.3	Q	unmodified flakes			
TT1-E/10-25	4	3.0	M	unmodified flakes			
TT1-E/25-30	12	6.8	C	unmodified flakes			
TT1-E/25-30	2	0.4	M	unmodified flakes			
TT1-E/45-60	1	0.5	I	unmodified flake			
TT1-W/0-5	1	7.3	C	scraper	UR	3	90
					UR	3	60
TT1-W/0-5	1	1.7	C	scraper frag.	UR	2	50
TT1-W/0-5	1	2.1	C	scraper frag.	UR	3	70
TT1-W/0-5	1	0.8	C	biface frag.	BR	2	60
TT1-W/0-5	1	2.5	C	retouched flake	UR	4	60
					UR	2	50
					UR	5	50
TT1-W/0-5	1	0.5	C	retouched flake frag.	UR	3	50
TT1-W/0-5	1	0.8	C	retouched flake frag.	UR	7	55
TT1-W/0-5	80	47.7	C	unmodified flakes			
TT1-W/0-5	5	1.8	Q	unmodified flakes			
TT1-W/0-5	2	0.7	O	unmodified flakes			
TT1-W/0-5	3	1.3	I	unmodified flakes			
TT1-W/0-5	2	3.6	M	unmodified flakes			
TT1-W/5-10	1	1.0	C	scraper frag.	UR	3	80
TT1-W/5-10	1	0.3	C	utilized flake frag.	Ut	3	70
TT1-W/5-10	1	5.2	M	utilized flake	Ut	2	45
TT1-W/5-10	49	35.1	C	unmodified flakes			
TT1-W/5-10	1	0.5	Q	unmodified flake			
TT1-W/5-10	6	7.4	M	unmodified flakes			
TT1-W/10-25	1	3.4	C	biface frag.	BR	3	70
TT1-W/10-25	1	0.2	C	biface frag.	BR	3	35

Table C3. (continued)

Provenience	N	Wt.	Mat.	Description	Utilized Edges Type	Shape	Angle
TT1-W/10-25	1	10.6	Q	retouched flake frag.	UR	2	45
TT1-W/10-25	1	55.3	C	core			
TT1-W/10-25	38	12.6	C	unmodified flakes			
TT1-W/10-25	1	0.2	O	unmodified flake			
TT1-W/10-25	3	1.7	I	unmodified flakes			
TT1-W/10-25	5	4.5	M	unmodified flakes			
TT1-W/15-30	13	5.4	C	unmodified flakes			
TT1-W/15-30	1	0.6	Q	unmodified flake			
TT1-W/30-45	4	1.4	C	unmodified flakes			
TT2-N/0-1	1	0.5	C	biface frag.	BR	2	45
TT2-N/0-1	17	6.0	C	unmodified flakes			
TT2-N/0-1	2	3.8	Q	unmodified flakes			
TT2-N/0-1	1	0.5	I	unmodified flake			
TT2-S/0-1	1	4.7	C	sidescraper	UR	2	60
					UR	2	45
TT2-S/0-1	9	4.7	C	unmodified flakes			
495N519W/0-5	1	0.7	C	scraper frag.	UR	3	60
495N519W/0-5	1	4.7	C	retouched flake	UR	7	55
495N519W/0-5	1	0.9	C	retouched flake frag.	UR	3	50
495N519W/0-5	1	2.0	C	retouched flake frag.	UR	2	55
495N519W/0-5	1	3.9	C	utilized flake	Ut	7	45
					Ut	3	65
495N519W/0-5	1	49.5	C	core			
495N519W/0-5	40	44.6	C	unmodified flakes			
495N519W/0-5	6	2.7	Q	unmodified flakes			
495N519W/0-5	1	0.3	I	unmodified flake			
495N519W/0-5	5	6.7	M	unmodified flakes			
495N519W/5-10	1	0.9	C	retouched flake frag.	UR	2	55

Table C3. (continued)

Provenience	N	Wt.	Mat.	Description	Utilized Edges Type	Shape	Angle
					UR	3	70
495N519W/5-10	20	6.8	C	unmodified flakes			
495N519W/5-10	2	1.4	Q	unmodified flakes			
495N519W/5-10	1	3.8	M	unmodified flake			
495N519W/10-15	1	0.7	C	crude biface frag.	BR	3	70
495N519W/10-15	1	248.4	C	hammerstone			
495N519W/10-15	17	13.8	C	unmodified flakes			
495N519W/15-20	1	3.5	C	retouched flake frag.	UR	5	75
					UR	1	80
					UR	3	90
495N519W/15-20	1	6.1	Q	retouched flake	UR	7	50
495N519W/15-20	10	16.8	C	unmodified flakes			
495N519W/20-25	10	24.4	C	unmodified flakes			
495N519W/20-25	2	9.3	Q	unmodified flakes			
499N460W/0-1	1	1.3	C	utilized flake frag.	Ut	2	45
499N460W/0-1	2	2.5	C	unmodified flakes			
499N461W/0-1	1	1.0	C	utilized flake frag.	Ut	3	45
499N461W/0-1	4	2.6	C	unmodified flakes			
499N461W/0-1	1	0.2	O	unmodified flake			
499N500W/0-10	1	0.9	C	retouched flake frag.	UR	7	80
499N500W/0-10	1	3.1	C	utilized flake	Ut	2	30
499N500W/0-10	54	24.6	C	unmodified flakes			
499N500W/0-10	3	0.7	O	unmodified flakes			
499N500W/0-10	1	0.3	I	unmodified flake			
499N500W/0-10	1	0.3	M	unmodified flake			
499N500W/10-15	1	0.8	C	biface frag.	BR	3	30
499N500W/10-15	1	0.4	C	biface frag.	BR	2	55
499N500W/10-15	1	9.0	C	core			

Table C3. (continued)

Provenience	N	Wt.	Mat.	Description	Utilized Edges		
					Type	Shape	Angle
499N500W/10-15	15	11.6	C	unmodified flakes			
499N500W/10-15	1	0.4	Q	unmodified flake			
499N500W/10-15	1	0.2	M	unmodified flake			
499N500W/15-20	1	2.4	M	utilized flake	Ut	4	60
499N500W/15-20	25	11.1	C	unmodified flakes			
499N500W/15-20	2	0.9	Q	unmodified flakes			
499N500W/15-20	1	1.2	M	unmodified flake			
499N500W/20-30	14	6.3	C	unmodified flakes			
499N500W/20-30	1	0.4	Q	unmodified flake			
499N500W/20-30	1	3.1	C	core frag.			
499N500W/30-35	5	4.0	C	unmodified flakes			
499N500W/35-40	1	1.8	C	retouched flake	UR	3	65
					UR	2	40
499N500W/35-40	2	1.0	C	unmodified flakes			
499N500W/35-40	1	0.4	Q	unmodified flake			
499N501W/0-5	1	2.1	C	biface frag.	BR	3	55
499N501W/0-5	1	5.3	C	crude biface (preform)			
499N501W/0-5	1	1.4	C	retouched flake frag.	UR	7	55
499N501W/0-5	1	0.7	C	retouched flake frag.	UR	3	70
499N501W/0-5	1	0.6	C	utilized flake	Ut	2	40
499N501W/0-5	1	1.8	I	utilized flake	Ut	3	25
499N501W/0-5	1	15.2	C	core			
499N501W/0-5	82	44.0	C	unmodified flakes			
499N501W/0-5	1	0.4	Q	unmodified flake			
499N501W/0-5	1	0.1	O	unmodified flake			
499N501W/0-5	7	6.3	I	unmodified flakes			
499N501W/0-5	10	28.9	M	unmodified flakes			
499N501W/5-10	1	0.6	C	retouched flake frag.	UR	2	60

Table C3. (continued)

Provenience	N	Wt.	Mat.	Description	Utilized Edges		
					Type	Shape	Angle
					UR	2	70
499N501W/5-10	32	19.1	C	unmodified flakes			
499N501W/5-10	1	0.7	Q	unmodified flake			
499N501W/5-10	5	2.1	M	unmodified flakes			
499N501W/10-15	1	2.3	C	utilized flake	Ut	9	60
499N501W/10-15	23	13.9	C	unmodified flakes			
499N501W/10-15	3	0.7	Q	unmodified flakes			
499N501W/10-15	4	4.3	M	unmodified flakes			
499N501W/15-20	1	0.3	C	biface frag.	BR	3	35
499N501W/15-20	1	3.3	C	utilized flake	Ut	3	50
499N501W/15-20	1	1.0	C	utilized flake	Ut	3	25
499N501W/15-20	22	8.7	C	unmodified flakes			
499N501W/15-20	3	4.0	Q	unmodified flakes			
499N501W/15-20	2	1.0	I	unmodified flakes			
499N501W/15-20	2	1.9	M	unmodified flakes			
499N501W/20-25	1	4.2	C	retouched flake	UR	4	70
499N501W/20-25	1	2.2	C	retouched flake frag.	UR	7	40
499N501W/20-25	15	8.5	C	unmodified flakes			
499N501W/20-25	1	0.6	I	unmodified flake			
499N501W/20-25	1	1.3	M	unmodified flake			
499N501W/25-30	9	11.2	C	unmodified flakes			
499N501W/25-30	1	0.1	Q	unmodified flake			
499N502W/0-5	1	1.2	C	biface frag.	BR	3	30
499N502W/0-5	1	0.6	C	biface frag.	BR	3	60
499N502W/0-5	1	0.5	C	biface frag.	BR	6	60
499N502W/0-5	1	0.8	C	retouched flake frag.	UR	7	55
499N502W/0-5	1	1.1	C	utilized flake	Ut	2	40
499N502W/0-5	1	0.6	C	utilized flake frag.	Ut	3	20

Table C3. (continued)

Provenience	N	Wt.	Mat.	Description	Utilized Edges Type	Shape	Angle
499N502W/0-5	38	15.0	C	unmodified flakes	Ut	2	55
499N502W/0-5	2	2.5	Q	unmodified flakes			
499N502W/0-5	2	0.6	M	unmodified flakes			
499N502W/5-10	1	9.0	C	endscraper	UR	3	80
					UR	7	80
499N502W/5-10	1	2.7	C	retouched flake	UR	7	45
499N502W/5-10	1	1.9	C	utilized flake	Ut	3	50
					Ut	3	30
499N502W/5-10	1	4.7	C	utilized flake	Ut	3	40
499N502W/5-10	1	0.2	C	utilized	Ut	2	20
499N502W/5-10	1	12.7	C	core			
499N502W/5-10	1	1.7	C	core			
499N502W/5-10	37	33.5	C	unmodified flakes			
499N502W/5-10	7	9.2	Q	unmodified flakes			
499N502W/5-10	4	2.5	M	unmodified flakes			
499N502W/10-15	1	3.2	M	crude biface (preform)			
499N502W/10-15	1	0.6	C	retouched flake frag.	UR	2	70
499N502W/10-15	36	30.7	C	unmodified flakes			
499N502W/10-15	4	8.5	Q	unmodified flakes			
499N502W/10-15	3	7.6	M	unmodified flakes			
499N502W/15-20	1	0.9	C	biface (preform?) frag			
499N502W/15-20	1	11.3	C	core			
499N502W/15-20	18	10.1	C	unmodified flakes			
499N502W/15-20	1	1.3	M	unmodified flake			
499N502W/20-25	1	0.6	C	utilized flake	Ut	3	20
499N502W/20-25	12	7.7	C	unmodified flakes			
499N502W/20-25	1	0.2	I	unmodified flake			

Table C3. (continued)

Provenience	N	Wt.	Mat.	Description	Utilized Edges Type	Shape	Angle
499N502W/25-30	1	0.3	C	biface frag.	BR	2	50
499N502W/25-30	1	2.6	C	utilized flake	Ut	2	70
					Ut	4	25
					Ut	3	30
499N502W/25-30	15	5.1	C	unmodified flakes			
499N502W/25-30	1	0.2	Q	unmodified flake			
499N502W/25-30	1	1.1	M	unmodified flake			
499N503W/0-5	1	9.0	C	endscraper	UR	3	70
					UR	7	75
499N503W/0-5	1	33.9	M	sidescraper	UR	3	70
					UR	3	60
499N503W/0-5	1	5.5	Q	retouched flake	UR	8	60
499N503W/0-5	1	0.1	C	utilized flake frag.	Ut	2	30
499N503W/0-5	40	41.4	C	unmodified flakes			
499N503W/0-5	1	0.2	Q	unmodified flake			
499N503W/0-5	1	0.2	M	unmodified flake			
499N503W/5-10	1	1.1	C	biface frag.	BR	3	60
499N503W/5-10	1	0.8	C	retouched flake frag.	UR	7	80
499N503W/5-10	29	20.3	C	unmodified flakes			
499N503W/5-10	3	15.7	M	unmodified flakes			
499N503W/10-15	1	5.2	M	endscraper	UR	3	90
					UR	3	60
					UR	3	90
499N503W/10-15	1	1.9	C	biface frag.	BR	3	45
499N503W/10-15	1	5.3	C	retouched flake	BR	3	55
499N503W/10-15	1	0.2	C	utilized flake frag.	Ut	3	70
499N503W/10-15	30	19.3	C	unmodified flakes			
499N503W/10-15	2	2.4	Q	unmodified flakes			

Table C3. (continued)

Provenience	N	Wt.	Mat.	Description	Utilized Edges Type	Shape	Angle
499N503W/15-20	1	20.8	M	endscraper	UR	3	80
499N503W/15-20	1	4.2	C	core frag.			
499N503W/15-20	39	23.2	C	unmodified flakes			
499N503W/15-20	1	0.5	Q	unmodified flake			
499N503W/15-20	1	0.6	I	unmodified flake			
499N503W/15-20	3	2.7	M	unmodified flakes			
499N503W/20-25	8	2.7	C	unmodified flakes			
499N503W/20-25	1	0.7	Q	unmodified flake			
499N503W/20-25	3	8.5	M	unmodified flakes			
499N503W/25-30	8	2.7	C	unmodified flakes			
499N504W/0-5	1	2.3	C	biface frag.	BR	3	40
499N504W/0-5	1	1.7	C	utilized flake	Ut	2	30
499N504W/0-5	11	5.6	C	unmodified flakes			
499N504W/0-5	3	2.3	M	unmodified flakes			
499N504W/5-10	1	0.3	O	biface frag.	BR	3	35
499N504W/5-10	1	2.1	C	ovate biface frag.	BR	3	60
499N504W/5-10	1	0.5	C	retouched flake	UR	2	80
499N504W/5-10	1	0.5	C	retouched flake frag.	UR	3	60
499N504W/5-10	1	0.3	C	utilized flake frag.	Ut	2	70
499N504W/5-10	56	29.2	C	unmodified flakes			
499N504W/5-10	5	7.9	Q	unmodified flakes			
499N504W/5-10	1	0.4	I	unmodified flake			
499N504W/5-10	8	12.7	M	unmodified flakes			
499N504W/10-15	1	6.4	C	scraper	UR	8	40
					UR	7	75
499N504W/10-15	1	0.2	C	retouched flake frag.	BR	2	40
499N504W/10-15	1	1.2	C	utilized flake	Ut	2	30
499N504W/10-15	35	16.4	C	unmodified flakes			

Table C3. (continued)

Provenience	N	Wt.	Mat.	Description	Utilized Edges Type	Shape	Angle
499N504W/10-15	1	0.5	I	unmodified flake			
499N504W/10-15	4	2.4	Q	unmodified flakes			
499N504W/15-20	1	1.2	C	sidescraper frag.	UR	2	60
					UR	2	60
499N504W/15-20	1	2.3	C	retouched flake	UR	5	90
					UR	3	70
499N504W/15-20	1	1.1	C	retouched flake frag.	UR	3	65
499N504W/15-20	1	0.7	C	utilized flake	Ut	3	20
499N504W/15-20	1	4.5	C	utilized flake	Ut	2	50
					Ut	3	40
499N504W/15-20	17	10.9	C	unmodified flakes			
499N504W/15-20	2	1.1	Q	unmodified flakes			
499N504W/20-25	1	3.5	C	core or crude biface frag.	UR	7	60
499N504W/20-25	1	0.4	C	utilized flake frag.	Ut	3	40
499N504W/20-25	16	7.2	C	unmodified flakes			
499N504W/20-25	1	0.1	Q	unmodified flake			
499N504W/20-25	1	1.1	M	unmodified flake			
499N504W/25-30	1	1.0	C	retouched flake frag.	UR	3	80
499N504W/25-30	28	13.4	C	unmodified flakes			
499N504W/25-30	1	0.1	Q	unmodified flake			
499N504W/30-35	2	0.5	C	unmodified flakes			
499N505W/0-5	8	6.1	C	unmodified flakes			
499N505W/0-5	4	1.1	Q	unmodified flakes			
499N505W/0-5	1	2.3	M	unmodified flake			
499N505W/5-10	1	0.5	C	small biface frag.	BR	3	70
499N505W/5-10	1	1.4	C	retouched flake frag.	UR	2	50
499N505W/5-10	54	42.7	C	unmodified flakes			
499N505W/5-10	1	1.0	O	unmodified flake			

Table C3. (continued)

Provenience	N	Wt.	Mat.	Description	Utilized Edges Type	Shape	Angle
499N505W/5-10	6	9.5	Q	unmodified flakes			
499N505W/5-10	1	1.3	I	unmodified flake			
499N505W/5-10	2	2.9	M	unmodified flakes			
499N505W/10-15	1	1.6	C	scraper frag.	UR	2	70
499N505W/10-15	1	3.2	C	biface frag.	BR	2	55
499N505W/10-15	1	1.9	C	biface frag.	BR	2	55
499N505W/10-15	1	0.3	C	scraper frag.	UR	2	60
499N505W/10-15	1	0.6	C	utilized flake frag.	Ut	4	35
499N505W/10-15	63	44.8	C	unmodified flakes			
499N505W/10-15	5	6.7	Q	unmodified flakes			
499N505W/10-15	2	4.5	M	unmodified flakes			
499N505W/15-20	20	10.7	C	unmodified flakes			
499N505W/15-20	3	2.0	Q	unmodified flakes			
499N505W/15-20	2	2.3	M	unmodified flakes			
499N505W/20-25	12	6.1	C	unmodified flakes			
499N505W/20-25	1	2.1	Q	unmodified flake			
499N505W/25-30	10	3.4	C	unmodified flakes			
499N506W/0-5	16	9.5	C	unmodified flakes			
499N506W/0-5	1	0.6	Q	unmodified flake			
499N506W/0-5	2	1.7	M	unmodified flakes			
499N506W/5-10	1	1.5	C	biface frag.	BR	3	45
499N506W/5-10	45	30.8	C	unmodified flakes			
499N506W/5-10	4	4.0	Q	unmodified flakes			
499N506W/5-10	4	2.1	M	unmodified flakes			
499N506W/10-15	1	31.6	M	end-and-side scraper	UR	2	80
					UR	3	90
					UR	4	60
499N506W/10-15	1	0.4	C	biface frag.	BR	-	60

Table C3. (continued)

Provenience	N	Wt.	Mat.	Description	Utilized Edges		
					Type	Shape	Angle
499N506W/10-15	1	0.9	C	utilized flake frag.	Ut	3	25
499N506W/10-15	34	29.4	C	unmodified flakes			
499N506W/10-15	2	0.6	Q	unmodified flakes			
499N506W/10-15	1	1.0	M	unmodified flake			
499N506W/15-20	25	13.4	C	unmodified flakes			
499N506W/20-25	17	24.0	C	unmodified flakes			
499N506W/20-25	1	0.1	O	unmodified flake			
499N506W/20-25	1	0.2	I	unmodified flake			
499N506W/20-25	1	2.0	Q	unmodified flake			
499N506W/20-25	2	1.0	M	unmodified flakes			
499N506W/25-30	2	0.8	C	unmodified flakes			
499N506W/30-35	7	4.5	C	unmodified flakes			
499N506W/30-35	1	0.4	O	unmodified flake			
499N512W/0-5	10	3.2	C	unmodified flakes			
499N512W/0-5	1	5.1	Q	unmodified flake			
499N512W/5-10	1	2.5	C	core frag.			
499N512W/5-10	11	16.4	C	unmodified flakes			
499N512W/10-15	1	7.1	C	endscraper	UR	3	75
					UR	7	70
499N512W/10-15	1	6.0	C	retouched flake	UR	2	60
499N512W/10-15	1	0.2	C	retouched flake frag.	UR	2	65
499N512W/10-15	1	6.0	C	retouched flake	UR	4	40
499N512W/10-15	1	0.5	C	utilized flake frag.	Ut	2	60
499N512W/10-15	1	0.1	C	utilized flake frag.	Ut	3	20
499N512W/10-15	58	55.7	C	unmodified flakes			
499N512W/10-15	4	6.5	Q	unmodified flakes			
499N512W/10-15	4	4.6	M	unmodified flakes			
499N512W/15 (Item 1)	1	22.3	C	core			

Table C3. (continued)

Provenience	N	Wt.	Mat.	Description	Utilized Edges Type	Shape	Angle
499N512W/15-20	1	4.1	C	endscraper	UR	3	80
					UR	3	50
499N512W/15-20	1	7.2	C	crude endscraper	UR	7	60
499N512W/15-20	44	36.7	C	unmodified flakes			
499N512W/15-20	1	0.2	Q	unmodified flake			
499N512W/15-20	1	0.2	I	unmodified flake			
499N512W/15-20	3	1.6	M	unmodified flakes			
499N512W/20-25	1	3.3	C	spurred endscraper	UR	3	70
499N512W/20-25	1	9.2	C	crude endscraper	UR	3	80
499N512W/20-25	1	7.1	C	core frag.			
499N512W/20-25	29	54.8	C	unmodified flakes			
499N512W/20-25	2	2.2	Q	unmodified flakes			
499N512W/25-30	1	8.0	C	crude biface frag.	BR	3	55
499N512W/25-30	21	9.4	C	unmodified flakes			
499N512W/25-30	3	2.0	I	unmodified flakes			
499N512W/25-30	3	4.4	Q	unmodified flakes			
499N512W/25-30	2	1.3	M	unmodified flakes			
499N512W/30-35	1	6.4	C	core			
499N512W/30-35	12	11.6	C	unmodified flakes			
499N512W/30-35	1	0.2	O	unmodified flake			
499N512W/30-35	1	0.2	Q	unmodified flake			
499N512W/30-35	2	0.3	M	unmodified flakes			
499N512W/35-40	7	3.3	C	unmodified flakes			
499N512W/35-40	1	0.5	O	unmodified flake			
499N512W/35-40	1	0.6	Q	unmodified flake			
499N512W/40-45	9	8.5	C	unmodified flakes			
499N512W/40-45	2	1.2	Q	unmodified flakes			
499N512W/40-45	1	0.5	I	unmodified flake			

Table C3. (continued)

Provenience	N	Wt.	Mat.	Description	Utilized Edges		
					Type	Shape	Angle
499N512W/45-50	7	7.7	C	unmodified flakes			
499N512W/45-50	1	3.7	Q	unmodified flake			
499N512W/45-50	1	0.3	I	unmodified flake			
499N512W/45-50	2	0.9	M	unmodified flakes			
499N513W/0-5	1	0.4	Q	retouched flake frag.	UR	2	60
499N513W/0-5	1	5.7	C	retouched flake	UR	4	65
499N513W/0-5	1	14.8	C	sidescraper	UR	7	70
					UR	7	90
499N513W/0-5	1	16.3	C	multi-facetted core			
499N513W/0-5	1	0.7	C	retouched tool frag. (drill?)	BR	2	70
499N513W/0-5	29	28.2	C	unmodified flakes			
499N513W/0-5	2	0.8	I	unmodified flakes			
499N513W/0-5	4	6.8	Q	unmodified flakes			
499N513W/0-5	4	1.4	M	unmodified flakes			
499N513W/5-10	1	2.2	C	retouched flake	UR	3	90
499N513W/5-10	1	0.6	C	retouched biface frag.	BR	4	70
499N513W/5-10	1	1.3	C	utilized flake	Ut	4	40
					Ut	4	30
499N513W/5-10	1	1.0	C	utilized flake frag.	Ut	2	30
499N513W/5-10	1	0.4	C	utilized flake frag.	Ut	3	40
499N513W/5-10	1	0.7	C	biface frag.	BR	7	70
499N513W/5-10	1	15.2	C	retouched flake	UR	3	90
499N513W/5-10	1	5.6	C	small multi-facetted core			
499N513W/5-10	76	78.6	C	unmodified flakes			
499N513W/5-10	10	17.6	Q	unmodified flakes			
499N513W/5-10	1	0.4	I	unmodified flake			
499N513W/5-10	4	2.5	M	unmodified flakes			
499N513W/10-15	1	0.6	C	retouched flake	UR	3	20

Table C3. (continued)

					Utilized Edges		
Provenience	N	Wt.	Mat.	Description	Type	Shape	Angle
499N513W/10-15	1	0.2	C	retouched flake frag.	BR	2	40
499N513W/10-15	1	9.6	C	core frag.			
499N513W/10-15	8	2.8	C	unmodified flakes			
499N513W/10-15	1	0.4	I	unmodified flake			
499N513W/15-20	1	3.3	C	core frag.			
499N513W/15-20	1	8.9	C	scraper	UR	3	70
499N513W/15-20	33	13.4	C	unmodified flakes			
499N513W/15-20	1	7.5	C	utilized flake	Ut	7	45
499N513W/15-20	2	0.8	Q	unmodified flakes			
499N513W/15-20	1	0.8	M	unmodified flake			
499N513W/20-25	1	2.0	C	biface frag.	BR	3	45
499N513W/20-25	1	1.2	C	scraper frag.	UR	7	65
499N513W/20-25	26	33.7	C	unmodified flakes			
499N513W/20-25	2	6.3	Q	unmodified flakes			
499N513W/25-30	1	2.1	C	utilized flake frag.	Ut	4	45
499N513W/25-30	33	21.7	C	unmodified flakes			
499N513W/25-30	1	1.2	Q	unmodified flake			
499N513W/25-30	1	0.4	I	unmodified flake			
499N513W/25-30	2	2.8	M	unmodified flakes			
499N513W/30-35	1	2.6	C	retouched flake frag.	UR	3	65
499N513W/30-35	14	8.3	C	unmodified flakes			
499N513W/30-35	2	4.3	Q	unmodified flakes			
499N513W/30-35	1	5.3	I	unmodified flake			
499N513W/30-35	1	0.3	M	unmodified flake			
499N513W/35-40	1	0.8	C	utilized flake	Ut	7	30
499N513W/35-40	19	15.3	C	unmodified flakes			
499N513W/35-40	1	0.5	Q	unmodified flake			
499N513W/35-40	1	1.3	I	unmodified flake			

Table C3. (continued)

Provenience	N	Wt.	Mat.	Description	Utilized Edges Type	Shape	Angle
499N513W/35-40	1	1.6	M	unmodified flake			
499N513W/40-45 (south half)	1	6.0	C	scraper	UR	7	65
499N513W/40-45 (south half)	8	3.1	C	unmodified flakes			
499N513W/40-45 (south half)	2	0.7	M	unmodified flakes			
499N514W/0-5	1	0.2	C	biface frag.	BR	6	80
499N514W/0-5	1	2.2	C	retouched flake	UR	7	55
499N514W/0-5	1	1.0	C	retouched flake frag. with graving spur	UR	5	65
					UR	7	75
					UR	1	-
499N514W/0-5	1	28.6	C	core			
499N514W/0-5	1	6.3	C	core			
499N514W/0-5	67	79.9	C	unmodified flakes			
499N514W/0-5	2	0.6	O	unmodified flakes			
499N514W/0-5	2	2.5	I	unmodified flakes			
499N514W/0-5	2	5.7	Q	unmodified flakes			
499N514W/0-5	5	4.9	M	unmodified flakes			
499N514W/5-10	1	0.6	C	biface frag.	BR	3	35
499N514W/5-10	1	0.6	C	retouched flake frag.	UR	4	65
499N514W/5-10	1	2.3	C	retouched flake frag.	UR	3	80
499N514W/5-10	1	1.9	C	utilized flake	Ut	4	30
499N514W/5-10	1	1.3	C	retouched flake frag.	UR	6	35
499N514W/5-10	1	1.1	C	utilized flake frag.	Ut	4	55
499N514W/5-10	42	28.2	C	unmodified flakes			
499N514W/5-10	1	0.2	O	unmodified flake			
499N514W/5-10	1	0.3	I	unmodified flake			
499N514W/5-10	1	0.3	Q	unmodified flake			
499N514W/5-10	5	4.3	M	unmodified flakes			
499N514W/10-15	1	0.6	C	retouched flake	UR	3	70

Table C3. (continued)

Provenience	N	Wt.	Mat.	Description	Utilized Edges Type	Shape	Angle
499N514W/10-15	1	0.4	M	retouched flake frag.	UR	2	40
499N514W/10-15	28	19.4	C	unmodified flakes			
499N514W/10-15	2	1.3	Q	unmodified flakes			
499N514W/10-15	2	0.7	M	unmodified flakes			
499N514W/15-20	37	23.4	C	unmodified flakes			
499N514W/15-20	1	0.6	Q	unmodified flake			
499N514W/15-20	1	0.8	M	unmodified flake			
499N514W/20-25	1	0.8	C	utilized flake	Ut	5	50
499N514W/20-25	21	17.3	C	unmodified flakes			
499N514W/20-25	1	0.3	Q	unmodified flake			
499N514W/25-30	18	8.0	C	unmodified flakes			
499N514W/25-30	1	0.2	M	unmodified flake			
499N514W/25-30	1	0.3	Q	unmodified flake			
499N515W/0-5	1	0.4	C	small biface frag (point preform?)	BR	2	40
499N515W/0-5	1	0.3	C	retouched tool frag. (battered edge)	BR	2	60
499N515W/0-5	1	0.5	C	utilized flake frag.	Ut	4	30
499N515W/0-5	1	3.7	C	crude biface (probable point preform)			
499N515W/0-5	1	0.4	C	utilized flake frag	Ut	2	60
499N515W/0-5	1	1.3	C	retouched flake frag.	UR	2	75
					Ut	3	35
499N515W/0-5	87	45.8	C	unmodified flakes			
499N515W/0-5	3	1.3	Q	unmodified flakes			
499N515W/0-5	1	0.1	I	unmodified flake			
499N515W/0-5	2	0.7	M	unmodified flakes			
499N515W/5-10	1	36.6	M	discoidal scraper	UR	7	65

Table C3. (continued)

Provenience	N	Wt.	Mat.	Description	Utilized Edges Type	Shape	Angle
					UR	7	90
499N515W/5-10	1	6.5	C	retouched flake frag.	UR	7	65
499N515W/5-10	1	8.2	C	retouched flake	BR	7	60
499N515W/5-10	1	1.5	C	retouched flake	UR	7	60
499N515W/5-10	1	15.2	C	retouched flake	UR	4	50
499N515W/5-10	55	32.7	C	unmodified flakes			
499N515W/5-10	2	0.7	Q	unmodified flakes			
499N515W/5-10	1	0.3	O	unmodified flake			
499N515W/5-10	7	5.1	M	unmodified flakes			
499N515W/10-15	1	4.7	C	sidescraper	UR	4	80
499N515W/10-15	1	0.5	C	retouched flake frag.	UR	3	55
499N515W/10-15	23	15.6	C	unmodified flakes			
499N515W/10-15	1	9.7	Q	unmodified flake			
499N515W/10-15	1	1.6	I	unmodified flake			
499N515W/10-15	2	3.9	M	unmodified flakes			
499N515W/15-20	11	10.9	C	unmodified flakes			
499N515W/15-20	1	0.5	Q	unmodified flake			
499N515W/15-20	2	0.7	M	unmodified flakes			
499N515W/20-25	1	0.9	C	small biface frag.	BR	7	50
					BR	2	50
499N515W/20-25	5	1.3	C	unmodified flakes			
499N515W/25-30	7	3.1	C	unmodified flakes			
499N515W/25-30	1	1.3	M	unmodified flake			
499N516W/0-5	1	19.2	C	core			
499N516W/0-5	1	0.7	C	retouched flake frag.	UR	3	60
499N516W/0-5	1	1.7	Q	retouched flake	BR	7	65
499N516W/0-5	1	1.2	C	utilized flake	Ut	4	60
499N516W/0-5	1	4.9	C	retouched flake	UR	3	50

Table C3. (continued)

Provenience	N	Wt.	Mat.	Description	Utilized Edges		
					Type	Shape	Angle
					Ut	2	60
499N516W/0-5	43	32.0	C	unmodified flakes			
499N516W/0-5	4	6.6	Q	unmodified flakes			
499N516W/0-5	1	0.3	I	unmodified flake			
499N516W/0-5	2	3.4	M	unmodified flakes			
499N516W/10-15	1	3.6	C	retouched flake	UR	7	50
					UR	1	-
					BR	2	55
499N516W/10-15	1	3.3	C	crude biface frag			
499N516W/10-15	1	0.4	C	retouched flake frag.	UR	3	40
499N516W/10-15	29	17.8	C	unmodified flakes			
499N516W/10-15	3	7.1	Q	unmodified flakes			
499N516W/10-15	2	0.3	O	unmodified flakes			
499N516W/10-15	1	0.3	M	unmodified flake			
499N516W/15-20	1	1.7	C	core frag.			
499N516W/15-20	1	1.3	C	utilized flake frag.	Ut	2	30
499N516W/15-20	16	12.7	C	unmodified flakes			
499N516W/15-20	1	0.9	M	unmodified flake			
499N516W/20-25	1	0.3	C	utilized flake frag.	Ut	3	50
499N516W/20-25	8	1.9	C	unmodified flakes			
499N516W/20-25	1	0.2	Q	unmodified flake			
499N517W/0-5	1	4.7	C	denticulate sidescraper	UR	7	80
499N517W/0-5	1	11.0	C	denticulate sidescraper	UR	7	70
499N517W/0-5	1	7.2	C	sidescraper frag.	UR	4	75
					UR	5	90
499N517W/0-5	1	9.0	C	end- and sidescraper frag.	UR	2	75
					UR	2	80
					UR	7	65

Table C3. (continued)

Provenience	N	Wt.	Mat.	Description	Utilized Edges Type	Shape	Angle
499N517W/0-5	1	0.6	C	biface frag.	BR	3	65
499N517W/0-5	1	1.1	C	utilized flake (with spur)	Ut	7	50
					Ut	1	-
					Ut	2	50
499N517W/0-5	1	3.5	C	utilized flake	Ut	2	40
499N517W/0-5	1	0.4	C	utilized flake frag.	Ut	3	20
499N517W/0-5	1	3.7	Q	utilized flake	Ut	3	40
499N517W/0-5	1	8.9	C	core			
499N517W/0-5	1	11.6	C	core frag.			
499N517W/0-5	56	53.7	C	unmodified flakes			
499N517W/0-5	3	2.6	Q	unmodified flakes			
499N517W/0-5	6	15.7	M	unmodified flakes			
499N517W/5-10	1	15.8	C	core scraper	UR	7	75
					UR	7	75
499N517W/5-10	1	4.2	C	utilized blade-like flake	Ut	2	50
					Ut	4	60
499N517W/5-10	1	2.0	C	utilized flake	Ut	4	35
499N517W/5-10	22	24.3	C	unmodified flakes			
499N517W/5-10	1	0.7	Q	unmodified flake			
499N517W/5-10	5	6.0	M	unmodified flakes			
499N517W/10-15	1	6.2	C	core frag.			
499N517W/10-15	1	5.2	C	utilized flake	Ut	2	30
499N517W/10-15	31	12.8	C	unmodified flakes			
499N517W/10-15	2	0.6	Q	unmodified flakes			
499N517W/10-15	3	2.4	M	unmodified flakes			
499N517W/15-20	1	11.3	C	core scraper	UR	7	75
					UR	3	80
499N517W/15-20	1	4.9	C	retouched flake frag.	BR	2	70

Table C3. (continued)

Provenience	N	Wt.	Mat.	Description	Utilized Edges Type	Shape	Angle
499N517W/15-20	1	0.7	C	biface frag.	BR	3	60
499N517W/15-20	1	21.7	C	core frag.			
499N517W/15-20	12	3.9	C	unmodified flakes			
499N517W/15-20	1	1.7	Q	unmodified flake			
499N517W/15-20	2	3.3	M	unmodified flakes			
499N517W/20-25	1	2.4	C	small scraper	UR	3	50
499N517W/20-25	1	2.1	C	utilized flake	Ut	3	15
499N517W/20-25	13	8.5	C	unmodified flakes			
499N518W/0-5	1	2.3	C	retouched flake	BR	2	50
					Ut	2	30
499N518W/0-5	1	0.5	C	biface frag.	BR	2	40
499N518W/0-5	1	3.9	C	retouched flake	UR	2	80
					UR	5	65
499N518W/0-5	1	2.0	C	retouched flake frag.	UR	5	70
499N518W/0-5	1	3.3	I	sidescraper frag.	UR	2	60
499N518W/0-5	1	49.4	C	core			
499N518W/0-5	56	47.4	C	unmodified flakes			
499N518W/0-5	1	0.2	I	unmodified flake			
499N518W/0-5	1	0.5	Q	unmodified flake			
499N518W/0-5	10	15.2	M	unmodified flakes			
499N518W/5-10	1	6.7	M	endscraper	UR	3	90
					UR	3	75
499N518W/5-10	1	1.3	Q	bifacial drill frag.	BR	2	90
499N518W/5-10	1	2.4	C	utilized flake	Ut	3	20
499N518W/5-10	1	4.0	C	utilized flake frag.	Ut	3	60
499N518W/5-10	1	19.2	Q	flake with crude bifacial retouch (blank?)			
499N518W/5-10	29	25.0	C	unmodified flakes			

Table C3. (continued)

Provenience	N	Wt.	Mat.	Description	Utilized Edges		
					Type	Shape	Angle
499N518W/5-10	1	0.2	Q	unmodified flake			
499N518W/5-10	2	3.0	M	unmodified flakes			
499N518W/10-15	1	1.7	C	utilized flake frag.	Ut	3	60
499N518W/10-15	1	15.1	C	core frag.			
499N518W/10-15	10	7.0	C	unmodified flakes			
499N518W/10-15	1	4.0	Q	unmodified flake			
499N518W/10-15	1	0.5	M	unmodified flake			
499N518W/15-20	1	0.4	C	retouched flake frag.	UR	3	65
499N518W/15-20	10	6.1	C	unmodified flakes			
499N518W/15-20	1	0.8	Q	unmodified flake			
499N518W/15-20	1	1.0	M	unmodified flake			
499N518W/20-25	2	0.8	C	unmodified flakes			
499N518W/20-25	1	0.2	I	unmodified flake			
500N460W/0-5	3	1.4	C	unmodified flakes			
500N461W/0-5	5	2.7	C	unmodified flakes			
500N480W/0-5	1	1.3	C	utilized flake	Ut	3	20
500N480W/0-5	1	1.1	C	utilized flake	Ut	3	40
500N500W/0-5	1	2.8	C	core frag.			
500N500W/0-5	1	1.9	M	utilized flake	Ut	3	30
500N500W/0-5	92	46.2	C	unmodified flakes			
500N500W/0-5	2	0.5	O	unmodified flakes			
500N500W/0-5	4	3.5	Q	unmodified flakes			
500N500W/0-5	16	12.5	M	unmodified flakes			
500N500W/5-10	1	39.2	C	core			
500N500W/5-10	1	3.3	C	core frag.			
500N500W/5-10	15	9.7	C	unmodified flakes			
500N500W/10-15	21	21.9	C	unmodified flakes			
500N500W/10-15	1	1.2	Q	unmodified flake			

Table C3. (continued)

Provenience	N	Wt.	Mat.	Description	Utilized Edges Type	Shape	Angle
500N500W/15-20	6	3.8	C	unmodified flakes			
500N500W/15-20	1	0.1	O	unmodified flake			
500N500W/20-25	17	10.7	C	unmodified flakes			
500N500W/25-30	10	2.8	C	unmodified flakes			
500N500W/25-30	1	0.3	Q	unmodified flake			
500N500W/25-30	2	1.4	M	unmodified flakes			
500N501W/0-5	1	1.8	I	scraper frag.	UR	7	65
500N501W/0-5	1	6.5	Q	retouched flake frag.	UR	2	80
500N501W/0-5	1	7.9	C	retouched flake	UR	4	65
					UR	2	85
500N501W/0-5	1	1.8	C	retouched flake frag.	UR	7	75
500N501W/0-5	1	2.0	C	utilized flake	Ut	2	60
500N501W/0-5	1	3.5	C	utilized flake	Ut	3	60
500N501W/0-5	1	21.0	C	core			
500N501W/0-5	1	9.6	C	core frag.			
500N501W/0-5	89	61.4	C	unmodified flakes			
500N501W/0-5	3	2.1	Q	unmodified flakes			
500N501W/0-5	18	23.0	M	unmodified flakes			
500N501W/5-10	14	5.5	C	unmodified flakes			
500N501W/5-10	2	5.0	M	unmodified flakes			
500N501W/10-15	1	1.3	C	retouched flake frag.	BR	2	70
					UR	2	60
500N501W/10-15	16	9.8	C	unmodified flakes			
500N501W/10-15	3	5.8	M	unmodified flakes			
500N501W/10.5 (Item 2)	1	0.7	C	unmodified flake			
500N501W/15-20	1	4.5	C	crude biface (point preform)			
500N501W/15-20	1	3.4	C	core frag.			
500N501W/15-20	11	3.2	C	unmodified flakes			

Table C3. (continued)

Provenience	N	Wt.	Mat.	Description	Utilized Edges Type	Shape	Angle
500N501W/15-20	2	1.3	I	unmodified flakes			
500N501W/20-25	1	0.6	C	retouched flake frag.	UR	3	80
500N501W/20-25	1	0.5	C	utilized flake frag.	Ut	4	55
500N501W/20-25	10	4.6	C	unmodified flakes			
500N501W/20-25	2	1.6	Q	unmodified flakes			
500N501W/25-30	1	1.3	C	retouched flake with graving spur	UR	4	90
					UR	4	80
					UR	1	70
500N501W/25-30	1	2.0	Q	utilized flake frag.	Ut	2	60
500N501W/25-30	10	4.4	C	unmodified flakes			
500N501W/25-30	2	0.3	Q	unmodified flakes			
500N502W/0-5	1	5.0	C	endscraper on small bifacial core	BR	3	90
500N502W/0-5	1	0.5	C	retouched flake frag.	UR	5	60
500N502W/0-5	1	7.0	C	core			
500N502W/0-5	1	2.4	C	utilized flake	Ut	3	60
500N502W/0-5	1	3.7	C	utilized flake	Ut	4	70
500N502W/0-5	33	18.7	C	unmodified flakes			
500N502W/0-5	2	2.2	Q	unmodified flakes			
500N502W/0-5	3	12.3	M	unmodified flakes			
500N502W/5-10	1	0.9	C	retouched flake frag.	UR	2	80
					UR	4	70
500N502W/5-10	1	1.0	C	retouched flake	UR	7	50
500N502W/5-10	1	0.3	C	utilized flake frag.	Ut	3	55
500N502W/5-10	1	1.8	C	utilized flake frag.	Ut	2	80
500N502W/5-10	1	6.5	C	utilized flake	Ut	3	60
					Ut	4	40
500N502W/5-10	1	12.0	C	core			

Table C3. (continued)

Provenience	N	Wt.	Mat.	Description	Utilized Edges		
					Type	Shape	Angle
500N502W/5-10	35	24.2	C	unmodified flakes			
500N502W/5-10	3	5.5	Q	unmodified flakes			
500N502W/5-10	1	0.2	I	unmodified flake			
500N502W/5-10	8	18.3	M	unmodified flakes			
500N502W/10-15	1	1.2	C	utilized flake	Ut	2	50
500N502W/10-15	1	0.8	C	utilized flake frag.	Ut	3	20
500N502W/10-15	19	4.8	C	unmodified flakes			
500N502W/10-15	3	1.0	I	unmodified flakes			
500N502W/10-15	2	2.8	M	unmodified flakes			
500N502W/Feat. 1	1	0.1	C	unmodified flake			
500N502W/15-20	22	13.3	C	unmodified flakes			
500N502W/15-20	2	2.0	M	unmodified flakes			
500N502W/20-25	15	9.5	C	unmodified flakes			
500N502W/20-25	3	1.6	Q	unmodified flakes			
500N502W/20-25	2	9.0	M	unmodified flakes			
500N502W/25-30	8	7.5	C	unmodified flakes			
500N502W/30-35	1	0.6	C	unmodified flake			
500N502W/30-35	1	0.3	Q	unmodified flake			
500N503W/0-5	1	50.7	C	core scraper	BR	7	80
500N503W/0-5	1	0.5	C	biface frag.	BR	2	70
500N503W/0-5	1	0.3	O	scraper frag.	UR	3	70
500N503W/0-5	1	8.2	C	retouched flake	UR	7	65
500N503W/0-5	1	13.3	M	utilized flake frag.	Ut	3	45
500N503W/0-5	1	2.1	Q	utilized flake	Ut	3	30
500N503W/0-5	1	1.5	C	utilized flake frag.	Ut	2	40
500N503W/0-5	1	0.4	C	utilized flake frag.	Ut	2	80
500N503W/0-5	1	1.5	C	utilized flake frag.	Ut	5	70
					Ut	5	50

Table C3. (continued)

Provenience	N	Wt.	Mat.	Description	Utilized Edges Type	Shape	Angle
500N503W/0-5	79	72.1	C	unmodified flakes			
500N503W/0-5	7	8.7	Q	unmodified flakes			
500N503W/0-5	12	20.7	M	unmodified flakes			
500N503W/5-10	1	2.3	C	crude biface frag (point preform?)			
500N503W/5-10	1	0.2	C	retouched flake frag.	UR	2	70
500N503W/5-10	23	13.6	C	unmodified flakes			
500N503W/5-10	3	3.4	Q	unmodified flakes			
500N503W/5-10	5	1.9	M	unmodified flakes			
500N503W/10-15	16	5.3	C	unmodified flakes			
500N503W/15-20	1	2.5	M	utilized flake	Ut	4	60
500N503W/15-20	14	18.0	C	unmodified flakes			
500N503W/15-20	1	0.7	I	unmodified flake			
500N503W/15-20	1	0.8	M	unmodified flake			
500N503W/20-25	1	9.5	C	utilized flake frag.	Ut	3	75
500N503W/20-25	8	4.3	C	unmodified flakes			
500N503W/25-30	2	0.9	C	unmodified flakes			
500N504W/0-5	1	6.3	C	retouched flake frag.	UR	7	70
500N504W/0-5	1	2.2	C	retouched flake frag.	UR	7	80
500N504W/0-5	1	0.9	C	retouched flake frag.	UR	2	70
500N504W/0-5	1	1.2	C	retouched flake frag.	UR	3	55
500N504W/0-5	1	0.4	C	retouched flake frag.	UR	4	70
500N504W/0-5	1	0.9	M	retouched flake frag.	UR	5	70
					UR	1	-
					Ut	2	40
500N504W/0-5	1	2.0	C	utilized flake frag.	Ut	3	30
500N504W/0-5	1	1.4	C	scraper frag.	BR	3	90
500N504W/0-5	75	46.9	C	unmodified flakes			

Table C3. (continued)

Provenience	N	Wt.	Mat.	Description	Utilized Edges Type	Shape	Angle
500N504W/0-5	4	1.4	Q	unmodified flakes			
500N504W/0-5	2	1.4	I	unmodified flakes			
500N504W/0-5	10	25.2	M	unmodified flakes			
500N504W/5-10	1	3.3	C	thin ovate biface frag.	BR	3	40
500N504W/5-10	1	1.9	C	biface frag (point preform?)	BR	2	40
500N504W/5-10	1	0.9	C	retouched flake frag.	UR	2	40
500N504W/5-10	1	1.2	C	utilized flake frag.	Ut	9	50
500N504W/5-10	40	19.2	C	unmodified flakes			
500N504W/5-10	8	4.7	Q	unmodified flakes			
500N504W/5-10	1	0.1	O	unmodified flake			
500N504W/5-10	2	2.0	I	unmodified flakes			
500N504W/5-10	5	1.8	M	unmodified flakes			
500N504W/10-15	28	16.2	C	unmodified flakes			
500N504W/10-15	2	2.1	Q	unmodified flakes			
500N504W/10-15	2	8.6	M	unmodified flakes			
500N504W/15-20	1	15.7	M	sidescraper	UR	2	65
500N504W/15-20	1	16.0	C	core			
500N504W/15-20	15	8.1	C	unmodified flakes			
500N504W/15-20	1	0.4	I	unmodified flake			
500N504W/20-25	1	6.4	C	small scraper	UR	3	70
500N504W/20-25	15	7.5	C	unmodified flakes			
500N504W/20-25	2	0.7	Q	unmodified flakes			
500N504W/20-25	1	0.4	O	unmodified flake			
500N504W/25-30	1	1.5	C	retouched flake (exhausted	UR	4	80
				scraper 'slug')	UR	4	90
500N504W/25-30	13	4.8	C	unmodified flakes			
500N504W/25-30	1	0.2	Q	unmodified flake			
500N504W/25-30	1	0.1	I	unmodified flake			

Table C3. (continued)

Provenience	N	Wt.	Mat.	Description	Utilized Edges Type	Shape	Angle
500N504W/25-30	4	1.8	M	unmodified flakes			
500N505W/0-5	1	11.7	C	crude bifacial core			
500N505W/0-5	8	10.3	C	unmodified flakes			
500N505W/0-5	2	1.3	I	unmodified flakes			
500N505W/0-5	1	1.1	M	unmodified flake			
500N505W/5-10	1	4.6	C	retouched flake	UR	6	60
500N505W/5-10	1	4.8	C	utilized flake	Ut	3	40
500N505W/5-10	1	3.1	C	core frag.			
500N505W/5-10	1	0.8	C	retouched flake frag.	UR	4	60
500N505W/5-10	54	36.9	C	unmodified flakes			
500N505W/5-10	1	0.3	Q	unmodified flake			
500N505W/5-10	5	12.9	M	unmodified flakes			
500N505W/10-15	1	0.5	C	retouched flake (tiny endscraper)	UR	3	70
500N505W/10-15	1	1.9	C	retouched flake frag.	UR	3	70
500N505W/10-15	40	30.3	C	unmodified flakes			
500N505W/10-15	1	2.7	Q	unmodified flake			
500N505W/10-15	3	12.3	M	unmodified flakes			
500N505W/15-20	1	1.9	C	biface frag.	BR	2	60
					BR	2	40
500N505W/15-20	1	0.7	C	utilized flake frag.	Ut	2	50
500N505W/15-20	1	9.7	C	core frag.			
500N505W/15-20	20	23.4	C	unmodified flakes			
500N505W/15-20	1	0.2	Q	unmodified flake			
500N505W/15-20	1	0.4	I	unmodified flake			
500N505W/15-20	3	4.9	M	unmodified flakes			
500N505W/20-25	24	15.8	C	unmodified flakes			
500N505W/20-25	1	0.5	Q	unmodified flake			

Table C3. (continued)

Provenience	N	Wt.	Mat.	Description	Utilized Edges Type	Shape	Angle
500N505W/20-25	1	0.3	O	unmodified flake			
500N505W/25-30	1	2.4	C	retouched flake frag.	UR	5	60
500N505W/25-30	15	7.7	C	unmodified flakes			
500N505W/25-30	2	0.5	Q	unmodified flakes			
500N505W/25-30	2	0.5	I	unmodified flakes			
500N505W/25-30	1	0.7	M	unmodified flake			
500N505W/30-35	1	2.6	C	biface frag.	BR	3	55
500N505W/30-35	1	0.6	C	retouched flake frag.	UR	2	60
500N505W/30-35	1	4.1	C	core frag.			
500N505W/30-35	8	2.9	C	unmodified flakes			
500N505W/30-35	1	0.8	M	unmodified flake			
500N506W/0-5	3	3.3	C	unmodified flakes			
500N506W/0-5	2	4.3	M	unmodified flakes			
500N506W/5-10	1	1.1	C	biface frag.	BR	2	70
					BR	3	50
500N506W/5-10	1	5.5	M	retouched flake	UR	7	70
500N506W/5-10	1	1.3	C	utilized flake frag.	Ut	8	40
500N506W/5-10	46	22.5	C	unmodified flakes			
500N506W/5-10	3	1.6	Q	unmodified flakes			
500N506W/5-10	7	5.1	M	unmodified flakes			
500N506W/10-15	1	32.9	M	sidescraper	UR	4	70
500N506W/10-15	1	1.5	C	retouched flake frag.	UR	7	60
500N506W/10-15	1	25.0	C	core			
500N506W/10-15	45	24.7	C	unmodified flakes			
500N506W/10-15	2	4.0	Q	unmodified flakes			
500N506W/10-15	6	15.0	M	unmodified flakes			
500N506W/15-20	1	0.2	C	biface frag. (probable point)	BR	2	30
500N506W/15-20	1	1.9	C	utilized flake	Ut	2	40

Table C3. (continued)

Provenience	N	Wt.	Mat.	Description	Utilized Edges Type	Shape	Angle
500N506W/15-20	26	18.5	C	unmodified flakes			
500N506W/15-20	2	1.4	Q	unmodified flakes			
500N506W/15-20	2	0.6	I	unmodified flakes			
500N506W/15-20	1	4.0	M	unmodified flake			
500N506W/20-25	1	1.4	C	retouched flake frag.	UR	5	70
500N506W/20-25	15	8.5	C	unmodified flakes			
500N506W/20-25	1	0.4	Q	unmodified flake			
500N506W/20-25	1	0.5	M	unmodified flake			
500N506W/25-30	1	3.7	C	endscraper	UR	3	80
500N506W/25-30	10	6.9	C	unmodified flakes			
500N506W/25-30	1	0.2	I	unmodified flake			
500N506W/30-35	8	2.4	C	unmodified flakes			
500N512W/0-5	1	2.8	C	retouched flake	UR	2	80
500N512W/0-5	1	0.1	C	unmodified flake			
500N512W/5-10	1	1.5	C	scraper frag.	UR	8	80
500N512W/5-10	1	2.5	C	retouched flake frag.	BR	3	60
500N512W/5-10	1	1.1	C	utilized flake	Ut	2	90
					Ut	9	20
500N512W/5-10	1	4.5	C	crude bifacial core			
500N512W/5-10	23	15.0	C	unmodified flakes			
500N512W/5-10	3	6.8	M	unmodified flakes			
500N512W/10-15	1	0.4	C	biface tip	BR	2	40
					BR	2	50
500N512W/10-15	1	1.3	O	retouched flake	UR	2	60
500N512W/10-15	1	5.9	C	utilized flake	Ut	2	70
500N512W/10-15	1	0.6	C	utilized flake frag.	Ut	2	50
500N512W/10-15	1	1.7	C	crude bifacial core			
500N512W/10-15	1	107.7	C	core			

Table C3. (continued)

Provenience	N	Wt.	Mat.	Description	Utilized Edges Type	Shape	Angle
500N512W/10-15	1	43.0	C	core			
500N512W/10-15	86	72.8	C	unmodified flakes			
500N512W/10-15	3	1.0	Q	unmodified flakes			
500N512W/10-15	1	0.9	I	unmodified flake			
500N512W/10-15	13	15.8	M	unmodified flakes			
500N512W/15-20	1	0.7	C	retouched flake	UR	2	70
					Ut	4	40
500N512W/15-20	1	1.2	C	utilized flake	Ut	3	40
500N512W/15-20	1	8.9	C	core			
500N512W/15-20	43	38.1	C	unmodified flakes			
500N512W/15-20	1	0.2	I	unmodified flake			
500N512W/15-20	2	1.8	M	unmodified flakes			
500N512W/20-25	1	6.5	C	small core			
500N512W/20-25	24	40.6	C	unmodified flakes			
500N512W/20-25	1	0.3	Q	unmodified flake			
500N512W/20-25	1	0.4	I	unmodified flake			
500N512W/20-25	7	21.4	M	unmodified flakes			
500N512W/25-30	1	0.8	C	biface frag.	BR	2	60
500N512W/25-30	12	11.2	C	unmodified flakes			
500N512W/25-30	1	0.4	Q	unmodified flake			
500N512W/25-30	1	0.2	I	unmodified flake			
500N512W/25-30	1	0.3	M	unmodified flake			
500N512W/30-35	1	4.3	C	retouched flake	BR	4	55
500N512W/30-35	3	0.5	C	unmodified flakes			
500N512W/30-35	3	7.1	M	unmodified flakes			
500N513W/0-5	1	0.4	C	retouched flake frag.	UR	2	70
500N513W/0-5	8	3.7	C	unmodified flakes			
500N513W/5-10	1	1.2	C	retouched flake frag. (small	UR	3	65

Table C3. (continued)

Provenience	N	Wt.	Mat.	Description	Utilized Edges		
					Type	Shape	Angle
				sidescraper)	UR	2	70
500N513W/5-10	1	3.9	C	retouched flake frag.	UR	4	70
					UR	7	65
500N513W/5-10	1	4.1	C	biface frag. (preform broken in manufacture)			
500N513W/5-10	33	31.0	C	unmodified flakes			
500N513W/5-10	1	0.4	Q	unmodified flake			
500N513W/5-10	3	4.5	M	unmodified flakes			
500N513W/10-15	1	0.8	C	retouched flake frag.	UR	4	90
500N513W/10-15	1	0.4	C	biface frag.	BR	3	30
500N513W/10-15	1	1.8	C	biface frag. (point preform?)			
500N513W/10-15	50	32.9	C	unmodified flakes			
500N513W/10-15	1	1.2	Q	unmodified flake			
500N513W/10-15	1	2.3	I	unmodified flake			
500N513W/10-15	5	2.4	M	unmodified flakes			
500N513W/15-20	1	3.9	I	utilized flake	Ut	4	60
500N513W/15-20	44	31.9	C	unmodified flakes			
500N513W/15-20	2	1.5	Q	unmodified flakes			
500N513W/15-20	4	1.6	I	unmodified flakes			
500N513W/15-20	7	9.1	M	unmodified flakes			
500N513W/20-25	1	13.0	C	core			
500N513W/20-25	25	19.5	C	unmodified flakes			
500N513W/20-25	1	0.2	Q	unmodified flake			
500N513W/20-25	2	1.5	M	unmodified flakes			
500N513W/25-30	12	5.7	C	unmodified flakes			
500N513W/25-30	1	0.1	O	unmodified flake			
500N513W/30-35	5	1.7	C	unmodified flakes			
500N513W/30-35	1	0.2	Q	unmodified flake			

Table C3. (continued)

Provenience	N	Wt.	Mat.	Description	Utilized Edges		
					Type	Shape	Angle
500N513W/30-35	2	1.6	M	unmodified flakes			
500N514W/0-5	1	4.8	C	biface (ovate point preform)	BR	3	40
500N514W/0-5	1	4.4	C	small scraper (irregular	UR	7	90
				multi-spurred)	UR	4	90
500N514W/0-5	1	3.0	I	utilized flake	Ut	2	50
500N514W/0-5	1	9.4	C	utilized flake frag.	Ut	2	40
500N514W/0-5	1	0.6	C	utilized flake	Ut	2	30
500N514W/0-5	52	59.7	C	unmodified flakes			
500N514W/0-5	3	1.3	Q	unmodified flakes			
500N514W/0-5	10	49.4	M	unmodified flakes			
500N514W/5-10	1	93.7	C	hammerstone			
500N514W/5-10	1	3.0	Q	biface frag.	BR	3	40
					BR	3	50
500N514W/5-10	1	3.6	C	retouched flake frag.	UR	2	65
500N514W/5-10	1	0.4	C	utilized flake frag.	Ut	2	45
					Ut	2	60
500N514W/5-10	1	1.8	C	utilized flake	Ut	7	60
500N514W/5-10	1	0.8	C	utilized flake frag.	Ut	8	20
500N514W/5-10	1	27.3	C	core			
500N514W/5-10	66	33.4	C	unmodified flakes			
500N514W/5-10	4	3.2	Q	unmodified flakes			
500N514W/5-10	1	0.3	I	unmodified flake			
500N514W/5-10	7	5.5	M	unmodified flakes			
500N514W/10-15	1	0.8	C	retouched flake (multiple graver)	UR	7	40
500N514W/10-15	1	8.8	C	retouched flake	UR	2	70
500N514W/10-15	1	0.3	C	utilized flake frag.	Ut	3	70
					Ut	2	60

Table C3. (continued)

Provenience	N	Wt.	Mat.	Description	Utilized Edges Type	Shape	Angle
500N514W/10-15	1	11.1	C	core frag.			
500N514W/10-15	53	39.2	C	unmodified flakes			
500N514W/10-15	2	1.8	I	unmodified flakes			
500N514W/10-15	1	0.9	M	unmodified flake			
500N514W/15-20	1	1.7	C	retouched flake frag.	UR	6	65
500N514W/15-20	1	2.0	C	utilized flake	Ut	2	20
500N514W/15-20	1	2.5	C	utilized flake	Ut	2	30
500N514W/15-20	31	37.2	C	unmodified flakes			
500N514W/15-20	1	0.3	Q	unmodified flake			
500N514W/15-20	2	0.9	I	unmodified flakes			
500N514W/15-20	4	3.6	M	unmodified flakes			
500N514W/20-25	1	2.2	C	utilized flake	Ut	2	40
					Ut	2	50
500N514W/20-25	1	2.6	C	utilized flake frag.	Ut	2	50
500N514W/20-25	14	7.9	C	unmodified flakes			
500N514W/20-25	1	0.6	O	unmodified flake			
500N514W/20-25	2	8.2	M	unmodified flakes			
500N514W/25-30	1	2.7	C	crude biface frag. (fire-shattered preform?)			
500N514W/25-30	10	6.2	C	unmodified flakes			
500N515W/0-5	1	22.5	C	retouched flake	UR	8	55
500N515W/0-5	1	1.9	C	retouched flake frag.	UR	7	60
500N515W/0-5	1	0.6	C	utilized flake frag.	Ut	3	60
500N515W/0-5	77	54.9	C	unmodified flakes			
500N515W/0-5	3	3.8	Q	unmodified flakes			
500N515W/0-5	2	0.9	M	unmodified flakes			
500N515W/5-10	1	1.5	I	retouched flake	UR	2	55
500N515W/5-10	1	0.3	C	biface frag.	BR	3	40

Table C3. (continued)

Provenience	N	Wt.	Mat.	Description	Utilized Edges Type	Shape	Angle
500N515W/5-10	1	7.8	C	crude biface (preform)			
500N515W/5-10	32	18.1	C	unmodified flakes			
500N515W/5-10	1	0.1	Q	unmodified flake			
500N515W/5-10	1	0.1	O	unmodified flake			
500N515W/5-10	1	2.4	M	unmodified flake			
500N515W/10-15	1	13.6	I	sidescraper	UR	7	55
					BR	7	65
500N515W/10-15	1	3.7	C	biface frag.	BR	3	70
500N515W/10-15	1	4.1	C	retouched flake frag.	UR	2	65
					UR	3	40
500N515W/10-15	1	4.2	C	retouched flake	UR	3	45
500N515W/10-15	1	2.1	C	retouched flake frag.	BR	2	50
500N515W/10-15	1	49.0	Q	core frag.			
500N515W/10-15	36	33.6	C	unmodified flakes			
500N515W/10-15	4	12.9	Q	unmodified flakes			
500N515W/10-15	1	0.1	O	unmodified flake			
500N515W/10-15	5	2.2	M	unmodified flakes			
500N515W/15-20	1	1.9	C	retouched flake	UR	2	60
					UR	2	60
500N515W/15-20	23	24.4	C	unmodified flakes			
500N515W/15-20	2	2.4	Q	unmodified flakes			
500N515W/15-20	1	0.1	O	unmodified flake			
500N515W/15-20	5	4.3	M	unmodified flakes			
500N515W/20-25	26	15.7	C	unmodified flakes			
500N515W/20-25	3	0.6	Q	unmodified flakes			
500N515W/25-30	7	4.4	C	unmodified flakes			
500N515W/25-30	2	2.9	M	unmodified flakes			
500N516W/0-5	1	1.3	C	retouched flake frag.	BR	3	40

Table C3. (continued)

Provenience	N	Wt.	Mat.	Description	Utilized Edges		
					Type	Shape	Angle
500N516W/0-5	1	0.5	C	retouched flake frag.	BR	3	45
500N516W/0-5	1	0.9	C	utilized flake frag.	Ut	2	20
500N516W/0-5	1	0.6	C	utilized flake frag.	Ut	2	20
500N516W/0-5	1	22.0	C	core			
500N516W/0-5	54	61.5	C	unmodified flakes			
500N516W/0-5	2	0.7	Q	unmodified flakes			
500N516W/0-5	5	11.6	M	unmodified flakes			
500N516W/5-10	28	27.0	C	unmodified flakes			
500N516W/5-10	1	1.9	Q	unmodified flake			
500N516W/5-10	2	1.1	M	unmodified flakes			
500N516W/10-15	1	2.9	C	utilized flake	Ut	3	40
500N516W/10-15	1	8.5	C	utilized flake	Ut	4	65
					Ut	3	70
500N516W/10-15	1	2.4	C	utilized blade	Ut	2	35
					Ut	3	30
500N516W/10-15	1	79.2	M	core			
500N516W/10-15	28	22.3	C	unmodified flakes			
500N516W/10-15	4	3.1	Q	unmodified flakes			
500N516W/10-15	3	4.0	M	unmodified flakes			
500N516W/15-20	1	2.3	C	retouched flake	UR	4	50
500N516W/15-20	1	0.5	C	retouched flake frag.	UR	7	65
500N516W/15-20	19	35.0	C	unmodified flakes			
500N516W/15-20	1	0.4	Q	unmodified flake			
500N516W/15-20	1	0.1	O	unmodified flake			
500N516W/15-20	1	7.0	M	unmodified flake			
500N516W/20-25	1	0.6	O	utilized flake	Ut	7	60
500N516W/20-25	12	12.6	C	unmodified flakes			
500N516W/25-30	7	4.7	C	unmodified flakes			

Table C3. (continued)

Provenience	N	Wt.	Mat.	Description	Utilized Edges Type	Shape	Angle
500N517W/0-5	1	5.8	C	utilized flake	Ut	2	80
500N517W/0-5	1	2.3	C	utilized flake	Ut	3	30
500N517W/0-5	1	7.8	C	core			
500N517W/0-5	42	35.7	C	unmodified flakes			
500N517W/0-5	1	0.4	Q	unmodified flake			
500N517W/0-5	1	0.1	O	unmodified flake			
500N517W/0-5	2	1.0	M	unmodified flakes			
500N517W/5-10	1	10.4	C	retouched flake	UR	3	70
500N517W/5-10	43	22.0	C	unmodified flakes			
500N517W/5-10	5	2.0	Q	unmodified flakes			
500N517W/5-10	1	0.2	O	unmodified flake			
500N517W/5-10	1	0.3	I	unmodified flake			
500N517W/5-10	5	3.3	M	unmodified flakes			
500N517W/10-15	1	3.6	C	utilized flake	Ut	3	60
500N517W/10-15	1	4.4	C	utilized flake frag.	Ut	3	65
500N517W/10-15	1	1.0	C	utilized flake frag.	Ut	3	60
500N517W/10-15	1	5.9	C	bifacial core frag.			
500N517W/10-15	21	21.8	C	unmodified flakes			
500N517W/10-15	5	3.2	Q	unmodified flakes			
500N517W/10-15	2	1.0	M	unmodified flakes			
500N517W/15-20	1	12.6	C	endscraper	UR	3	60
500N517W/15-20	1	9.8	C	utilized flake	Ut	4	45
500N517W/15-20	25	9.3	C	unmodified flakes			
500N517W/15-20	1	0.1	Q	unmodified flake			
500N517W/15-20	2	0.9	M	unmodified flakes			
500N517W/20-25	11	4.5	C	unmodified flakes			
500N517W/20-25	2	0.3	Q	unmodified flakes			
500N517W/20-25	3	1.5	M	unmodified flakes			

Table C3. (continued)

Provenience	N	Wt.	Mat.	Description	Utilized Edges Type	Shape	Angle
500N517W/25-30	1	4.2	C	ovate biface frag.	BR	3	60
500N517W/25-30	11	7.3	C	unmodified flakes			
500N517W/25-30	1	4.3	Q	unmodified flake			
500N517W/25-30	1	0.5	M	unmodified flake			
500N518W/0-5	1	2.2	C	utilized flake	Ut	4	55
500N518W/0-5	1	0.5	C	utilized flake	Ut	3	65
500N518W/0-5	1	10.3	C	core			
500N518W/0-5	36	31.3	C	unmodified flakes			
500N518W/0-5	1	2.4	Q	unmodified flake			
500N518W/0-5	1	0.2	O	unmodified flake			
500N518W/0-5	5	5.3	M	unmodified flakes			
500N518W/5-10	1	2.0	C	utilized flake	Ut	5	65
					Ut	4	70
500N518W/5-10	1	2.2	C	utilized flake	Ut	2	45
500N518W/5-10	22	31.2	C	unmodified flakes			
500N518W/5-10	2	4.4	Q	unmodified flakes			
500N518W/5-10	1	0.4	M	unmodified flake			
500N518W/10-15	1	93.2	M	core			
500N518W/10-15	24	13.0	C	unmodified flakes			
500N518W/10-15	1	0.3	Q	unmodified flake			
500N518W/10-15	1	0.3	I	unmodified flake			
500N518W/10-15	4	16.3	M	unmodified flakes			
500N518W/15-20	11	6.0	C	unmodified flakes			
500N518W/15-20	1	1.4	M	unmodified flake			
503N515W/0-5	1	28.2	Q	utilized flake	Ut	3	70
503N515W/0-5	8	7.4	C	unmodified flakes			
503N515W/0-5	4	1.5	Q	unmodified flakes			
503N515W/5-10	1	1.0	C	biface frag. (burned point?)	BR	2	60

Table C3. (continued)

Provenience	N	Wt.	Mat.	Description	Utilized Edges Type	Shape	Angle
503N515W/5-10	1	2.3	C	scraper frag.	UR	3	70
503N515W/5-10	1	5.8	C	retouched flake	UR	7	50
503N515W/5-10	1	9.8	C	utilized flake	Ut	2	65
					Ut	2	50
503N515W/5-10	1	6.2	C	utilized flake	Ut	2	70
503N515W/5-10	54	43.4	C	unmodified flakes			
503N515W/5-10	5	13.4	Q	unmodified flakes			
503N515W/5-10	2	1.1	I	unmodified flakes			
503N515W/5-10	2	2.9	M	unmodified flakes			
503N515W/10-15	1	1.3	C	utilized flake	Ut	3	70
503N515W/10-15	1	70.9	C	core			
503N515W/10-15	51	24.6	C	unmodified flakes			
503N515W/10-15	3	3.7	Q	unmodified flakes			
503N515W/10-15	1	0.4	O	unmodified flake			
503N515W/10-15	1	0.5	I	unmodified flake			
503N515W/10-15	8	3.0	M	unmodified flakes			
503N515W/15-20	42	19.9	C	unmodified flakes			
503N515W/15-20	1	0.3	Q	unmodified flake			
503N515W/15-20	1	0.2	V	unmodified flake			
503N515W/15-20	3	1.3	I	unmodified flakes			
503N515W/15-20	1	0.3	M	unmodified flake			
503N515W/20-25	1	1.6	C	retouched flake frag.	UR	3	55
503N515W/20-25	1	2.9	C	retouched flake frag.	UR	3	70
503N515W/20-25	1	0.4	C	retouched flake frag. (graver)	UR	1	20
503N515W/20-25	29	23.1	C	unmodified flakes			
503N515W/20-25	5	4.2	M	unmodified flakes			
503N515W/25-30	1	1.0	C	retouched flake frag.	UR	6	40
503N515W/25-30	27	19.6	C	unmodified flakes			

Table C3. (continued)

Provenience	N	Wt.	Mat.	Description	Utilized Edges Type	Shape	Angle
503N515W/25-30	1	1.4	M	unmodified flake			
503N569W/0-5	3	0.7	C	unmodified flakes			
503N569W/5-10	1	0.8	C	unmodified flake			
503N569W/5-10	1	1.4	M	unmodified flake			
503N569W/10-15	2	0.6	C	unmodified flakes			
503N569W/10-15	1	0.6	Q	unmodified flake			
504N515W/0-5	3	2.0	C	unmodified flakes			
504N515W/0-5	1	0.2	M	unmodified flake			
504N515W/5-10	1	0.5	C	utilized flake frag.	Ut	6	30
504N515W/5-10	1	1.5	C	utilized flake	Ut	3	70
504N515W/5-10	1	0.6	C	utilized flake	Ut	3	20
504N515W/5-10	64	32.2	C	unmodified flakes			
504N515W/5-10	7	3.7	Q	unmodified flakes			
504N515W/5-10	4	1.4	I	unmodified flakes			
504N515W/5-10	11	19.6	M	unmodified flakes			
504N515W/10-15	1	0.4	C	retouched flake frag.	BR	2	45
504N515W/10-15	1	1.7	C	retouched flake	UR	7	60
504N515W/10-15	1	0.8	C	utilized flake frag.	Ut	3	30
504N515W/10-15	1	8.6	C	core			
504N515W/10-15	43	19.9	C	unmodified flakes			
504N515W/10-15	2	1.6	Q	unmodified flakes			
504N515W/10-15	6	3.6	M	unmodified flakes			
504N515W/15-20	1	3.2	C	sidescraper frag.	UR	2	90
504N515W/15-20	31	14.5	C	unmodified flakes			
504N515W/15-20	4	1.6	Q	unmodified flakes			
504N515W/15-20	2	13.4	M	unmodified flakes			
504N515W/20-25	1	1.2	C	retouched flake frag.	UT	3	60
504N515W/20-25	1	2.1	C	utilized flake	Ut	2	45

Table C3. (continued)

Provenience	N	Wt.	Mat.	Description	Utilized Edges Type	Shape	Angle
504N515W/20-25	17	24.2	C	unmodified flakes			
504N515W/25-30	1	4.6	C	bifacial core frag.			
504N515W/25-30	12	4.6	C	unmodified flakes			
504N515W/25-30	1	0.6	Q	unmodified flake			
504N515W/25-30	1	0.8	I	unmodified flake			
504N515W/25-30	4	8.5	M	unmodified flakes			
504N569W/0-5	1	0.9	C	unmodified flake			
504N569W/0-5	1	0.3	M	unmodified flake			
504N569W/5-10	1	0.2	O	unmodified flake			
505N515W/0-5	1	0.4	C	retouched flake frag.	UR	2	40
					UR	2	60
505N515W/0-5	1	4.6	M	biface frag.	BR	3	45
505N515W/0-5	1	5.3	Q	retouched flake	BR	7	80
505N515W/0-5	1	0.7	C	retouched flake frag.	UR	2	55
505N515W/0-5	1	0.6	C	retouched flake frag.	UR	2	50
505N515W/0-5	1	0.6	C	retouched flake frag.	UR	2	40
					UR	2	30
505N515W/0-5	1	0.5	C	retouched flake frag.	UR	2	60
505N515W/0-5	67	71.4	C	unmodified flakes			
505N515W/0-5	10	4.0	Q	unmodified flakes			
505N515W/0-5	3	1.5	I	unmodified flakes			
505N515W/0-5	8	6.3	M	unmodified flakes			
505N515W/10-15	1	0.3	C	biface frag.	BR	3	60
505N515W/10-15	33	17.6	C	unmodified flakes			
505N515W/10-15	3	0.8	Q	unmodified flakes			
505N515W/10-15	1	0.2	I	unmodified flake			
505N515W/10-15	6	2.5	M	unmodified flakes			
505N515W/15-20	1	1.3	C	retouched flake frag.	UR	3	90

Table C3. (continued)

Provenience	N	Wt.	Mat.	Description	Utilized Edges Type	Shape	Angle
505N515W/15-20	1	0.7	C	utilized flake frag.	Ut	2	40
505N515W/15-20	1	0.7	C	utilized flake frag.	Ut	3	50
505N515W/15-20	1	1.1	C	utilized flake	Ut	3	30
505N515W/15-20	1	61.8	C	core			
505N515W/15-20	30	25.1	C	unmodified flakes			
505N515W/15-20	2	5.7	Q	unmodified flakes			
505N515W/15-20	2	0.6	O	unmodified flakes			
505N515W/15-20	1	1.1	I	unmodified flake			
505N515W/15-20	6	4.2	M	unmodified flakes			
505N515W/20-25	31	18.9	C	unmodified flakes			
505N515W/20-25	1	0.2	Q	unmodified flake			
505N515W/20-25	4	2.1	I	unmodified flakes			
505N515W/20-25	3	2.4	M	unmodified flakes			
505N515W/25-30	1	4.7	C	core frag.			
505N515W/25-30	20	12.4	C	unmodified flakes			
505N515W/25-30	1	0.2	Q	unmodified flake			
505N515W/25-30	5	8.5	M	unmodified flakes			
506N515W/0-5	1	10.5	C	core			
506N515W/0-5	49	20.7	C	unmodified flakes			
506N515W/0-5	3	2.1	Q	unmodified flakes			
506N515W/0-5	1	0.9	V	unmodified flake			
506N515W/0-5	1	0.1	O	unmodified flake			
506N515W/0-5	1	0.4	M	unmodified flake			
506N515W/5-10	1	4.3	C	sidescraper	UR	3	60
					UR	4	50
506N515W/5-10	1	1.0	C	retouched flake	UR	3	55
506N515W/5-10	1	12.1	C	core			
506N515W/5-10	40	28.9	C	unmodified flakes			

Table C3. (continued)

Provenience	N	Wt.	Mat.	Description	Utilized Edges Type	Shape	Angle
506N515W/5-10	6	3.9	Q	unmodified flakes			
506N515W/5-10	1	1.7	I	unmodified flake			
506N515W/5-10	2	1.3	M	unmodified flakes			
506N515W/10-15	1	2.0	C	scraper frag.	UR	3	70
506N515W/10-15	1	3.1	C	retouched flake	UR	7	60
506N515W/10-15	28	26.8	C	unmodified flakes			
506N515W/10-15	2	0.7	Q	unmodified flakes			
506N515W/10-15	4	7.0	M	unmodified flakes			
506N515W/15-20	18	8.1	C	unmodified flakes			
506N515W/15-20	3	1.8	M	unmodified flakes			
506N515W/20-25	1	16.9	M	utilized flake	Ut	3	60
506N515W/20-25	19	8.9	C	unmodified flakes			
506N515W/20-25	1	0.3	I	unmodified flake			
506N515W/20-25	1	0.9	M	unmodified flake			
506N515W/25-30	1	2.3	C	utilized flake frag.	Ut	3	90
506N515W/25-30	7	2.8	C	unmodified flakes			
506N515W/25-30	1	0.5	Q	unmodified flake			
506N515W/25-30	1	0.6	I	unmodified flake			
506N515W/30-35	5	2.9	C	unmodified flakes			
511N514W/0-5	1	1.4	C	biface frag.	BR	3	45
					BR	3	60
511N514W/0-5	39	28.9	C	unmodified flakes			
511N514W/0-5	2	0.8	Q	unmodified flakes			
511N514W/0-5	1	0.1	I	unmodified flake			
511N514W/0-5	6	25.3	M	unmodified flakes			
511N514W/10-15	1	0.9	Q	retouched flake frag.	UR	2	90
511N514W/10-15	64	33.7	C	unmodified flakes			
511N514W/10-15	3	3.9	M	unmodified flakes			

Table C3. (continued)

Provenience	N	Wt.	Mat.	Description	Utilized Edges Type	Shape	Angle
511N514W/15-20	1	4.6	C	utilized flake	Ut	2	50
511N514W/15-20	2	49.0	M	core			
511N514W/15-20	18	11.2	C	unmodified flakes			
511N514W/15-20	4	3.3	M	unmodified flakes			
511N514W/20-25	1	2.3	C	utilized flake	Ut	2	40
511N514W/20-25	1	14.1	C	bifacial core			
511N514W/20-25	12	11.6	C	unmodified flakes			
511N514W/20-25	2	1.0	M	unmodified flakes			
511N514W/25-30	9	10.7	C	unmodified flakes			
511N514W/25-30	1	3.9	I	unmodified flake			
511N514W/30-35	5	6.8	C	unmodified flakes			
511N514W/30-35	3	0.5	I	unmodified flakes			
511N514W/30-35	1	0.6	M	unmodified flake			
511N515W/0-5	1	8.3	C	biface (dart point preform)			
511N515W/0-5	39	24.8	C	unmodified flakes			
511N515W/0-5	3	1.8	Q	unmodified flakes			
511N515W/0-5	4	1.7	I	unmodified flakes			
511N515W/0-5	5	5.4	M	unmodified flakes			
511N515W/5-10	20	17.4	C	unmodified flakes			
511N515W/5-10	2	2.1	Q	unmodified flakes			
511N515W/5-10	4	8.5	M	unmodified flakes			
511N515W/10-15	1	2.7	C	utilized flake	Ut	2	20
511N515W/10-15	1	2.6	C	retouched flake frag.	UR	2	60
					Ut	8	20
511N515W/10-15	18	8.4	C	unmodified flakes			
511N515W/10-15	1	0.2	Q	unmodified flake			
511N515W/10-15	2	1.0	M	unmodified flakes			
511N515W/15-20	16	7.6	C	unmodified flakes			

Table C3. (continued)

Provenience	N	Wt.	Mat.	Description	Utilized Edges Type	Shape	Angle
511N515W/15-20	3	1.8	Q	unmodified flakes			
511N515W/15-20	4	2.1	M	unmodified flakes			
511N515W/20-25	5	1.6	C	unmodified flakes			
511N515W/20-25	2	0.6	Q	unmodified flakes			
511N515W/25-30	1	2.7	C	triangular biface (reworked	BR	2	55
				point tip?)	BR	2	50
511N515W/25-30	1	5.7	C	biface frag.	BR	3	55
511N515W/25-30	7	2.7	C	unmodified flakes			
511N515W/25-30	1	0.6	Q	unmodified flake			
511N515W/25-30	1	0.5	I	unmodified flake			
511N515W/25-30	2	1.0	M	unmodified flakes			
512N514W/0-5	1	23.0	C	core			
512N514W/0-5	1	0.4	C	retouched flake frag.	UR	2	55
512N514W/0-5	25	18.4	C	unmodified flakes			
512N514W/0-5	1	0.2	Q	unmodified flake			
512N514W/0-5	1	0.2	O	unmodified flake			
512N514W/0-5	6	48.2	M	unmodified flakes			
512N514W/5-10	1	0.4	O	biface frag.	BR	3	80
512N514W/5-10	1	4.8	C	biface frag. (preform)			
512N514W/5-10	1	2.1	C	bifacial core frag.			
512N514W/5-10	1	0.7	C	utilized flake frag.	Ut	3	30
512N514W/5-10	35	18.5	C	unmodified flakes			
512N514W/5-10	2	3.7	Q	unmodified flakes			
512N514W/5-10	3	2.6	M	unmodified flakes			
512N514W/10-15	1	11.2	C	end- and sidescraper	UR	3	90
					UR	2	40
512N514W/10-15	26	13.4	C	unmodified flakes			
512N514W/10-15	1	0.3	Q	unmodified flake			

Table C3. (continued)

Provenience	N	Wt.	Mat.	Description	Utilized Edges Type	Shape	Angle
512N514W/10-15	1	0.3	I	unmodified flake			
512N514W/15-20	1	0.3	C	biface frag.	BR	2	40
512N514W/15-20	1	3.7	C	retouched flake (convergent	UR	2	85
				sidescraper)	UR	2	80
512N514W/15-20	1	7.9	C	retouched flake frag.	UR	2	60
512N514W/15-20	1	5.3	C	retouched flake frag.	UR	7	50
512N514W/15-20	17	9.6	C	unmodified flakes			
512N514W/15-20	2	0.3	Q	unmodified flakes			
512N514W/15-20	3	1.5	M	unmodified flakes			
512N514W/20-25	1	2.8	C	retouched flake frag.	UR	3	70
					Ut	2	60
512N514W/20-25	15	7.0	C	unmodified flakes			
512N514W/20-25	1	1.4	Q	unmodified flake			
512N514W/20-25	1	0.5	I	unmodified flake			
512N514W/25-30	1	0.2	C	utilized flake frag.	Ut	2	40
512N514W/25-30	11	3.9	C	unmodified flakes			
512N514W/25-30	1	0.3	Q	unmodified flake			
512N514W/25-30	1	0.9	M	unmodified flake			
512N514W/30-35	1	0.8	C	utilized flake	Ut	2	30
512N514W/30-35	6	1.7	C	unmodified flakes			
512N514W/30-35	2	0.9	Q	unmodified flakes			
512N515W/0-5	1	54.1	C	core			
512N515W/0-5	12	4.6	C	unmodified flakes			
512N515W/0-5	2	1.1	I	unmodified flakes			
512N515W/5-10	23	23.6	C	unmodified flakes			
512N515W/5-10	1	0.2	Q	unmodified flake			
512N515W/5-10	1	0.2	I	unmodified flake			
512N515W/5-10	3	1.3	M	unmodified flakes			

Table C3. (continued)

Provenience	N	Wt.	Mat.	Description	Utilized Edges Type	Shape	Angle
512N515W/10-15	1	0.3	C	biface frag.	BR	2	40
512N515W/10-15	22	12.0	C	unmodified flakes			
512N515W/10-15	2	4.2	Q	unmodified flakes			
512N515W/10-15	2	2.3	I	unmodified flakes			
512N515W/10-15	2	0.4	M	unmodified flakes			
512N515W/15-20	1	20.7	C	scraper	UR	7	70
512N515W/15-20	1	8.2	M	retouched flake	BR	3	60
512N515W/15-20	1	0.4	C	biface frag.	BR	3	45
512N515W/15-20	24	18.0	C	unmodified flakes			
512N515W/15-20	4	4.2	Q	unmodified flakes			
512N515W/15-20	2	1.6	I	unmodified flakes			
512N515W/15-20	1	0.4	M	unmodified flake			
512N515W/20-25	18	16.0	C	unmodified flakes			
512N515W/20-25	3	1.4	M	unmodified flakes			
512N515W/25-30	1	0.9	C	utilized flake	Ut	2	15
					Ut	3	20
512N515W/25-30	8	2.9	C	unmodified flakes			
512N515W/25-30	1	0.3	Q	unmodified flake			
512N515W/25-30	1	0.4	O	unmodified flake			
512N515W/30-35	11	4.9	C	unmodified flakes			
512N515W/30-35	2	2.2	Q	unmodified flakes			
512N515W/37.5 (Item 1, Feat. 4)	1	0.8	C	unmodified flake			
512N515W/ (west wall)	2	5.6	C	unmodified flakes			
512N515W/ (west wall)	2	1.6	M	unmodified flakes			
512N516W/0-5	1	3.9	C	utilized flake	Ut	2	60
					Ut	3	50
512N516W/0-5	23	11.6	C	unmodified flakes			
512N516W/0-5	1	0.4	Q	unmodified flake			

Table C3. (continued)

Provenience	N	Wt.	Mat.	Description	Utilized Edges Type	Shape	Angle
512N516W/0-5	2	6.2	M	unmodified flakes			
512N516W/5-10	15	15.3	C	unmodified flakes			
512N516W/5-10	3	7.5	M	unmodified flakes			
512N516W/10-12 (Feat. 5)	1	0.1	C	unmodified flake			
512N516W/10-15	1	1.1	C	retouched flake frag.	UR	2	60
512N516W/10-15	30	18.4	C	unmodified flakes			
512N516W/10-15	2	1.3	Q	unmodified flakes			
512N516W/10-15	2	4.0	M	unmodified flakes			
512N516W/15-20	1	68.3	C	core			
512N516W/15-20	20	9.5	C	unmodified flakes			
512N516W/15-20	3	2.9	Q	unmodified flakes			
512N516W/20-25	1	0.8	C	biface frag.	BR	3	80
512N516W/20-25	13	4.4	C	unmodified flakes			
512N516W/20-25	1	0.2	Q	unmodified flake			
512N516W/20-25	1	0.1	O	unmodified flake			
512N516W/20-25	2	4.1	M	unmodified flakes			
512N516W/25-30	1	1.9	C	retouched flake frag.	UR	3	30
512N516W/25-30	1	0.9	C	utilized flake	Ut	3	60
512N516W/25-30	15	36.1	C	unmodified flakes			
512N516W/25-30	2	2.3	M	unmodified flakes			
512N516W/30-35	1	0.4	C	retouched flake frag.	UR	2	90
512N516W/30-35	8	1.6	C	unmodified flakes			
512N516W/30-35	1	0.2	M	unmodified flake			

APPENDIX D.

CERAMIC DATA

Table D1
Inventory of painted ceramics

Provenience[1]	Chup B/W bowl	Chup B/W jar	Chup B/W Indet	San Andr R/T	Thr Riv R/T	Thr Riv Ware	Linc B/R	Red-wash Brn	Mim B/W	Mim-Mang B/W	Red Mesa B/W	Gal B/W	St John Poly	Play Incd	Unid Paint
TT1-E/0-5	–	2	–	–	–	–	–	–	–	1	–	–	–	–	–
TT1-E/5-10	–	2	–	–	–	–	–	–	–	–	–	–	–	–	–
TT1-W/0-5	–	1	–	–	–	–	–	–	–	–	–	–	–	–	–
TT1-W/10-25	–	–	–	–	–	1	–	–	–	–	–	–	–	–	–
499N500W/0-5	2	–	–	–	–	–	–	–	–	–	–	–	–	–	–
499N500W/10-15	2	–	–	–	–	–	–	–	–	–	–	–	–	–	–
499N502W/0-5	–	–	–	–	–	–	–	1	–	–	–	–	–	–	–
499N502W/5-10	–	1	–	–	–	–	–	–	–	–	–	–	–	–	–
499N503W/0-5	–	1	–	–	–	–	–	–	–	–	–	–	–	–	–
499N503W/5-10	–	3	–	–	–	–	–	–	–	–	–	–	–	–	–
499N504W/0-5	–	1	–	1	–	–	–	–	–	–	–	–	–	–	–
499N504W/15-20	1	–	–	–	–	–	–	–	–	–	–	–	–	–	–
499N505W/0-5	1	–	–	–	–	–	–	–	–	–	–	–	–	–	–
499N505W/15-20	1	–	–	–	–	–	–	–	–	–	–	–	–	–	–
499N512W/10-15	3	–	–	–	–	–	–	–	–	–	–	1	–	4	–
499N512W/15-20	1	–	–	–	–	–	–	–	–	–	–	–	–	–	–
499N512W/20-25	–	1	–	–	–	–	–	–	–	–	–	–	–	–	–
499N512W/25-30	–	1	–	–	–	–	–	–	–	–	–	–	–	–	–
499N513W/0-5	–	1	–	–	–	–	–	–	–	–	–	–	–	–	–
499N513W/5-10	–	7	–	–	–	1	–	–	–	–	–	–	–	–	–
499N513W/15-20	–	1	–	–	–	–	1	–	–	–	–	–	–	–	–
499N513W/20-25	2	–	–	–	–	–	–	–	–	–	–	–	–	–	–
499N514W/0-5	1	4	–	3	–	–	–	–	–	–	–	–	–	–	–
499N514W/5-10	–	4	–	–	–	–	–	–	–	–	–	–	–	–	–
499N514W/15-20	–	1	–	–	–	–	–	–	–	–	–	–	–	–	–
499N515W/0-5	–	3	–	–	2	2	–	–	–	–	–	–	–	–	–

Table D1. (continued)

Provenience[1]	Chup B/W bowl	Chup B/W jar	Chup B/W Indet	San Andr R/T	Thr Riv R/T	Thr Riv Ware	Linc B/R	Red-wash Brn	Mim B/W	Mim-Mang B/W	Red Mesa B/W	Gal B/W	St John Poly	Play Incd	Unid Paint
499N515W/5-10	-	1	-	-	-	-	-	-	-	1	-	-	-	-	-
499N515W/15-20	-	1	-	-	-	-	-	-	-	-	-	-	-	-	-
499N515W/20-25	-	-	-	1	-	-	-	-	-	-	-	-	-	-	-
499N516W/0-5	-	1	-	-	-	-	-	-	-	-	-	-	-	-	-
499N516W/10-15	-	-	-	-	1	-	-	-	-	-	-	-	-	-	-
499N516W/15-20	-	-	-	-	-	-	-	1	-	-	-	-	-	-	-
499N517W/0-5	-	2	-	-	1	1	-	-	-	-	-	-	-	-	-
499N517W/5-10	-	1	-	-	-	-	-	-	-	-	-	-	-	-	-
499N517W/10-15	-	1	-	-	-	-	-	-	-	-	-	-	-	-	-
499N517W/15-20	-	-	-	-	-	-	-	-	-	-	1	-	-	-	-
499N518W/0-5	-	3	-	-	-	-	-	-	-	-	-	-	-	-	-
499N518W/5-10	-	1	-	-	-	-	-	-	-	-	-	-	-	-	-
499N518W/10-15	-	-	1	-	-	-	-	-	-	-	-	-	-	-	-
499N518W/15-20	-	-	-	-	-	1	-	-	-	-	-	-	-	-	-
500N500W/0-5	-	3	-	-	-	-	-	-	-	-	-	-	-	-	-
500N500W/20-25	-	1	-	-	-	-	-	-	-	-	-	-	-	-	-
500N501W/20-25	-	-	-	-	-	1	-	-	-	-	-	-	-	-	-
500N502W/0-5	-	1	-	-	-	-	-	-	-	-	-	-	-	-	-
500N502W/5-10	1	-	-	-	-	-	-	-	-	-	-	-	-	-	-
500N502W/20-25	-	1	-	-	-	-	-	-	-	-	-	-	-	-	-
500N503W/0-5	-	1	-	-	-	-	-	-	-	-	-	-	-	-	-
500N504W/5-10	-	-	1	-	-	-	-	-	-	-	-	-	-	-	-
500N506W/10-15	-	2	-	-	-	1	1	-	-	-	-	-	-	-	-
500N506W/20-25	-	1	-	-	-	-	-	-	-	-	-	-	-	-	-
500N512W/5-10	-	-	-	-	-	-	-	-	-	-	-	1	-	1	-
500N512W/10-15	1	2	-	-	-	1	-	-	-	-	-	-	-	-	-
500N512W/15-20	1	1	-	-	-	-	-	-	-	-	-	-	-	-	-
500N512W/25-30	-	-	-	-	-	1	-	-	-	-	-	-	-	-	-

Table D1. (continued)

Provenience[1]	Chup B/W bowl	Chup B/W jar	Chup B/W Indet	San Andr R/T	Thr Riv R/T	Thr Riv Ware	Linc B/R	Red-wash Brn	Mim B/W	Mim-Mang B/W	Red Mesa B/W	Gal B/W	St John Poly	Play Incd	Unid Paint
500N513W/5-10	-	2	1	-	-	-	-	-	-	1	-	-	1	-	-
500N513W/10-15	-	4	-	-	-	-	-	-	-	-	-	-	-	-	-
500N513W/15-20	1	1	-	-	-	-	-	-	-	-	-	-	-	-	-
500N513W/25-30	-	-	-	-	-	-	-	-	-	-	-	-	1	-	-
500N514W/0-5	-	3	-	2	2	2	-	-	-	2	1	-	1	-	-
500N514W/5-10	1	6	-	3	-	1	-	-	-	-	-	-	-	-	1
500N514W/10-15	-	-	-	1	-	1	-	-	-	-	-	-	-	-	1
500N514W/15-20	-	1	-	-	-	-	-	-	-	-	-	-	-	-	-
500N515W/0-5	-	-	-	-	1	-	-	-	-	-	-	-	-	-	-
500N515W/15-20	-	-	-	-	1	-	-	-	-	-	-	-	-	-	-
500N516W/0-5	1	3	-	-	-	-	-	-	-	-	-	-	1	-	-
500N517W/10-15	-	1	-	-	-	-	-	-	-	-	-	-	-	-	-
500N518W/10-15	-	1	-	-	-	-	-	-	-	-	-	-	-	-	-
500N518W/15-20	-	1	-	-	-	-	-	-	-	-	-	-	-	-	-
503N515W/0-5	-	1	-	-	-	-	-	-	-	-	-	-	-	-	-
503N515W/5-10	-	1	-	-	-	-	-	-	-	-	-	-	-	-	-
503N515W/10-15	-	-	-	-	-	1	-	-	-	-	-	-	-	-	-
503N515W/25-30	-	-	-	-	-	1	-	-	-	-	-	-	-	-	-
504N515W/0-10	-	-	1	-	-	1	-	-	-	-	-	-	-	-	-
504N515W/10-15	-	1	-	-	1	-	-	-	-	-	-	-	-	-	-
504N569W/0-5	-	-	1	-	-	-	-	-	-	-	-	-	-	-	-
505N514W/surf.	-	-	-	-	1	-	-	-	-	-	-	-	-	-	-
505N515W/10-15	-	1	-	-	1	-	-	-	-	-	-	-	-	-	-
505N515W/15-20	-	1	-	-	-	1	-	-	-	-	-	-	-	-	-
505N515W/20-25	-	-	-	-	1	-	-	-	-	-	-	-	-	-	-
506N515W/5-10	-	1	-	-	-	-	-	-	-	-	-	-	-	-	-
506N515W/10-15	-	1	-	1	-	-	-	-	-	-	-	-	-	-	-
506N515W/15-20	-	-	-	-	-	-	-	1	-	-	-	-	-	-	-

Table D1. (continued)

Provenience[1]	Chup B/W bowl	Chup B/W jar	Chup B/W Indet	San Andr R/T	Thr Riv R/T	Thr Riv Ware	Linc B/R	Red-wash Brn	Mim B/W	Mim-Mang B/W	Red Mesa B/W	Gal B/W	St John Poly	Play Incd	Unid Paint
510N516W/surf.	-	-	-	-	-	1	-	-	-	1	-	-	-	-	-
511N514W/0-5	-	1	-	-	-	-	-	-	-	-	-	-	-	-	-
511N514W/5-10	-	-	-	-	-	1	-	-	-	1	-	-	-	-	-
511N514W/10-15	-	-	-	-	-	-	-	1	-	-	-	-	-	-	-
511N514W/15-20	-	-	-	-	-	-	-	-	-	1	-	-	-	-	-
511N514W/20-25	-	1	-	-	-	-	-	-	-	-	-	-	-	-	-
511N515W/0-5	1	-	-	-	-	-	-	-	-	-	-	-	-	-	-
512N514W/0-5	-	3	-	-	-	-	-	-	-	-	-	-	-	-	-
512N514W/5-10	-	-	-	-	-	-	-	-	-	-	-	-	-	1	-
512N514W/15-20	-	-	-	-	-	-	-	-	-	1	-	-	-	-	-
512N514W/20-25	-	1	-	-	-	-	-	-	-	1	-	-	-	-	-
512N514W/30-35	-	1	-	-	-	-	-	-	-	-	-	-	-	-	-
512N515W/0-5	-	1	-	-	-	-	-	-	-	-	-	-	-	-	-
512N515W/10-15	-	-	-	-	-	-	-	-	1	2	-	-	-	-	-
512N516W/5-10	-	-	1	-	-	-	-	-	-	-	-	-	-	-	1
512N516W/10-15	-	2	-	-	-	-	-	1	-	-	-	-	-	-	-
512N516W/15-20	-	-	-	-	-	-	-	-	1	-	-	-	-	-	-
Surface	6	14	-	-	-	-	-	-	-	-	-	-	-	-	1

[1]We are grateful to Regge N. Wiseman of the Museum of New Mexico for providing the data tabulated in this table.

Table D2
Inventory of utility wares

Provenience[1]	Jornada	Roswell	South Pecos	McKenz	El Paso	Corrug	Unid
TT1-E/0-5	2	-	6	12	1	-	-
TT1-E/5-10	1	-	1	6	-	-	1
TT1-E/10-25	-	-	1	1	-	-	-
TT1-E/15-30	-	-	1	-	-	-	-
TT1-E/45-60	-	1	-	-	-	-	-
TT1-W/0-5	6	2	3	1	1	-	-
TT1-W/5-10	2	1	2	-	1	-	-
TT1-W/10-25	1	-	2	-	-	-	-
TT1-W/15-30	-	-	-	1	-	-	-
495N519W/0-5	1	1	3	-	1	-	-
495N519W/5-10	2	-	2	-	-	-	-
495N519W/10-15	1	-	-	1	-	-	-
495N519W/15-20	1	1	-	-	-	-	1
499N500W/0-5	-	-	1	-	1	-	-
499N501W/5-10	1	-	-	-	-	-	-
499N501W/10-15	1	-	-	-	-	-	-
499N501W/15-20	1	-	-	-	-	-	-
499N502W/0-5	-	-	1	-	-	-	-
499N502W/5-10	-	1	-	-	-	-	-
499N503W/0-5	-	-	1	-	-	-	-
499N503W/10-15	-	-	1	-	-	-	-
499N504W/0-5	1	1	1	-	-	-	-
499N504W/5-10	2	-	-	2	-	-	-
499N504W/10-15	1	-	-	-	-	-	-
499N504W/15-20	1	-	-	-	1	-	-
499N505W/0-5	1	-	-	-	-	-	-
499N505W/5-10	1	1	-	-	-	-	-
499N505W/10-15	2	-	-	-	-	-	-
499N505W/15-20	-	-	-	2	-	-	-
499N506W/5-10	1	-	2	1	-	-	-
499N506W/10-15	3	3	-	-	1	-	-
499N506W/15-20	1	1	1	-	-	-	-
499N506W/25-30	-	-	-	1	-	-	-
499N512W/10-15	7	-	3	4	1	-	-
499N512W/15-20	3	4	8	2	-	-	-
499N512W/20-25	2	-	1	-	2	-	-
499N512W/25-30	-	1	-	1	-	-	-
499N512W/40-45	-	-	1	-	-	-	-
499N512W/ South wall	-	-	1	-	-	-	-
499N513W/5-10	4	-	5	5	1	1	-
499N513W/10-15	-	-	1	-	-	-	-
499N513W/15-20	2	-	2	-	-	-	-
499N513W/20-25	2	-	-	-	-	-	-
499N514W/0-5	4	1	9	2	1	-	-

Table D2. (continued)

Provenience[1]	Jornada	Roswell	South Pecos	McKenz	El Paso	Corrug	Unid
499N514W/5-10	3	2	7	-	3	-	1
499N514W/10-15	3	1	1	-	-	-	-
499N514W/15-20	1	-	2	1	-	-	-
499N515W/0-5	4	-	5	9	1	-	-
499N515W/5-10	3	1	2	2	1	-	-
499N515W/15-20	-	1	-	-	-	-	-
499N515W/25-30	-	-	1	-	-	-	-
499N516W/0-5	2	1	-	-	-	-	1
499N516W/10-15	-	-	1	-	-	-	-
499N516W/15-20	1	-	3	-	-	-	-
499N517W/0-5	2	1	2	1	1	-	1
499N517W/5-10	-	3	2	-	-	-	-
499N517W/10-15	3	-	3	-	-	-	-
499N517W/15-20	1	-	1	1	1	-	-
499N517W/20-25	-	-	1	-	-	-	-
499N518W/0-5	4	1	3	1	-	-	-
499N518W/5-10	-	1	2	-	-	-	-
499N518W/10-15	1	-	1	-	-	-	-
499N518W/15-20	-	-	1	-	-	-	-
500N500W/0-5	1	-	-	-	-	-	-
500N500W/5-10	1	-	-	-	-	-	-
500N501W/0-5	1	-	-	-	-	-	-
500N501W/10-15	1	1	-	-	-	-	-
500N501W/15-20	-	-	1	-	-	-	-
500N502W/0-5	-	-	1	-	-	-	-
500N502W/5-10	1	1	1	-	-	-	-
500N502W/10-15	1	1	-	-	-	-	-
500N502W/15-20	1	-	-	-	-	-	-
500N503W/0-5	1	-	1	1	-	-	-
500N503W/5-10	1	1	-	-	-	-	-
500N504W/0-5	-	-	3	-	-	-	-
500N505W/0-5	-	-	-	-	2	-	-
500N505W/5-10	1	-	-	-	-	-	-
500N505W/10-15	1	-	-	-	-	-	-
500N505W/15-20	2	-	-	-	-	-	-
500N505W/20-25	-	-	-	1	-	-	-
500N505W/25-30	1	-	-	-	-	-	-
500N506W/5-10	2	1	1	-	1	-	-
500N506W/10-15	2	2	-	1	-	-	-
500N512W/10-15	4	-	-	3	-	-	-
500N512W/15-20	1	-	1	3	-	-	-
500N512W/25-30	-	-	2	-	-	-	-
500N512W/30-35	-	-	1	-	-	-	-
500N513W/5-10	1	1	1	1	-	-	-
500N513W/10-15	-	1	2	5	-	-	-
500N513W/15-20	1	1	4	-	-	-	-
500N513W/20-25	1	-	-	1	-	-	-

Table D2. (continued)

Provenience[1]	Jornada	Roswell	South Pecos	McKenz	El Paso	Corrug	Unid
500N513W/25-30	-	-	-	1	-	-	-
500N513W/30-35	-	1	-	-	-	-	-
500N514W/0-5	3	-	1	6	1	-	-
500N514W/5-10	4	3	6	8	1	-	1
500N514W/10-15	1	-	4	1	-	-	-
500N514W/15-20	3	-	1	-	-	-	-
500N514W/20-25	-	-	-	1	-	-	-
500N515W/0-5	2	-	2	2	-	-	-
500N515W/5-10	3	1	1	-	-	-	-
500N515W/10-15	3	-	5	-	1	-	-
500N515W/15-20	-	2	3	-	-	-	-
500N515W/20-25	-	-	1	-	-	-	-
500N515W/25-30	-	-	1	-	-	-	-
500N516W/0-5	5	2	2	3	-	-	-
500N516W/5-10	2	2	3	2	1	-	-
500N516W/10-15	2	-	3	-	-	-	-
500N516W/15-20	1	-	4	-	-	-	-
500N516W/20-25	-	1	1	-	-	-	-
500N516W/25-30	-	-	2	-	-	-	-
500N517W/0-5	2	-	5	1	-	-	-
500N517W/5-10	4	1	4	1	-	-	-
500N517W/10-15	-	1	2	-	-	-	-
500N517W/15-20	-	-	2	1	-	-	-
500N517W/20-25	-	1	-	1	1	-	-
500N517W/25-30	-	-	1	-	1	-	-
500N518W/0-5	1	-	2	-	-	-	-
500N518W/5-10	1	-	1	-	-	-	-
500N518W/10-15	-	-	1	-	-	-	-
500N518W/15-20	1	-	-	-	-	-	-
503N515W/5-10	1	-	5	1	-	-	-
503N515W/10-15	2	1	2	1	-	-	-
503N515W/15-20	-	-	2	-	-	-	-
503N515W/20-25	1	-	1	-	-	-	-
503N515W/25-30	1	-	-	-	-	-	-
503N568W/5-10	1	-	-	-	-	-	-
503N569W/10-15	-	-	-	-	-	-	1
504N515W/0-10	4	1	2	-	-	-	-
504N515W/10-15	2	-	7	-	-	-	-
504N515W/15-20	-	-	1	-	-	-	-
504N515W/20-25	-	-	3	-	-	-	-
505N515W/0-5	2	1	4	1	-	-	1
505N515W/10-15	-	-	6	-	-	-	-
505N515W/15-20	1	-	1	-	-	-	-
505N515W/20-25	1	-	-	-	-	-	-
505N515W/25-30	-	-	1	-	-	-	-
506N515W/0-5	1	-	-	-	-	-	-
506N515W/5-10	3	-	-	-	-	-	-

Table D2. (continued)

Provenience[1]	Jornada	Roswell	South Pecos	McKenz	El Paso	Corrug	Unid
506N515W/10-15	-	2	1	-	-	-	-
506N515W/15-20	-	-	1	-	-	-	-
506N515W/25-30	-	-	3	-	-	-	-
511N514W/5-10	-	1	1	-	-	-	-
511N514W/10-15	1	-	1	-	1	-	-
511N514W/15-20	-	-	1	1	-	-	-
511N514W/20-25	1	-	-	-	-	-	-
511N514W/30-35	2	-	-	-	-	-	-
511N515W/0-5	3	-	2	-	-	-	-
511N515W/5-10	1	-	-	1	-	-	-
511N515W/10-15	-	-	1	-	-	-	1
512N514W/0-5	1	-	-	-	-	-	-
512N514W/5-10	-	-	3	-	-	-	-
512N514W/15-20	-	-	-	1	-	-	-
512N514W/20-25	-	-	1	1	-	-	-
512N515W/0-5	-	1	-	-	-	-	-
512N515W/5-10	2	-	-	-	-	-	-
512N515W/10-15	2	1	-	-	-	-	-
512N515W/15-20	4	-	2	-	-	-	-
512N515W/20-25	-	1	-	-	-	-	-
512N515W/25-30	-	-	-	1	-	-	-
512N516W/0-5	-	-	-	1	-	-	-
512N516W/5-10	1	-	-	-	-	-	-
512N516W/10-15	-	1	1	-	-	-	-
512N516W/15-20	-	-	1	-	-	-	-
512N516W/20-25	-	-	-	-	-	-	1
512N516W/30-35	-	1	-	-	-	-	-
Surface	12	5	16	2	1	-	-

[1]We are grateful to Regge N. Wiseman of the Museum of New Mexico for providing the data tabulated in this table.

APPENDIX E.

SURFACE-COLLECTED ARTIFACTS

Table E1
Inventory of prehistoric artifacts from surface of Garnsey Spring campsite

Square	N	Description
1	1	crude biface, chalky pink-tan fine-grained igneous
	3	small cores, milky grey iron-stained chalcedony
	1	spall, yellow-tan chert
2	1	small, steep spurred scraper, yellow-tan chert
	1	crude scraper, milky chalcedony
	13	spalls, milky chalcedony
	3	spalls, grey chalcedony
	3	spalls, brown chert
	2	spalls, red chert
	2	spalls, mottled grey chert
	2	spalls, purple quartzite
	1	spall, light quartzite
	1	spall, pink chert
	1	spall, obsidian
3	1	large spurred endscraper, tan chert with chalcedony mottles
	1	thumb-scraper, banded grey chert
	1	crude scraper, milky chalcedony
	1	finely retouched flake, brown chert
	16	spalls, milky chalcedony
	12	spalls, purple quartzite
	3	spalls, brown chert
	3	spalls, mottled grey chert
	2	spalls, black chert
	2	spalls, light quartzite
	2	spalls, sedimentary
	1	spall, black igneous
	1	spall, grey chalcedony
	1	spall, red chert
	1	spall, pink chert
	2	spalls, yellow chert
	1	spall, moss agate(?)
4	1	large biface midsection, tan chert with chalcedony mottles
	1	retouched flake, banded grey chert
	9	spalls, mottled grey chert
	7	spalls, milky chalcedony
	6	spalls, red chert (Alibates)
	1	spall, brown chert
	2	spalls, tan chalcedony
	2	spalls, purple quartzite
	2	spalls, black basalt

Table E1. (continued)

Square	N	Description
	2	spalls, sedimentary
	1	spall, light quartzite
	1	spall, yellow-tan chert
	1	spall, red basalt
	1	spall, obsidian
5	1	small, broadly side-notched point, chert (Alibates)
	1	large spurred endscraper, fingerprint chert
	1	core, tan chert with chalcedony mottles
	4	spalls, milky chalcedony
	2	spalls, mottled grey chert
	1	spall, purple quartzite
6	1	sherd, Chupadero B/W
	1	large steep endscraper, tan chert with chalcedony mottles
	6	spalls, milky chalcedony
	1	spall, red chert (Alibates)
	1	spall, white chert
	1	spall, grey chert
	1	spall, sandstone
7	1	crude scraper, milky chalcedony
	1	retouched flake, mottled grey chert
	16	spalls, milky chalcedony
	2	spalls (Alibates)
	2	spalls, red chert
	4	spalls, mottled grey chert
	2	spalls, purple quartzite
	1	spall, black igneous
8	1	large spurred endscraper, black basalt
	1	sidescraper, yellow-tan chert
	1	sidescraper, milky chalcedony
	13	spalls, milky chalcedony
	4	spalls, purple quartzite
	4	spalls, tan chert with chalcedony mottles
	3	spalls, mottled grey chert
	2	spalls, yellow quartzite
	2	spalls, tan chert
	1	spall, grey quartzite
	1	spall (Alibates)
	1	spall, fingerprint chert

Table E1. (continued)

Square	N	Description
9	1	small triangular point with basal notch, pink chert
	1	large spurred endscraper, milky chalcedony
	1	sidescraper, banded grey chert
	1	retouched flake, tan chert with chalcedony mottles
	1	retouched flake, grey quartzite
	1	lateral frag. of small corner-notched point, pink chert
	1	small scraper, milky chalcedony
	1	graver, quartzite
	2	biface frags., mottled grey chert
	22	spalls, milky chalcedony
	16	spalls, red-pink chert
	13	spalls, mottled grey chert
	9	spalls, light quartzite
	5	spalls, black igneous
	5	spalls, obsidian
	4	spalls, tan chalcedony
	4	spalls, tan chert with chalcedony mottles
	2	spalls, brown chert
	2	spalls, vein quartz
	1	spall, purple quartzite
	1	spall, petrified wood
10	2	small triangular side-notched points, grey chert
	1	crude scraper, black basalt
	1	point midsection, obsidian
	1	crude scraper, milky chalcedony
	2	crude scrapers, chalky igneous
	1	retouched, spurred flake, grey chert
	1	retouched, spurred flake, red chert
	1	retouched, spurred flake, quartzite
	1	core, brown chert
	1	drill(?) midsection, grey chert
	1	utilized flake, yellow chert
	3	utilized flakes, grey chert
	1	utilized flake, grey chalcedony
	1	small scraper, grey chalcedony
	22	spalls, milky chalcedony
	21	spalls, grey mottled chert
	13	spalls, red chert
	12	spalls, grey chalcedony
	9	spalls, purple quartzite
	5	spalls, obsidian
	4	spalls, black igneous
	4	spalls, sedimentary
	3	spalls, brown-yellow chert
	2	spalls, yellow chalcedony
	1	spall, light quartzite

Table E1. (continued)

Square	N	Description
	1	spall, tan chert with chalcedony mottles
11	1	sherd, Chupadero B/W
	1	sherd, brownware
	1	crude scraper, black basalt
	2	retouched flakes, pink chert
	2	cores, milky chalcedony
	6	spalls, milky chalcedony
	2	spalls, grey mottled chert
	2	spalls, tan chert with chalcedony mottles
	2	spalls, black igneous
	1	spall, red chert
	1	spall, obsidian
12	1	crude biface, mottled grey chert
	1	biface fragment, red chert
	1	retouched flake, milky chalcedony
	18	spalls, milky chalcedony
	7	spalls, grey mottled chert
	3	spalls, grey basalt
	4	spalls, grey chalky chert
	2	spalls, black chert
	2	spalls, purple quartzite
	1	spall, red chert
13	2	retouched flakes, tan chert with chalcedony mottles
	1	retouched flake, milky chalcedony
	1	utilized flake, grey mottled chert
	8	spalls, tan chert with chalcedony mottles
	9	spalls, milky chalcedony
	6	spalls, red chert
	2	spalls, purple quartzite
	1	spall, black igneous
	1	spall, oolitic chert
	1	steep scraper, pink chert
14	2	retouched flakes, mottled grey chert
	2	retouched flakes, white chert
	4	crude biface frags., mottled grey chert
	1	retouched flake, brown chert
	41	spalls, milky chalcedony
	13	spalls, grey mottled chert
	7	spalls, pink chert
	5	spalls, tan chert with chalcedony mottles
	4	spalls, purple quartzite
	2	spalls, black igneous
	2	spalls, grey chalcedony
	1	spall, brown chert

Table E1. (continued)

Square	N	Description
	1	spall, sedimentary
	1	spall, obsidian
15	1	expanded-stemmed point, tan chalcedony
	1	small triangular point frag., grey chalcedony
	1	unifacial lanceolate point <u>or</u> channel flake, tan chert
	3	biface frags., grey mottled chert
	1	small nosed scraper, tan chert with chalcedony mottles
	1	scraper frag., milky chalcedony
	1	retouched bladelet, mottled grey chert
	1	retouched flake (concave), mottled grey chert
	1	large scraper, purple quartzite
	1	utilized spurred flake, milky chalcedony
	1	utilized flake, light quartzite
	1	core, purple quartzite
	1	core,milky chalcedony
	1	crude biface, pink chert
	2	retouched flakes, mottled grey chert
	3	utilized flakes, grey chalcedony
	1	point midsection, red chert
	1	scraper frag., mottled grey chert
	49	spalls, mottled grey chert
	22	spalls, milky chalcedony
	18	spalls, grey and tan chalcedony
	8	spalls, purple quartzite
	5	spalls, light quartzite
	11	spalls, white chert-chalcedony
	10	spalls, yellow-brown chert
	33	spalls, red chert
	2	spalls, red basalt
	2	spalls, oolitic(?) chert
	1	spall, tan chert with chalcedony mottles
	10	spalls, black igneous
16	1	large spurred endscraper, red basalt
	1	sidescraper, tan chert with chalcedony mottles
	1	nosed scraper, milky chalcedony
	1	retouched flake, grey mottled chert
	1	spall, milky chalcedony
17	1	lanceolate point, mottled tan-blue chert
	1	sherd, Chupadero B/W
	2	retouched flakes, milky chalcedony
	1	crude biface, sedimentary
	1	utilized flake, grey mottled chert
	1	core, mottled grey chert
	1	core, sedimentary
	3	spalls, milky chalcedony

Table E1. (continued)

Square	N	Description
	4	spalls, grey mottled chert
	2	spalls, tan chalcedony
	1	spall, white chert
	1	spall, sedimentary
	1	spall, quartzite
	1	spall, black igneous
18	1	large spurred endscraper, rhyolite
	1	sherd, Chupadero B/W
	13	spalls, milky chalcedony
	9	spalls, grey mottled chert
	2	spalls, red chert
	2	spalls, black igneous
	1	spall, brown chert
	1	spall, purple quartzite
19	1	point midsection, brown chert
	1	rimsherd, Chupadero B/W
	1	scraper, milky Chalcedony
	1	retouched flake, tan chalcedony
	1	retouched flake, milky chalcedony
	1	core, milky chalcedony
	1	crude biface, sandstone
	1	utilized flake, milky chalcedony
	23	spalls, milky chalcedony
	12	spalls, mottled grey chert
	4	spalls, purple quartzite
	1	spall, yellow quartzite
	4	spalls, sedimentary
	1	spall, tan chert with chalcedony mottles
	2	spalls, black igneous
	1	spall, black mottled chert
20	1	point midsection, red chert
	1	point tip, milky chalcedony
	1	small biface, obsidian
	1	small biface, grey chalcedony
	1	steep nosed scraper, tan chert with chalcedony mottles
	1	spurred endscraper, tan chert with chalcedony mottles
	1	spurred endscraper, grey mottled chert
	2	retouched flakes, tan chalcedony
	1	retouched flake, mottled grey chert
	1	crude biface, milky chalcedony
	1	utilized flake (concave), mottled grey chert
	5	cores, milky chalcedony
	40	spalls, milky chalcedony
	24	spalls, mottled grey chert
	17	spalls, red chert

Table E1. (continued)

Square	N	Description
	10	spalls, purple quartzite
	5	spalls, black igneous
	4	spalls, sedimentary
	5	spalls, grey and tan chalcedony
	4	spalls, brown chert
	2	spalls, fingerprint chert
	1	spall, tan chert with chalcedony mottles
	1	spall, light quartzite
	1	spall, red basalt
	1	spall, obsidian (utilized)
21	4	spalls, mottled grey chert
	2	spalls, red basalt
	2	spalls, black igneous
	1	spall, purple quartzite
	1	spall, milky chalcedony
	1	spall, pink chert
	1	spall, tan chalcedony
	1	spall, tan chert with chalcedony mottles
22	1	small side-notched point, tan chalcedony
	1	sherd, Chupadero B/W
	1	crude biface, brown chert
	1	core, milky chalcedony
	8	spalls, milky chalcedony
	2	spalls, grey mottled chert
	3	spalls, black igneous
	1	spall, black chert
	1	spall, red chert
23	1	retouched flake, mottled grey chert
	1	utilized flake, mottled grey chert
	7	spalls, milky chalcedony
	3	spalls, red chert
	2	spalls, mottled grey chert
	2	spalls, grey chalcedony
	2	spalls, purple quartzite
	1	spall, light quartzite
	1	spall, red basalt
	1	spall, obsidian
24	2	sherds, Chupadero B/W
	1	sherd, brownware
	1	large biface, mottled grey chert
	3	cores, mottled grey chert
	1	core, purple quartzite
	1	core, milky chalcedony
	1	utilized flake, mottled grey chert

Table E1. (continued)

Square	N	Description
	1	bladelet, yellow quartzite (utilized)
	1	retouched (?) flake, mottled grey chert
	21	spalls, mottled grey chert
	9	spalls, purple quartzite
	8	spalls, milky chalcedony
	3	spalls, grey chalcedony
	4	spalls, red chert
	1	spall, brown chert
	3	spalls, tan chert with chalcedony mottles
	2	spalls, sedimentary
	2	spalls, black igneous
	1	spall, obsidian with red bands
	1	spall, red basalt
	1	spall, vein quartz
	2	bone frags.
25	2	sherds, Chupadero B/W
	1	retouched flake, black fine-grained igneous
	1	retouched flake, fingerprint chert
	1	large scraper (chopper), weathered sedimentary
	1	sherd, brownware
	1	point tip, white chert
	1	denticulate retouched flake, purple quartzite
	2	retouched flakes, grey mottled chert
	1	retouched flake, red chert
	5	utilized flakes, milky chalcedony
	2	utilized flakes, tan chert with chalcedony mottles
	3	cores, milky chalcedony
	2	burned bone frags.
	3	spalls, light quartzite
	12	spalls, purple quartzite
	1	spall, red basalt
	1	spall, coarse igneous
	7	spalls, black fine-grained igneous
	9	spalls, sedimentary
	183	spalls, misc. cherts
26	1	crude biface, fingerprint chert
	1	retouched flake, mottled grey chert
	1	core, milky chalcedony
	1	core, sedimentary
	7	spalls, misc. cherts
	2	spalls, purple quartzite
	1	spall, black fine-grained igneous
27	1	broadly side-notched point, grey mottled chert
	1	broadly side-notched point, red chert
	1	large pebble chopper, sedimentary

Table E1. (continued)

Square	N	Description
	1	retouched flake, red chert
	1	core, milky chalcedony
	1	crude biface, mottled grey chert
	2	spalls, misc. chert
	1	spall, purple quartzite
	1	spall, red basalt
28	4	sherds, Chupadero B/W
	1	broadly corner-notched point, brown chert
	1	point tip, mottled grey chert
	3	utilized flakes, misc. chert
	1	core, milky chalcedony
	13	spalls, misc. chert
	1	spall, quartzite
29	1	retouched flake, grey chalcedony
	1	crude biface, mottled grey chert
	1	core, milky chalcedony
	1	core, mottled grey chert
	15	spalls, misc. chert
	3	spalls, purple quartzite
	2	spalls, black fine-grained igneous
	1	spall, obsidian
30	1	expanded-stemmed point, mottled grey chert
	1	beveled knife, purple quartzite
	1	chopper, milky chalcedony
	1	large denticulate retouched flake, purple quartzite
	1	retouched flake, purple quartzite
	3	crude bifaces, mottled grey chert
	1	core, milky chalcedony
	1	core, vein quartz
	1	core, mottled grey chert
	1	utilized flake, fingerprint chert
	1	utilized flake (concave), tan chert with chalcedony mottles
	47	spalls, misc. cherts
	3	spalls, purple quartzite
	1	spall, red basalt
	1	spall, vein quartz
31	1	metate frag., sandstone
	1	mano frag., coarse-grained igneous
	2	rimsherds, Chupadero B/W
	2	body sherds, Chupadero B/W
	25	sherds, brownware
	2	crude bifaces, tan chert with chalcedony mottles
	1	crude biface, grey quartzite

Table E1. (continued)

Square	N	Description
	1	large steep concave scraper, milky chalcedony
	1	large steep concave scraper, black fine-grained igneous
	1	steep scraper, tan chert with chalcedony mottles
	1	retouched flake, tan chert with chalcedony mottles
	1	retouched flake, obsidian
	2	utilized flakes, purple quartzite
	1	utilized flake, white chert
	8	cores, milky chalcedony
	1	core, mottled grey chert
	1	point preform (side-notched?), milky chalcedony
	1	crude biface frag., grey chalcedony
	4	utilized flakes, mottled grey chert
	116	spalls, misc. cherts
	12	spalls, purple quartzite
	4	spalls, light quartzite
	6	spalls, black fine-grained igneous
	3	spalls, red basalt
	1	spall, obsidian
	1	spall, sedimentary
32	1	retouched flake (concave-spurred), milky chalcedony
	8	spalls, misc. cherts
	1	spall, purple quartzite
33	1	spall, red basalt
	1	spall, purple quartzite
34	6	spalls, chert
	2	spalls, purple quartzite
	1	spall, sedimentary
35	2	sherds, brownware
	1	point tip, red chert
	1	retouched flake, white chalcedony
	1	retouched flake, milky chalcedony
	2	utilized flakes, tan chert with chalcedony mottles
	10	spalls, misc. cherts
36	1	basal point frag. (small side-notched), grey mottled chert
	1	point tip, red chert
	1	large scraper, purple quartzite
	1	spurred retouched flake, white chalcedony
	1	spurred retouched flake, mottled grey chert
	2	utilized flakes, tan chert with chalcedony mottles
	1	utilized flake, milky chalcedony
	1	core, red chert

Table El. (continued)

Square	N	Description
	71	spalls, misc. cherts
	4	spalls, purple quartzite
	1	spall, vein quartz
	3	spalls, black fine-grained igneous
37	3	spalls, misc. cherts
38	2	utilized flakes, chert
	2	spalls, misc. cherts
39	1	biface, mottled grey chert
	1	spall, misc. chert
40	1	utilized flake, red basalt
	2	spalls, misc. cherts
41	1	sherd, Chupadero B/W
	1	core, misc. chert
	1	core, purple quartzite
	1	spall, misc. chert
	1	spall, purple quartzite
	1	spall, sedimentary
42	1	spall, misc. chert
43	1	endscraper, mottled grey chert
	1	utilized flake, mottled grey chert
	4	spalls, misc. cherts
	1	spall, black igneous
	1	spall, rhyolite
44	1	utilized flake, purple quartzite
	1	spall, purple quartzite
	5	spalls, misc. cherts
	1	spall, rhyolite
	1	spall, obsidian
45	-	sterile
46	1	core, milky chalcedony
	4	spalls, misc. cherts
47	1	crude biface, tan chert with chalcedony mottles
	1	retouched flake, black igneous
	9	spalls, misc. cherts
	2	spalls, purple quartzite
48	1	core, red chert

Table E1. (continued)

Square	N	Description
	1	utilized flake, mottled grey chert
	4	spalls, misc. cherts
	1	spall, black igneous
	1	spall, light quartzite
49	1	retouched flake, tan chert
	1	spall, mottled grey chert

Table E2
Inventory of historic artifacts from surface of Garnsey Spring campsite. Nails not collected; items in ( ) discarded; ABM, made by automatic bottling machine; BIM, hand blown in mold.

Square	N	Description
1	-	sterile
2	-	sterile
3	-	sterile
4	-	sterile
5	-	sterile
6	-	sterile
7	-	sterile
8	1	brown glass neck ABM crown beer bottle
	25	(brown glass body sherds)
	1	.22 caliber long cartridge case with "U" headstamp
9	-	sterile
10	-	sterile
11	-	sterile
12	-	sterile
13	-	sterile
14	-	sterile
15	1	(light green glass body sherd)
	1	(purple glass body sherd)
16	1	purple glass neck BIM patent lip bottle
	1	(purple glass body sherd)
17	1	purple glass neck BIM whiskey lip bottle
	1	purple glass base BIM round bottle marked: "NBBG" 55
	19	(purple glass body sherds)
18	-	sterile

Table E2. (continued)

Square	N	Description
19	2	(purple glass body sherds)
20	1	clear glass base BIM round bottle
	1	clear glass embossed body sherd
	6	(clear glass body sherds)
	1	(purple glass body sherd)
21	-	sterile
22	-	sterile
23	-	sterile
24	1	brass Mason Jar lid
	1	glazed redware sherd
	16	painted porcelain body sherds
	1	white porcelain jar lid sherd
	31	(white porcelain body sherds)
	2	(white porcelain tiles)
	1	gilded button "Richard Hudnut, N.Y."
	1	clear glass neck ABM whiskey bottle
	1	clear glass embossed body sherd "..ORE, ..ELL ..GWORKS, .. N.M."
	2	clear glass bases BIM round bottle
	2	clear glass bases ABM oval bottle embossed "..ULL PIN.." on side, "PIX" on base
	96	(clear glass body and window sherds)
	1	brown glass neck large BIM jug
	1	brown glass base large BIM jug
	43	(brown glass body sherds)
	2	light green glass bases BIM round bottles, one embossed "90"
	1	light green glass base ABM rect. bottle, embossed: "8." C
	10	(light green glass body sherds)
	1	purple glass shoulder inkwell, embossed "..EDY & EDDY"
	1	purple glass base ABM rect. bottle
	1	purple glass base ABM oval bottle
	8	(purple glass body sherds)
	1	blue glass neck ABM screw top bottle
	1	blue glass base ABM round bottle
	3	(blue glass body sherds)
25	29	painted porcelain body sherds
	3	embossed porcelain rim sherds
	1	white porcelain base round jar, embossed "..LATUM ..ADE ..RK"

Table E2. (continued)

Square	N	Description
	1	white porcelain Mason Jar lid, embossed "GENUIN.."
	25	(white porcelain body sherds)
	1	(white porcelain tile)
	1	clear glass neck ABM non-crown soda bottle
	2	clear glass necks ABM early var. crown soda bottles
	1	clear glass base ABM round bottle, embossed "CON..NTS"
	1	clear glass basal body sherd ABM round bottle, embossed "CON.."
	1	clear glass base ABM oval bottle, embossed "..PIX.."
	2	clear glass body sherds, embossed "REG.. RE.."; "..UIS ..BS ..ARK ..ED"
	64	(clear glass body sherds)
	4	purple glass neck sherds ABM milk bottle
	2	purple glass necks BIM patent lip bottles
	2	purple glass necks ABM (pre-Owen) patent lip bottles
	1	purple glass base BIM oval bottle
	1	purple glass embossed body sherd
	24	(purple glass body sherds)
	1	light green glass neck BIM crown soda bottle
	2	light green glass necks ABM crown soda bottles
	2	light green glass bases ABM round bottles
	1	light green glass base BIM round ridged bottle
	20	(light green glass body sherds)
	6	(dark green glass body sherds)
	3	(brown glass body sherds)
	1	red glass button
	1	square tin canister lid
	1	tin spoon bowl
	3	metal crown bottle caps
	1	.38 caliber bullet
	2	.22 caliber cartridge cases, headstamped "U"
	1	.22 caliber cartridge case, headstamped "US"
26	1	dark green glass base ABM oval bottle, embossed: "FULL PINT" 6
	20	(dark green glass body sherds)
	19	(brown glass body sherds)
	6	(light green glass body sherds)
	1	purple glass body sherd
	1	clear glass window sherd
	1	brass suspender hook
27	1	brown glass intact ABM 14 cc medicine bottle, embossed "FRANKLIN PRODUCTS 1845"
28	1	clear glass neck ABM patent lip bottle
	1	light green glass base BIM Mason Jar

Table E2. (continued)

Square	N	Description
	1	purple glass base BIM rect. bottle, embossed "4 3/4"
	1	(brown glass body sherd)
29	2	purple glass necks ABM whiskey bottles
30	5	painted porcelain body sherds
	1	clear glass base ABM round bottle, embossed "CAPACITY ONE FULL QUART <7>"
	1	clear glass base ABM round bottle, embossed "10"
	1	clear glass neck ABM screw cap bottle
	6	clear glass embossed body sherds
	17	(clear glass body sherds)
	1	light green glass body ABM round bottle, base embossed " I " 570
	14	(light green glass body sherds)
	1	purple glass base ABM square bottle, embossed "PATENTED"
	1	purple glass base spinmold wine bottle
	2	purple glass embossed sherds.
	5	(purple glass body sherds)
	2	(brown glass body sherds)
	1	yellow glass body sherd
31	2	painted porcelain body sherds
	1	embossed porcelain body sherd
	5	(white porcelain body sherds)
	1	clear glass neck ABM whiskey bottle
	1	clear glass base ABM round bottle
	1	clear glass base BIM rect. bottle
	8	clear glass embossed body sherds
	84	(clear glass body sherds)
	1	brown glass neck ABM crown beer bottle
	1	brown glass base ABM round bottle
	38	(brown glass body sherds)
	1	purple glass neck ABM screw cap bottle
	1	purple glass base ABM oval bottle, embossed "..LYRIC"
	1	purple glass base BIM? round bottle
	29	(purple glass body sherds)
	1	light green glass base ABM Mason Jar
	4	light green glass bases ABM round bottle, one embossed "58"
	1	light green glass base BIM? round bottle, embossed "W F & S MIL 10"
	1	brass Mason Jar lid
	1	.22 caliber cartridge, headstamped "P"
	1	iron buckle
	22	(light green glass body sherds)

Table E2. (continued)

Square	N	Description
	7	(dark green glass body sherds)
32	3	(clear glass body sherds)
	1	(dark green glass body sherds)
	1	(white porcelain body sherd)
33	-	sterile
34	-	sterile
35	-	sterile
36	3	(white porcelain body sherds)
	1	(brown glass body sherd)
37	-	sterile
38	-	sterile
39	-	sterile
40	-	sterile
41	-	sterile
42	-	sterile
43	-	sterile
44	1	painted porcelain body sherd
	1	purple glass neck ABM milk bottle
	1	purple glass base (melted)
	1	gilded purse clasp

REFERENCES CITED

Beckett, Patrick H.
1974 A Tiwa Rabbit Hunt, as Held by the Tortugas Indains. Awanyu 2(1):40-46.

Bell, Robert E.
1958 Guide to the Identification of Certain American Indian Projectile Points. Oklahoma Anthropological Society Special Bulletin 1.

1960 Guide to the Identification of Certain American Indian Projectile Points. Oklahoma Anthropological Society Special Bulletin 2.

Binford, Lewis R.
1963 A Proposed Attribute List for the Description and Classification of Projectile Points. Museum of Anthropology, University of Michigan, Anthropological Papers 19:193-221.

Breternitz, David A.
1966 An Appraisal of Tree-Ring Dated Pottery in the Southwest. University of Arizona, Anthropological Papers 10.

Buffington, Lee C., and Carlton H. Herbel
1965 Vegetational Changes on a Semidesert Grassland Range from 1858 to 1963. Ecological Monographs 35:139-164.

Burns, Bruce A.
1977 Ceramic Section. In Caprock Water System Archaeological Project, Lea County, New Mexico, edited by J. Loring Haskell. Unpublished report on file at the Agency for Conservation Archaeology, Department of Anthropology, Eastern New Mexico University, Portales.

Cahen, D., and J. Moeyersons
1977 Subsurface Movements of Stone Artefacts and Their Implications for the Prehistory of Central Africa. Nature 166:812-815.

Collins, Michael B.
1968 The Andrews Lake Locality: New Archeological Data from the Southern Llano Estacado, Texas. Unpublished M.A. Thesis. Austin: University of Texas.

1971 A Review of Llano Estacado Archeology and Ethnohistory. Plains Anthropologist 16:85-104.

Cordell, Linda S., and Amy C. Earls
1982 The Rio Grande Glaze "Sequence" and the Mogollon. Paper presented at the 2nd Mogollon Conference, Las Cruces.

Court, Arnold
1974 The Climate of the Conterminous United States. In World Survey of Climatology, vol. 11, Climates of North America, edited by R. A. Bryson and F. K. Hare, pp. 193-266. Amsterdam: Elsevier Scientific Publishing Company.

Cushing, Edward J.
1967 Evidence for Differential Pollen Preservation in Late Quaternary Sediment in Minnesota. Review of Palaeobotany and Palynology 4:87-101.

Downton, W. J. S.
1975 The Occurrence of C_4 Photosynthesis among Plants. Photosynthetica 9(1):96-105.

Driesch, Angela von den
1976 A Guide to the Measurement of Animal Bones from Archaeological Sites. Peabody Museum of Archaeology and Ethnology, Harvard University, Peabody Museum Bulletin 1.

Eickmeier, W. G.
1978 Photosynthetic Pathway Distributions along an Aridity Gradient in Big Bend National Park, and Implications for Enhanced Resource Partitioning. Photosynthetica 12(3):290-297.

Folk, Robert L.
1968 Petrology of Sedimentary Rocks. Austin: Hemphills.

Fowler, Melvin L., and Robert L. Hall
1975 Archaeological Phases at Cahokia. Illinois Archaeological Survey Bulletin 10:1-14.

Fox, Daniel J., and Kenneth E. Guire
1976 Documentation for MIDAS. Ann Arbor: Statistical Research Laboratory, University of Michigan.

Gardner, J. L.
1951 Vegetation of the Creosotebush Area of the Rio Grande Valley in New Mexico. Ecological Monographs 21:379-403.

Gifford, Diane P.
1978 Ethnoarchaeological Observations of Natural Processes Affecting Cultural Materials. In Explorations in Ethnoarchaeology, edited by Richard A. Gould, pp. 77-101. Albuquerque: University of New Mexico Press.

Gross, Frederick A., and William A. Dick-Peddie
1979 A Map of Primeval Vegetation in New Mexico. Southwestern Naturalist 24:115-122.

Hafsten, Ulf
1961 Pleistocene Development of Vegetation and Climate in the Southern High Plains as Evidenced by Pollen Analysis. In Paleoecology of the Llano Estacado, assembled by Fred Wendorf, pp. 59-91. Fort Burgwin Research Center Publication 1.

Hall, Stephen A.
1977 Late Quaternary Sedimentation and Paleoecological History of Chaco Canyon, New Mexico. Geological Society of America Bulletin 88:1593-1618.

1981 Deteriorated Pollen Grains and the Interpretation of Quaternary Pollen Diagrams. Review of Palaeobotany and Palynology 32:193-206.

1982 Late Holocene Paleoecology of the Southern Plains. Quaternary Research 17:391-407.

Hammond, George P., and Agapito Rey
1966 The Rediscovery of New Mexico, 1580-1594. Albuquerque: University of New Mexico Press.

Hester, Thomas R., and Robert F. Heizer
1972 Problems in the Functional Interpretation of Artifacts: Scraper Planes from Mitla and Yagul, Oaxaca. Contributions of the University of California Archaeological Research Facility 14:107-123.

Holmer, Richard N., and Dennis G. Weder
1980 Common Post-Archaic Projectile Points of the Fremont Area. Utah Division of State History, Antiquities Section Selected Papers 7(16):55-68.

Horowitz, Aharon, Rex E. Gerald, and Michael S. Chaiffetz
1981 Preliminary Paleoenvironmental Implications of Pollen Analyzed from Archaic, Formative, and Historic Sites near El Paso, Texas. Texas Journal of Science 33:61-72.

Houghton, Frank E.
1974 The Climate of New Mexico. In Climates of the States, Vol. 2, Western States, by Officials of the United States National Oceanic and Atmospheric Administration, pp. 794-810. Port Washington, N.Y.: Water Information Center.

Jelinek, Arthur J.
1966 Correlation of Archeological and Palynological Data. Science 152:1507-1509.

1967 A Prehistoric Sequence in the Middle Pecos Valley, New Mexico. Museum of Anthropology, University of Michigan, Anthropological Papers 31.

Johnson, Eileen, Vance T. Holliday, Michael J. Kaczor, and Robert Stuckenrath
1977 The Garza Occupation of the Lubbock Lake Site. Bulletin of the Texas Archeological Society 48:83-109.

Keeley, Lawrence H.
1980 Experimental Determination of Stone Tool Uses: A Microwear Analysis. Chicago: University of Chicago Press.

Kelley, Jane Holden
1966 The Archaeology of the Sierra Blanca Region of Southeastern New Mexico. Unpublished Ph.D. Dissertation. Cambridge: Harvard University.

1979 The Sierra Blanca Restudy Project. In Jornada Mogollon Archaeology: Proceedings of the First Jornada Conference, edited by Patrick H. Beckett and Regge N. Wiseman, pp. 107-132. Las Cruces: Cultural Resources Management Division, Department of Sociology and Anthropology, New Mexico State University.

Kelley, Vincent C.
1971 Geology of the Pecos Country, Southeastern New Mexico. *New Mexico State Bureau of Mines and Mineral Resources Memoir* 24.

Klein, J., J. C. Lerman, P. E. Damon, and E. K. Ralph
1982 Calibration of Radiocarbon Dates: Tables Based on the Consensus Data of the Workshop on Calibrating the Radiocarbon Time Scale. *Radiocarbon* 24(2):103-150.

Lehmer, Donald J.
1948 The Jornada Branch of the Mogollon. *University of Arizona Social Science Bulletin* 17.

Leopold, Luna B., W. W. Emmett, and R. M. Myrick
1966 Channel and Hillslope Processes in a Semiarid Area, New Mexico. *U. S. Geological Survey Professional Paper* 352-G.

Leslie, Robert H.
1977 Projectile Point Types and Sequence of the Eastern Jornada Mogollon, Extreme Southeastern New Mexico. *Regional Archeological Symposium for Southeastern New Mexico and Western Texas, Transactions* 13:81-157.

Martin, Paul S.
1963 *The Last 10,000 Years, A Fossil Pollen Record of the American Southwest*. Tucson: University of Arizona Press.

1967 Pollen Analysis of Prehistoric Middens near Ft. Sumner, New Mexico. In A Prehistoric Sequence in the Middle Pecos Valley, New Mexico, by Arthur J. Jelinek, pp. 130-134. *Museum of Anthropology, University of Michigan, Anthropological Papers* 31.

Minnis, Paul E., and Richard I. Ford
n.d. Analysis of Plant Remains from Chimney Rock, Colorado. *Museum of Anthropology, University of Michigan, Ethnobotanical Laboratory Report* 460.

Minnis, Paul E., and Steven A. LeBlanc
1976 An Efficient, Inexpensive Arid Lands Flotation System. *American Antiquity* 41(4):491-493.

Nelson, Fred W., and Richard D. Holmes
1979 Trace Element Analysis of Obsidian Sources and Artifacts from Western Utah. *Utah Division of State History, Antiquities Section Selected Papers* 6(15):65-80.

Nie, N. H., C. H. Hull, J. G. Jenkins, K. Steinbrenner, and D. H. Bent
1975 SPSS: Statistical Package for the Social Sciences, 2nd edition. New York: McGraw-Hill.

O'Laughlin, Thomas C.
1980 The Keystone Dam Site and Other Archaic and Formative Sites in Northwest El Paso, Texas. University of Texas, El Paso Centennial Museum, Publications in Anthropology 8.

Ortiz, Alfonso
1969 The Tewa World. Chicago: University of Chicago Press.

Parry, William J.
1980 The Use of Edge Morphology and Other Attributes in Functional Classification of Chipped Stone Tools. Paper presented at the 45th Annual Meeting of the Society for American Archaeology, Philadelphia.

Payne, Sebastian
1969 A Metrical Distinction Between Sheep and Goat Metacarpals. In The Domestication and Exploitation of Plants and Animals, edited by Peter J. Ucko and G. W. Dimbleby, pp. 295-306. Chicago: Aldine.

Perino, Gregory
1968 Guide to the Identification of Certain American Indian Projectile Points. Oklahoma Anthropological Society Special Bulletin 3.

Ralph, E. K., H. N. Michael, and M. C. Han
1973 Radiocarbon Dates and Reality. MASCA Newsletter 9:1-20.

Reher, Charles A., and George C. Frison
1980 The Vore Site, 48CK302, a Stratified Buffalo Jump in the Wyoming Black Hills. Plains Anthropologist Memoir 16.

Runkles, Frank A.
1964 The Garza Site: A Neo-American Campsite Near Post, Texas. Bulletin of the Texas Archeological Society 35:101-126.

Sampson, Robert J.
1975 Surface II Graphics System. Kansas Geological Survey, Series on Spatial Analysis 1.

Speth, John D.

1983 Bison Kills and Bone Counts: Decision Making by Ancient Hunters. Chicago: University of Chicago Press.

Speth, John D., and William J. Parry

1978 Late Prehistoric Bison Procurement in Southeastern New Mexico: The 1977 Season at the Garnsey Site. Museum of Anthropology, University of Michigan, Technical Reports 8.

1980 Late Prehistoric Bison Procurement in Southeastern New Mexico: The 1978 Season at the Garnsey Site (LA-18399). Museum of Anthropology, University of Michigan, Technical Reports 12.

Spielmann, Katherine A.

1982 Inter-Societal Food Acquisition among Egalitarian Societies: An Ecological Study of Plains-Pueblo Interaction in the American Southwest. Unpublished Ph.D. Dissertation. Ann Arbor: University of Michigan.

Stockton, Eugene D.

1973 Shaw's Creek Shelter: Human Displacement of Artefacts and its Significance. Mankind 9(2):112-117.

Stuiver, Minze

1982 A High-Precision Calibration of the AD Radiocarbon Time Scale. Radiocarbon 24(1):1-26.

Suhm, Dee Ann, and Edward B. Jelks

1962 Handbook of Texas Archaeology: Type Descriptions. Texas Archeological Society Special Publication 1.

Syvertsen, J. P., G. L. Nickell, R. W. Spellenberg, and G. L. Cunningham

1976 Carbon Reduction Pathways and Standing Crop in Three Chihuahuan Desert Plant Communities. Southwestern Naturalist 21(3):311-320.

Thomas, David H.

1969 Great Basin Hunting Patterns: A Quantitative Method for Treating Faunal Remains. American Antiquity 34(4):392-401.

U. S. Department of Agriculture

1978 Potential Natural Vegetation, New Mexico. New Mexico Interagency Range Committee Report 11.

Von Eschen, G. F.
1961 The Climate of New Mexico. University of New Mexico, Bureau of Business Research, Business Information Series 37.

Whalen, Michael E.
1978 Settlement Patterns of the Western Hueco Bolson. University of Texas, El Paso Centennial Museum, Anthropological Paper 6.

1981 Origin and Evolution of Ceramics in Western Texas. Bulletin of the Texas Archeological Society 52:215-29.

Willey, Patrick S., and Jack T. Hughes
1978 The Deadman's Shelter Site. In Archaeology at MacKenzie Reservoir, edited by J. T. Hughes and P. S. Willey, pp. 149-190. Texas Historical Commission, Office of the State Archeologist, Archeological Survey Report 24.

Wilmsen, Edwin N.
1968 Functional Analysis of Flaked Stone Artifacts. American Antiquity 33(2):156-61.

Wiseman, Regge N.
1976 Multi-Disciplinary Investigations at the Smokey Bear Ruin (LA 2112), Lincoln County, New Mexico. COAS Publishing and Research Monograph 4.

Yellen, John E.
1977 Cultural Patterning in Faunal Remains: Evidence from the !Kung Bushmen. In Experimental Archaeology, edited by D. Ingersoll, J. Yellen, and W. Macdonald, pp. 271-331. New York: Columbia University Press.

York, John C., and William A. Dick-Peddie
1969 Vegetational Changes in Southern New Mexico During the Past Hundred Years. In Arid Lands in Perspective, edited by W. G. McGuinnes and B. J. Goldman, pp. 155-166. Tucson: University of Arizona Press.